Out of the Flames

‡

MICHAEL SERVETVS HIS... DE ARAGON

Out of the Flames

✦

The Remarkable Story of a Fearless
Scholar, a Fatal Heresy, and
One of the Rarest Books in the World

Lawrence and Nancy Goldstone

Broadway Books / New York

Broadway Books titles may be purchased for business or promotional use or for special sales. For information, please write to: Special Markets Department, Random House, Inc., 1540 Broadway, New York, NY 10036.

PRINTED IN THE UNITED STATES OF AMERICA

BROADWAY BOOKS and its logo, a letter B bisected on the diagonal, are trademarks of Broadway Books, a division of Random House, Inc.

Visit our website at www.broadwaybooks.com

First edition published 2002

Book design by Donna Sinisgalli
Map designed by Jackie Aher

Frontispiece: An early eighteenth-century engraving of Michael Servetus. There is no surviving image made during his lifetime

Library of Congress Cataloging-in-Publication Data

Goldstone, Lawrence, 1947–
Out of the flames : the remarkable story of a fearless scholar, a fatal heresy, and one of the rarest books in the world / Lawrence and Nancy Goldstone.—1st ed.
p. cm.
Includes bibliographical references.
1. Servetus, Michael, 1511?–1553. 2. Heretics, Christian—Europe—Biography. 3. Persecution—Europe—History—16th century. 4. Religious tolerance—History of doctrines—16th century. I. Goldstone, Nancy Bazelon. II. Title.

BX9869.S4 G57 2002
273'.6—dc21
[B]   2001056710

ISBN 0-7679-0836-8

1 3 5 7 9 10 8 6 4 2

For Emily

‡

CONTENTS

If, then, dead books may be committed to the flames, how much more live books, that is to say, men?

Matthieu Ory,
Inquisitor of Heretical Pravity
for the Realm of France,
Paris, 1544

ʃHORTLY AFTER NOON on a cold and rainy late October day in 1553, a procession began at the town hall of Geneva, in western Switzerland, on the border with France. At its head were the local dignitaries—magistrates in their robes and hats, members of the town council, clergymen in their gowns, and the *lieutenant-criminel*, the chief of police. Immediately behind them rode a wave of officers on horseback and a guard of mounted archers. Next came the citizens of the city, first the well-to-do burghers, then the tradespeople and artisans, and, finally, a mob of the city's lower classes. Their destination was a hillside at Champel, about a mile outside the city's walls.

In the midst of these fair-skinned Swiss, one man stood out, a prisoner. He was in his forties, dark, almost Moorish, dirty and weak, with a long, unkempt beard and ragged clothing. He was surrounded by a crowd of pastors exhorting him to confess his sins. An aging churchman walked next to him, whispering in his ear. The prisoner prayed silently in reply.

The prisoner's shabby appearance belied his status as one of Europe's leading physicians and preeminent thinkers. His name was Michael Servetus, and his crime was publishing a book that redefined Christianity in a more tolerant and inclusive way. Although this book contained, almost as an afterthought, a great scientific discovery—one which a century later would propel medicine into the modern age—on that October afternoon in 1553, no one in Geneva knew or cared.

Michael Servetus had risked life and position to publish this book. After running afoul of the Inquisition with an earlier version twenty years before, he had gone underground and, like Jean Valjean in *Les Misérables*, had risen again under an assumed identity to become a respected citizen of France. Noblemen traveled great distances to consult with "Dr. Villeneuve." But Michael Servetus was unwilling to live out his life without being true to his beliefs and his principles, so he wrote his book and had it printed and distributed.

Shortly after its publication, he had been arrested by the inquisitors of France and sentenced to death. On the eve of his execution, he had managed a daring escape and had eluded capture for months. He was on his way to Italy, where he would be safe, but chose instead to stop in Geneva. There, his dark skin betrayed him. He was recognized while praying in church and arrested.

Before his supporters could rally to his defense, Michael Servetus was thrown into a dark, airless, vermin-infested cell, where he was kept for seventy-five days, denied a change of clothes, bedding, and often food and water. His access to the outside world was limited to forced participation in a gaudy show trial, where he was to go head to head with his accuser, perhaps the greatest mind of the Reformation. He defended himself brilliantly, but the quality of his arguments never mattered. Servetus's fate had been sealed from the moment he was recognized. He was found guilty of the charges brought by a council and prosecutor hand picked by his archrival and sworn enemy, Jean Chauvin, an obscure failed humanist who had reinvented himself as the reformer John Calvin and risen to be virtual dictator of the great city.

On October 26, 1553, Michael Servetus was condemned "to be led to Champel and burned there alive on the next day together with his books."

Torture and cruelty were no strangers to sixteenth-century justice. There was a strict hierarchy of punishment, from relatively painless to gruesomely agonizing, depending on the severity of the crime. Slanderers had their tongues cut out, thieves were impaled. The penalty for murder—beheading—was considered relatively charitable.

But of all the punishments, the very worst was to be burned alive, and so this horror was reserved for the most terrible crime there was—heresy. Heretics were especially loathed because they put not only their own souls in mortal jeopardy, but also those of the otherwise innocent people infected by their teachings.

Hollywood has often used burnings as a special effect. The victim is led to a stake atop an immense pile of wood and trussed with ropes. Torches are brought; the pile of wood is set ablaze and huge flames immediately leap up, surrounding the body. The victim screams as the bonfire erupts and the flames leap higher and higher, burning furiously. The camera pans upward as the smoke rises into the sky, and it is understood that all is over, that the victim is past suffering.

Only Hollywood has gotten it wrong. It was never over quickly. The whole point of burning at the stake was to subject the condemned to prolonged, horrible, unendurable pain. That was the type of pain that awaited Michael Servetus—and he knew it.

When Servetus was led to the hill at Champel, the stake and pyre were made of fresh wood, green wood, newly cut branches with the leaves still attached. They sat him on a log and chained him to a post. His neck was bound with thick rope. On his head they put a crown made of straw, doused in sulphur. Chained to his side was what was thought to be the last available copy of his book, the rest having all been zealously hunted down and destroyed. The ideas were to be burnt along with the man. There was no escape.

The fire was lit. Green wood does not burn easily, does not roar up. It smokes and sputters, burning unevenly and slowly. And so Michael Servetus's life was not extinguished quickly in a blazing wall of fire. Rather, he was slowly roasted, agonizingly conscious the entire time, the fire creeping upward inch by inch. The flames licked at him, the sulphur dripped into his eyes, not for minutes but for a full half hour. "Poor me, who cannot finish my life in this fire," the spectators heard him moan. At last, he screamed a final prayer to God, and then his ashes commingled with those of his book.

‡

WHAT IS A BOOK? Paper, cardboard, vellum, calfskin, glue, ink? The embodiment of our ideas, the corporeal representation of our souls?

This is the story of one book—Michael Servetus's book—an old book, a rare book, a book that contained the mystery of a great scientific discovery. But unlike other old, rare books, this book was attacked almost from the moment of its publication, viciously and systematically, with the goal of total eradication, by forces of overwhelming power.

And yet, somehow, with no commensurate organized defense operating on its behalf, three copies survived. ‡

PART I

‡

Servetus

(1511–1553)

CHAPTER ONE

ⓂICHAEL SERVETUS WAS born Miguel Serveto Conesa alias Revés on Saint Michael's Day, September 29, 1511, in the small town of Villanueva de Sijena, in the province of Huesca. Huesca is in Aragon, at the northeast corner of Spain, just east of Navarre and about fifty miles south of the border with France. The house in which he was born still stands.

The Servetos were gentry of long standing. There is evidence of their having been given their title, *infanzones*, or nobles of the second category, as early as 1327. Miguel was the oldest of three sons. His father, Anthon, was a notary; his mother, Catalina Conesa, was also born of noble blood. The second son, Pedro, became a notary like his father; the youngest, Juan, stayed home and became a priest and was appointed rector of a nearby church.

The early sixteenth century was the crossroads where the medieval world, the Renaissance, the Inquisition, the New World, and the modern world all met. Although to most Americans the preeminent figure of the period was England's King Henry VIII, for most of his reign, Henry, despite the six wives, court intrigues, and general theatrics, was an afterthought in European politics. It was Charles V, the last of the Holy Roman Emperors, who dominated the stage. The Holy Roman Empire was the superpower of its time, stretching from Spain to the Balkans, from the Mediterranean to the Baltic.

Charles was a Hapsburg, born into one of the great ruling dynasties of Europe in 1500. His father was Philip the Fair, king of Castile, son of the emperor Maximilian, and his mother was Juana the Mad, daughter of Ferdinand and Isabella. Juana, unattractive and highly unstable, had fallen madly in love with a husband who couldn't stand her. When Philip took up with someone else, Juana retaliated by hacking off his mistress's hair at a public function. Philip got his revenge by locking up Juana in a tower in Spain, where she stayed for the next fifty years.

Then everyone died—Isabella in 1504, Philip two years later, Ferdinand in 1516, and Maximilian three years after that. Charles inherited everything. Before he had turned twenty, he ruled virtually all of Western Europe except England, France, and Portugal. Charles was smart, ambitious, fearless, and intensely Catholic.

Of the three remaining holdouts, France, under Francis I, was by far the most powerful. Six years older than Charles, Francis soon became his nemesis. The French monarch had been raised by a doting mother and sister (the bohemian Marguerite of Navarre) and was taught to be brave, romantic, and chivalrous. He was after Charles from the beginning. When he was twelve, he stole Charles's seven-year-old fiancée out from under his nose, an act that did nothing to improve relations with the future emperor.

Francis understood perfectly that Charles would have liked nothing better than to add France to his empire. But holding vast amounts of territory presents problems of its own, and Charles's resources were always stretched far too thin to mount a full-scale invasion of powerful France. Francis helped maintain this tenuous balance of power by attacking Charles's forces wherever he perceived them to be weak.

For years Charles and Francis tried alternately to outflank, outwit, or outfight each other. They used diplomacy, threats, love, and treachery. Each courted and threatened the pope. But while most of the world was consumed by the shifting alliances and machinations of these two Renaissance heavyweights, another force was at work, bubbling just under the surface. It was a force that was immense and inexorable, and it was made of paper.

‡

ABOUT HALF A CENTURY before, in the mid-1450s, an inventor had just finished a twenty-year struggle to perfect a new device that he was sure would make him a great fortune. The inventor was a shadowy figure—there is no surviving record of his birth, and no accurate image of him exists. He grew up in Mainz, about twenty-five miles west of Frankfurt in the Rhine River Valley. He seems to have been born of good family, but after some unrecorded transgression as a young man, he was forced to move to Strasbourg, about 100 miles to the south.

He seems, from the sketchy accounts that remain, to have been a disagreeable person. He worked in total secrecy—not even his next-door neighbors knew what he was up to. He borrowed heavily, putting off one creditor after another with vague promises of a vast return on investment. In fact, much of what we know about him has been gleaned from surviving court records of the many times he was sued by his partners, or unpaid bills from tax assessors or people to whom he owed money. Toward the end of this twenty-year quest, he seems to have become increasingly desperate, obsessed that someone would steal his idea or that others engaged in similar experiments would perfect the device before he did.

The inventor was Johann Gutenberg, and the invention was the process by which a book could be printed from movable type.

Although popular history often credits Gutenberg with single-handedly creating a new world of books and reading, he was merely responding to a demand that was already strong and growing fast. This was a venture much more entrepreneurial than scientific. When Gutenberg first began to tinker about with his printing apparatus in the 1430s, Europe was in the midst of a great post-plague commercial

Europe in 1520. France is virtually surrounded by territories of Charles V.

boom, with people becoming more mobile and worldlier than ever before. Literacy had been on the rise for decades, and new universities had begun to spring up in a number of major cities in Europe. Collecting books and establishing private libraries was now a popular pastime among the wealthy, and there were even glimmers of a thirst for reading material that was devoted to neither theology nor the better-known classics.

To meet this growing demand, publishers in the 1430s and 1440s had no alternative but to scramble about and try to produce as many books as possible using traditional methods. By far the most common of these was the use of scribes to create each copy of a book individually. More demand meant hiring more scribes—one publisher, Vespasiano da Bisticci, employed fifty at a time. But even this was not enough. New trainees were needed, but productive crafts like leather working, weaving, and metalsmithing paid much better than printing. Older scribes were having great difficulty inducing younger men to enter the profession.

Competition to draw from this limited labor pool grew intense, and the power of the scribes grew accordingly. In Paris, home of the most important university in Europe, there were so many of these Bob Cratchits hunched over their desks, copying one scholarly text after another, that they began to organize themselves into guilds.

The scribe system had other painfully obvious drawbacks. First and foremost, a book produced by a scribe was essentially a one-of-a-kind work of art. All calligraphers were hardly created equal, so the work of the more talented scribes was much more in demand, particularly among the aristocracy, than that of inferior artisans. In any case, a book copied by a scribe was a laborious effort, and necessarily limited by how many pages one man—no matter how adept—could produce in a day. Then there was the question of editing and correcting a product created without control or supervision. Error correction was tedious, requiring at a minimum the redrafting of an entire page. It clearly wouldn't do to have lines drawn through the text with little arrows pointing from additions in the margins to the correct spot on a page. As pressure to produce a greater volume of books increased, errors became more and more common—just how common depended upon the diligence or greed of the publisher—and neither buyer nor seller could really be sure that what was in a book, no matter how beautifully rendered, was an accurate reproduction of any given author's work.

Some publishers tried to get around the scribe problem by employing block printing. Block printing involved cutting away part of a wooden block's surface, leaving any desired text or illustration in relief. Ink was applied to the raised portions of the block, which was then pressed against the material being printed. Block printing, which began in Asia, had been used on textiles since about the fifth or sixth century and was being used to print books in China by the ninth. The Mongols used the technique for creating paper money in the thirteenth century. Block printing appeared around the same time in Italy. By the fourteenth century, German printers were using block printing for the text of illuminated manuscripts.

While the advantage of block printing was the ability to produce multiple copies from a single master, there were plenty of shortcomings here too. Creating the master copy was every bit as laborious as employing scribes, if not more so. Carving a block for each page of a four-hundred-page manuscript could take a sufficient amount of work to render all but the most timeless texts out of date. It was an approach that was only justified for texts for which the projected printing runs were quite large. And although the carvers could certainly choose hardwoods, such as oak or maple, wood is still porous, susceptible to wear, and difficult to clean, thus making it unwieldy to produce a large number of copies from a single block. Then, of course, there was the storage problem—what did you do with the blocks after you were done with them? Firewood was often the option of choice.

The inadequacies of both scribes and wood blocks in dealing with the burgeoning demand for printed material were as obvious to fifteenth-century entrepreneurs as the burgeoning demand for motor cars was to Henry Ford. Whoever came up with a better, more efficient, more cost-effective method of producing books was going to make lots and lots of money.

With the stakes this high, Gutenberg was not the only person drawn into the enterprise. All over Europe, inventors raced to come up with an idea that would work. In fact, to this day there are some who insist that there were crude versions of printing from movable type before Gutenberg's momentous achievement in 1455. Other scholars believe that some of these earlier versions were actually Gutenberg's own less sophisticated prototypes.

Since Gutenberg chose to be so secretive, there is no real record of his thought process or of the interim successes and failures he experienced in his two decades of work. It seems, however, that his first step was to create the type itself. This isn't surprising, since Gutenberg was familiar with goldsmithing, and metalsmiths had for some time used punches to deboss their work with an identifying mark. It obviously didn't take long for Gutenberg to realize that these punches could be made as easily in the shape of letters as anything else. Since 1440 is now generally accepted as the year in which he perfected typography, fifteen of the twenty years must have been devoted to figuring out how to make the type uniform. There was also the problem of utilizing the type in a practical and efficient manner.

Whatever the chronology, by 1450 Gutenberg was out of money again. He moved from Strasbourg back to Mainz, where he persuaded a local lawyer/financier named Johann Fust to become the latest in his string of partners. Fust advanced 800 guilders, a hefty sum, to allow Gutenberg to set up shop and buy tools and equipment, all of which were pledged to Fust as security for the loan, as was any product that Gutenberg might develop. Fust further agreed to loan Gutenberg 300 guilders a year for operating expenses. Instead, it seems, Fust loaned Gutenberg an additional 800 guilders in 1452. Whether or not Fust knew of Gutenberg's past associations before he put forth such a sum (which has been estimated at over one million dollars in today's currency) is unclear, but in any event, Fust turned out to be quite able to look after his own interests.

By 1453, Gutenberg had entirely reinvented the process of making books. There was not a single element of the printing process that he had not improved. He not only created the design of the type, he invented the mold used to make the actual letters, an ingenious sliding-walled box that would ensure that each letter was the exact same height as the rest, while accommodating the varying widths of different letters. He developed a linseed oil–based lampblack ink that would adhere to the typeface, transfer to the paper without smearing, and then dry uniform and black. He invented a jig to hold a page of letters, and then developed a press, modeled after a winepress, to hold the paper against the type and create a clean, sharp image. Gutenberg's method of printing was so ingenious, so elegant, that it remained largely undisturbed as the prevailing technology for more than four centuries.

All that was left was to pick a book on which to try the process. Since this was a commercial venture—posterity entered into his thinking very little, if at all—Gutenberg, not a particularly religious fellow himself, selected the Bible for his maiden effort because he thought it would be the easiest book to sell.

Gutenberg began producing printed pages sometime after 1452 and, after extensive tinkering and fine-tuning, was ready in early 1455 to show his work to the world. He took some unbound gatherings (groups of pages not yet bound into book form) to the Frankfurt Book Fair. The response was one of amazement.

Then, in November 1455, when the printing of all 1,286 pages of the new Bible had been completed and the commercial success of the venture assured, Fust sued for unpaid loans and compounded interest. Since Gutenberg had not had the time to actually sell any of his Bibles and realize any revenues, Fust won, foreclosed on the loans, and took over the entire operation, which he then put under the direction of his son-in-law, Peter Schoeffer, who, as it happened, was by trade a printer and whose most recent job had been working as Gutenberg's foreman.

When the completed Gutenberg Bible actually made its first appearance on the world stage, it was Johann Fust, not Johann Gutenberg, who introduced it. It sold out instantly and was immediately back-ordered. Not only did Fust and Schoeffer reap the profits of Gutenberg's invention, they did everything they could to perpetuate the notion that they had developed the process as well. In fairness, they did make some improvements. Schoeffer, for example, is generally credited with having invented the title page.

So successful were Fust and Schoeffer in convincing the world that the printing press was their own invention that in 1515, Fust's grandson, Johann Schoeffer, then head of the family printing business, had the following inserted in the colophon of one of their books (a colophon is an inscription on the last page stating facts relating to the publishing and printing of the work):

> Johann Fust, citizen of Mainz, foremost author of the said art, who in due course by his own genius began to think out and investigate the art of printing in the year of the Lord 1450 . . . and in the year 1452 perfected and by the favor of divine grace brought it to the work of printing, by the help, however, and with many necessary inventions of Peter Schoeffer of Gernsheim, his workman and adoptive son, to whom also he gave his daughter Christina Fust in marriage as a worthy reward of his labor and many inventions. And these two, Johann Fust and Peter Schoeffer, kept this art secret, all their workmen and servants being bound by oath not in any way to reveal it; but at last, from the year of the Lord 1462, through these same servants being spread into divers parts of the world, it received no small increase.

Gutenberg lived the rest of his life in obscurity. He continued to borrow money where he could and experiment to improve his art. In 1460, he produced a beautiful edition of the *Catholicon*, an encyclopedic dictionary by Johannus Balbus de Janua. Although this new book contained about the same amount of text as the Bible, Gutenberg had improved his type, and, at 746 pages, it was about a third smaller. The *Catholicon* was to be Gutenberg's last known work.

There is no firm record of when and where he died although it must have been around 1468. That is when a Mainz physician named Konrad Humery filed a legal action claiming that all of the late Johann Gutenberg's possessions, mostly printing materials, belonged to him as a result of unpaid debts.

Fust and Schoeffer reprinted the *Catholicon* in 1469.

‡

WITHIN MONTHS OF THE first printed Bible's appearance, printers were setting up shop all over Germany. Soon afterward, printing spread to Italy, France, Switzerland, the Netherlands, Spain, and England. Although, like Gutenberg's Bible, books were still laid out to approximate manuscripts as closely as possible (even Gutenberg had employed scribes to add lead letters and decorative borders to his pages once the ink had dried), improvements were made, mostly to make the operation more cost-effective. Paper was the most expensive element in the process, so typeface was made smaller to squeeze more words on a line and more lines on a page. New fonts, such as Nicolas Jenson's roman, were developed to replace Gutenberg's gothic, allowing for greater reduction still. Roman was also a crisper font and made reading easier on the eye.

Demand burgeoned and printed books became the new craze, particularly among the merchant class, which was growing in numbers, wealth, and influence as people in Europe moved about more freely and markets expanded to a continentwide scale. For this group, nouveau riche and desperate to be accepted, printed books were an announcement of arrival. For aristocrats with libraries, on the other hand—the old money—printed books were considered cheap and tawdry imitations compared to the beauty and stateliness of genuine handwritten manuscripts. Many an aristocratic bibliophile would no sooner have placed a printed book on his shelf next to a handcrafted manuscript than a modern collector would place a mass market paperback next to a Charles Dickens first edition.

Many of the first printed books were Bibles or other religious texts, such as missals, books of hours, or manuals for confessors. These were easy to sell—every church needed a Bible, for example. Although literacy in the second half of the fifteenth century was still largely confined to ecclesiastics, academics, and the monied elite, businessmen, along with bankers, lawyers, and magistrates, also began to read and clamored for books to help in the conduct of their day-to-day affairs. Interest quickly spread beyond treatises on law and jurisprudence to a demand for scientific and general knowledge. There were books on botany, agronomy, animal husbandry, and architecture. A market even grew up around the desire for the occasional "light read"—a tale of chivalry, perhaps. With the rise of secular reading, university towns had trouble attracting printers to service them. The quick guilder was to be made near the courts and business centers.

Tens of thousands of books were printed toward the end of the fifteenth century, and by 1500 more than three hundred presses had been set up across Europe. Still, books had largely remained the province of the wealthy, only trickling down to a now-thirsting populace. Guildsmen, the nascent urban middle class, and even wealthier members of the peasantry also wanted to avail themselves of the new knowledge but lacked the opportunity to do so. That was all to change in the very next year, because of one man, when the trickle became a flood.

‡

IN 1453, THE OTTOMAN TURKS overran the decaying Byzantine Empire and took Constantinople. The Ottomans were Muslims, originally followers of a Turkish warlord named Osman who, in the early 1300s, united the Turkish tribes around Nicaea, now Iznik in western Turkey. Descendants of Osman ruled in unbroken succession until 1922, presiding over what was to become one of the world's great empires. The boundaries of the Ottoman Empire shifted constantly, at one point stretching deep into central Asia, through the Balkans into Serbia, and across the Mediterranean.

The Byzantines, the last remnants of the Roman Empire, had long been champions of Greek culture, and Constantinople, their capital, was a hub of Greek scholarship. Some of those scholars were already in Italy when Constantinople fell, trying to cajole support for the defense of the empire, while others, leery about subjecting themselves to the hospitality of the onrushing Turks, took to boats and fled west. Many members of both groups, some with their entire personal libraries intact, settled in the thriving port of Venice, on the Adriatic Sea in northern Italy. One of these émigrés, Johannus Bessarion, the bishop of Nicaea, brought over more than five hundred Greek manuscripts, all of which he donated to his adopted city, an act for which, among other things, Pope Pius II demonstrated his gratitude by making Bessarion a cardinal. The Biblioteca Marciana, where his library ended up, suddenly held the largest collection of Greek manuscripts in Europe, and Venice was transformed into *the* center of classical learning. In 1469, printing arrived, and soon more books were being produced in the city than anywhere else on the continent.

‡

THE GROWTH OF LITERACY and the interest in books and in the Greek classics were a direct result of a major intellectual and literary movement called *humanism.*

For centuries, scholarship and learning had been dominated by a Church-controlled educational system called *scholasticism* (from the Latin *schola*, or school). In scholastic doctrine, all knowledge was divided into four strictly delineated areas—theology, philosophy, jurisprudence, and medicine—with an equally specific list of approved scholars or Latin versions of books as the unquestioned authorities for each. Every major university established in the Middle Ages was divided into faculties along scholastic lines.

In any of these faculties, a student would first undertake the *lectio*, a long, painstakingly detailed, closely supervised reading of one of the approved works, such as Euclid's geometry, or the writings of Saint Augustine or Thomas Aquinas. He would then engage in the *disputatio*, a debate using strict Aristotelian logic to examine some issue arising from the text. It was not permissible to question the overall veracity of the source—that was heresy—only the meaning of a particular passage or phrase. The *disputatio* itself was carefully monitored to ensure that no proscribed interpretations crept into the discussions.

Courses of study lasted for five, ten, even fifteen years. While the limitation on sources promoted exhaustive, even microscopic familiarity with those materials that were made available, after a while it was inevitable that all this intellectual inbreeding would result in *disputatios* that descended to minutiae. In the universities of the Middle Ages, it was not uncommon for students to spend weeks, even months, on such esoteric topics as whether or not God could reverse time or whether, as Alister McGrath noted in *In the Beginning*, "Christ could have become incarnate as a donkey, or perhaps a cucumber, rather than a man."

Church fathers were all too aware that it was far more important to set the boundaries within which debate might occur than to decide where within those boundaries to actually undertake it. As scholasticism matured, those boundaries were tightened so as to serve only to support the authority of the Church itself. Their raison d'être became the alignment of Christianity as defined in the Bible—more specifically the Vulgate, the officially recognized Latin translation completed in the fourth century by Saint Jerome—with the often shifting interpretations of Rome. In other words, canon law as set down by the pope and other Church leaders was irrefutable, even more irrefutable, for example, than the word of a king.

Humanism began at the same place as scholasticism—the teachings of the ancients—then spun off in a completely different direction. Unlike the cold, inward analysis of the scholastics, humanists looked outward to the realm of human experience and values. Minute examination of translated phrases as the sole tool of learning, humanists argued, distorted understanding of the nature of man and his place in God's universe. After all, Aristotelian logic is not a particularly useful vehicle for understanding poetry. Humanists thus encouraged breadth of scholarship as well as the reading of materials in their original languages.

The discipline had been around since Dante and Petrarch in the thirteenth and fourteenth centuries, beginning as an approved offshoot of scholasticism, exploring ancient secular values that did not conflict with Church teachings. By the early fifteenth century, however, humanism had broken away. Classical Greek had largely supplanted Latin as the language of choice, and humanist scholars were reading Plato, Homer, playwrights like Euripides, and the narratives of Plutarch and Xenophon.

Humanism encouraged free inquiry every bit as much as scholasticism discouraged it, and soon humanist thought began to work its way into the educational system. The term *studia humanitatis* came to mean a well-defined curriculum that included grammar, rhetoric, history, poetry, and moral philosophy, all based on Greek and Latin authors and classical texts. After a while, this expansion of learning piqued the interest of the more sophisticated elements of society at large, and a demand sprung up not only for the classics but also for books and reading in general.

The humanists' emphasis on the personal worth of the individual and the central importance of human values was eventually going to set itself in opposition to religious dogma. An uneasy truce developed between the Church and the humanist philosophers. Humanist scholars and writers were tolerated as long as they avoided direct challenges to either the Church's authority or its interpretation of theologic or scientific principles. In other words, they could write poetry but not question the nature of God. But as the essence of humanism involved intellectual speculation, this truce became more and more difficult to maintain.

✣

IN THE MID-1480S, an obscure young humanist scholar and Grecophile from an undistinguished family named Aldus Manutius secured a pleasant assignment as private tutor to the sons of the Princess of Carpi, the sister of one his classmates in Rome. Carpi was in north-central Italy, about two hundred miles west of Venice. Although Carpi itself was not a center of anything, the princess, something of a patron, often invited some of Venice's learned refugees to be her guests.

Aldus, for his part, found it difficult to properly instruct his charges in the classics. Many of the works of classical authors were not available at all, even in manuscript, and others only in uncertain translation. The visits to Carpi by all those walking textbooks gave him an idea. When he told the princess what he had in mind, she not only agreed, but even provided the seed money to get the venture off the ground.

In 1490, Aldus moved to Venice to establish a printing business. He set himself up in a large old house, in which he designated Greek as the official language, and converted the entire premises to a combination living quarters, editorial office, and factory.

Aldus was a genuine visionary, and nothing was going to come out of his press that did not fit that vision precisely. Developing a vision takes time and money, however, and Aldus was soon forced to supplement his initial stake from the princess by selling off an additional share of the business to a savvy venture capitalist named Andrea de Torresani. Torresani knew an exploding industry when he saw one. He had recently bought out Nicolas Jenson and his roman font, and Aldus's scheme seemed a good way to further expand his influence in the market. (Later on, in 1505, taking a cue from Peter Schoeffer, Aldus expanded *his* influence with Torresani by marrying his daughter.)

Aldus held strongly to the humanist view that a book should be read in the language in which it was written—"without intermediaries," as he put it—so he intended to publish his beloved Greeks in Greek. For his first work, therefore, he chose to publish a Greek lexicon, essentially a Greek–Latin dictionary and phrase book. He purchased fine linen and hemp paper from the Fabriano mills and mixed the ink on the premises. He was experimenting with Greek typefaces when he noticed that his chief compositor, a brilliant Cretan scholar named Marcus Musurus, had a beautiful, flowing handwriting. He copied Musurus's characters and, in 1494, published his lexicon. He followed that quickly with *Opusculum de Herone et Leandro* (*The Story of Hero and Leander*), and then, in 1495, he published a Greek grammar. Later that year, Aldus also published the first volume of what was to be a four-volume set of the works of Aristotle. Everything he printed sold out, and suddenly Aldus's notion of making the works of the ancients available to book buyers across Italy had leapt to the forefront of the printing stage.

For the remainder of the century, Aldus published classics, eventually adding Latin ones to those in Greek. For his Latin works, Aldus used the roman font developed by Jenson (now owned by his partner), adding some wrinkles of his own, such as small capitals. In all, he published thirty-eight titles. He expanded print runs from the usual 250 to 1,000 in order to better amortize his costs.

As the fifteenth century drew to a close, Aldus began to experiment, both with content and with style. As to the former, in December 1499 he published the *Hypnerotomachia Poliphili* (*Dream of Polifilo*) by a Dominican monk named Francesco Colonna. The story itself, of Polifilo's pursuit of his lover, Polia, through a fantastic world of buildings and gardens, is an amalgam of fable, history, architecture, and mathematics written in an odd hybrid of Latin and Italian. The *Hypnerotomachia* is one of the most beautiful of the Aldine books, done in a graceful typographical arrangement with many finely drawn illustrations. These illustrations, filled with fountains and obelisks, are unsub-

tly erotic (one, of Priapus, Greek god of procreation, is overtly porno-
graphic), and Colonna himself was a very un-Aldine type of author. He
was expelled from his order more than once for misdeeds and in 1516,
when he was in his eighties, was convicted of seducing a young girl.

The *Hypnerotomachia* was one of the few books printed by Aldus in
which he did not identify himself as the printer. Over the years it was
sometimes rumored to be mystical or satanic, filled with cryptic refer-

The Priapus woodcut from the Hypnerotomachia,
*arguably one of the most valuable book illustrations
in history*

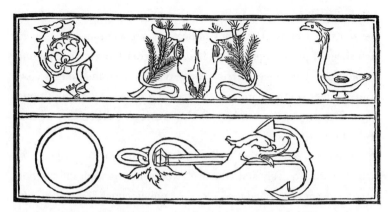

The Dolphin and Anchor (festina lente) *later adopted by Aldus as his printer's mark*

ences and hidden meanings. (Perhaps demonstrating the relative value of the occult and the erotic, it was the one famous woodcut that was most sought after, and today, after numerous snippings, there are almost no original volumes left with the notorious Priapus illustration intact.)

It was in another of those illustrations—the artist remains unknown—that Aldus noticed a drawing of a dolphin encircling the post of an anchor. The design was actually an *impresa*, a form of pictorial puzzle popular in Italy at the time. The picture illustrates a motto, in this case, *festina lente* ("Make haste slowly"), a saying of Augustus Caesar recorded by Suetonius. The anchor was symbolic of slowness and the dolphin of speed. One year later, Aldus would adopt this design as the emblem for the Aldine Press, and today it remains as perhaps the most famous printer's mark in all of publishing history.

But it was his experiments with style that were to complete Aldus's vision and result in an innovation that made Aldus Manutius one of the seminal forces in intellectual history.

Books may have gotten thinner thanks to improved typography, but they were no smaller. Printers, including Aldus, turned out only bulky, unwieldy folios or quartos, which were usually read on lecterns and therefore not terribly convenient as study aids.

Folio and *quarto* refer to the surface area of a page and thus the dimensions of a book. The terms indicate how many times a 32-by-21-inch sheet of printer's paper was folded in order to create a gathering. A folio was folded once, creating two leaves, which translated into four printed pages, and a quarto twice, creating four leaves or eight printed pages. The greater the number of folds, obviously, the smaller the size of the book.

Aldus realized that the smaller and more efficient you made the vehicle, the more quickly and effectively you could transmit information. In 1500, he commissioned the Bolognese punch-cutter Francesco Griffo to create a new typeface for books printed in Latin. It was to be narrower than roman type and slanted to resemble the cursive style that had originated in the papal chancery and that humanists were then using to correspond with one another. All lowercase letters were to be the same height and combined with the small roman capitals that Aldus had employed in his previous Latin editions. The new design, graceful and pleasing to the eye, allowed more words to fit on a page without sacrificing any ease in reading. Then, rather than producing two folds, Aldus folded his sheet three times, producing a gathering of eight leaves—octavo—or sixteen text-rich 5-by-8-inch pages. When he was done, Aldus had produced a book half the size of anything that had gone before without making it appreciably thicker, a handy volume that could fit perfectly into a saddlebag.

The Aldine octavos, produced without illustrations, were a huge and immediate success. The moment the works of Virgil, the first edition to be printed in the new format, came off the presses in 1501, books became democratized—lightweight, personal, and portable, suitable for home, office, or travel. Aldus obtained an official monopoly over the production of this type of book from the Venetian senate, but both the octavo form and italic type were almost instantly pirated by printers across Italy, Germany, and France, including Griffo, who was miffed at being cut out of the action. Within just a year or two octavos became the standard, and texts printed in one corner of Europe were now regularly shipped to another.

As his fame increased, Aldus's household expanded, to eventually include not only his family, but thirty-three translators, correctors, typesetters, and pressmen as well. He met once a day with the complete staff to discuss, in Greek (lapsing into any other language resulted in a fine), what to publish and who would do what on each project. It was as much think tank as printing house. Many of those attracted by the heady atmosphere were noted scholars in their own right, and clashes of temperament were inevitable.

In 1507, Aldus received a letter from the humanist scholar Desiderius Erasmus, in which Erasmus proposed that he come to Venice to supervise a new edition of his Latin translation of Euripides. Erasmus, later to gain the reputation as the greatest mind in Europe, was at the time only moderately well known. After the Euripides had been completed, Erasmus remained in the household, working on both other translations and on his own *Adagia* (*Adages*). Erasmus was unused to the feverish Aldine pace. Manuscript pages were grabbed up as soon as they were finished and rushed to be typeset with no chance for revision. "The labor was such that there was no time to scratch one's ears," he complained.

While Erasmus got along well with Aldus himself ("He is building up a library that has no other limits than the world itself," he wrote later), this bonhomie did not extend to other members of the firm. In *Opulentia Sordida* (*Stingy Wealth*), he called Torresani the prince of cheapskates, a man of riches who nonetheless let his guests go hungry on sour wine and thin soup. The food issue got him in trouble with Musurus as well. At Aldus's house, there was no breakfast, lunch was at one, and dinner, such as it was, not until ten. Erasmus eventually eschewed the common table and took his meals in his room. He wrote that during his stay at the Aldine Press he almost starved. Musurus replied that Erasmus drank enough for Geryon (a three-headed, triple-bodied monster slain by Hercules) but only did the work of half a man.

Still, the collaboration served both Erasmus and Aldus. The octavo *Collectanea Adagiorum*, essentially an annotated series of one-liners complete with genesis and commentary, was Erasmus's first big bestseller. The original edition, published some years earlier in Paris, had about eight hundred of these pithy little sayings, culled from old Greek and Latin texts. By the time the Aldus household was through bombarding him with new material, there were over 3,200. (When Erasmus finally left Venice, Aldus offered him some complimentary author copies. "Not unless you give me a horse as well," Erasmus replied, looking at the bulky volume.) Sixty different editions were to appear during Erasmus's lifetime, translated into English, Italian, German, and Dutch. The *Adagia*, in many ways, has never been out of print. From Erasmus we get "To champ at the bit"; "Where there is smoke there is fire"; "A necessary evil"; "Know thyself"; "One foot in the grave"; "Many hands make light work"; and that old standby, "To leave no stone unturned."

‡

FROM 1501 TO 1515, Aldus published forty-eight titles in octavo in Greek, Italian, and Latin. Among the works he chose to print were those of Petrarch, Horace, Ovid, Thucydides, and Plato, many for the first time. Aldine volumes remain some of the most simple and elegant in printing history. When he died in 1515, he lay in state in the church next to his house, and humanist scholars paid him homage by erecting stacks of Aldine octavos around the bier that held his body. According to his wish, Aldus Manutius was buried at Carpi.

Aldus changed the face of Western civilization even more profoundly than had Gutenberg. Aldine octavos were to the sixteenth century what personal computing was to the twentieth. Suddenly, more information was available to an individual reader than had previously been available to most institutions. Ordinary citizens were now linked across Europe. They read what they wanted, which meant that they could think what they wanted. Most of all, they had the power that came from the knowledge that there were others who thought like them.

Although Michael Servetus was born only ten years after the Aldine edition of Virgil was published, the world he entered was almost unrecognizable compared with that of his parents. The number of books in circulation in Europe had multiplied exponentially. Not only were the classics now translated and disseminated among a widespread multitude of new (usually young) readers, but it soon occurred to this new generation—as it has to another generation five hundred years later—that you could send information out just as easily as you could take it in. Books could be written as well as read—if you had something to say you could have your ideas disseminated just as widely as those of Aristotle. All you needed was an idea or a point of view to try and capture the attention of the world. And if what was in your book was radical, controversial, revolutionary, or even heretical, so be it. There was no longer any effective power to stop it. ‡

HUESCA, WHERE MIGUEL Serveto grew up, while technically a part of Spain, was heavily influenced both by France to
the north and the independent kingdom of Navarre less than
twenty miles to the west. Navarre was ruled by the Albrets, a
noble French family that later in the century would spawn the great
king Henri IV. In 1512, the ruthless and powerful Ferdinand, king of
Aragon, Charles V's grandfather, who had wanted Navarre for some
time, convinced his son-in-law, Henry VIII (married to his daughter,
Catherine of Aragon), to invade France by way of northern Spain.
While their combined armies were passing through Navarre, Ferdinand
conveniently used the English troops to help seize the kingdom for
Spain. The part of Navarre south of the Pyrenees was annexed to
Castile soon after. (Ferdinand eventually double-crossed Henry by
making a secret, separate peace with the French king Louis XII. Henry
promptly retaliated by making his own secret peace with Louis, throw-
ing in the hand of his beautiful younger sister, Mary, in marriage.)

Even after the annexation, the culture of Navarre remained much
more French than Spanish. This wasn't surprising, as Spain was considered a country of inferiors. The Spanish were also seen as having
something of a racial problem. There were more Jews and Muslims in
Spain than almost anywhere else in Europe, and the Spanish Inquisition had compounded the problem by at first allowing them to remain
in Spain if they converted to Christianity. Still, the converted Muslims

and Jews, who believed in a single deity, found it particularly difficult to accept the doctrine of the Trinity.

This created a class of titular Catholics whom the rest of Europe derisively called *Marranos*—a word that in Spanish means hog, pig, or someone without principles—an epithet that soon slid over to cover Spaniards of any stripe. There was a sixteenth-century joke that made the rounds: "A Spaniard, after having confessed all his sins, returned to the confessor to say that he had forgotten one small sin (*peccadiglio*), namely, that he did not believe in God." A celebrated Italian poet, Ludovico Ariosto, came up with the phrase *peccadiglio di Spagna*, which compared anyone who did not believe in Christ and the unity of the Father, the Son, and the Holy Spirit to a Spaniard. The Spanish, of course, later rectified their error of tolerance by the wholesale slaughter of any Jews or Muslims who had foolishly thought to remain in Spain, but it didn't do any good. The slurs stuck.

Whereas Isaac Newton's mother thought he was a simpleton because he could not seem to concentrate on farm chores and chose to lie around and read or stare into space all day, there was never any question in Huesca that Anthon Serveto's eldest son was a prodigy. The nurturing of gifted children has not changed all that much in five hundred years. Then, like now, they tended to get the best teachers, were doted on by parents and other adults, resented by less talented siblings, looked on as being somewhat odd by their peers, and, in general, grew up to believe that they were better, smarter, and more worthy than anyone else.

Of all his exceptional talents, it was Miguel's facility with languages that was initially most striking. By the time he was thirteen years old, in addition to his native language, he could read French, Greek, Latin, and, most significantly, Hebrew. In most of Christian Europe, Hebrew was a forbidden language. It was considered dangerous, mystical, and subversive. The Church was adamantly against it: knowledge of Hebrew meant that the Old Testament could be read in its original form without resorting to approved translations. The French would not openly teach Hebrew until 1531, when Francis I, in a particularly tolerant mood, and under pressure from French intellectuals, opened the *Lecteurs Royaux* in Paris for the study of classical languages and included Hebrew in the curriculum.

But the rules of Christendom tended to blur in rural Spain, whose society, despite the Inquisition, reflected countless centuries of Jewish and Muslim cultural influence. Miguel evidently studied under, or at least was acquainted with, someone of Semitic origin since Hebrew, when it was taught at all, was almost always taught in secret, and by a Jew. Because of Servetus's views on the Trinity, his enemies would later hypothesize that he was himself a Jew, but there is nothing to indicate that this was so.

It is much more likely that Miguel, growing up in a time of political and religious upheaval, was bombarded by heterodoxy on all sides. He watched the Jews and Muslims resist Catholicism and the Navarrese resist Spain, both powerless minorities fighting a desperate battle for freedom. He learned to identify with the outcast long before he was to discover that he would be one himself.

‡

MEANWHILE, THE INFORMATION revolution of the sixteenth century surged ahead. Books continued to flood Europe. There were the classics, of course, and how-to books on subjects like agronomy and navigation. But most popular were the books by the new, young authors who commented on the pressing issues of the day, and no issue was more pressing than the scandalous state of the Church.

This was a rich topic with no shortage of material upon which to draw. Corruption in Rome had reached unprecedented, almost laughable levels. Everything had a price. The popes used their powers to grant dispensations, create ecclesiastic offices, levy tithes, and elevate favorites to continually replenish coffers drained by debauchery and excess. In the recent past, there was the single-minded, fiendish hedonism so casually and regularly practiced by Pope Alexander VI (r. 1493–1503) and his family, the Borgias. "The exceptional infamy that attaches to Alexander VI is largely due to the fact that he did not add hypocrisy to his other vices," observed a bishop at the time.

Born Rodrigo Borgia, Pope Alexander bought the papacy by promising one of the other candidates a high position and all the gold and silver that could be stuffed into the saddlebags of four mules if he would not pursue the office. He was described by a contemporary as "a handsome man with a pleasant look and a honeyed tongue, who lures women to love him, and attracts those on whom he casts his eyes more powerfully than a magnet draws iron." An earlier pope, Pius II, had had to admonish Rodrigo for participating in an orgy in a Sienese garden when he was a young cardinal. As pope, Alexander carried on his sexual exploits with undiminished vigor.

But rampant sensuality was only one aspect of Alexander's personality. He was also a fond parent. When Alexander's youngest son, Cesare, killed his older brother, Giovanni, in order to get ahead in the world, Alexander mourned his eldest son for six months. Then, in order to demonstrate to Cesare that the incident was forgotten, he allowed him to murder his brother-in-law, Alfonso, who was sure to object to Cesare's desire to engage in an incestuous relationship with his sister Lucrezia, a woman of singular beauty, with long golden hair. A while later Alexander had to make provision for a mysterious *infans Romanus* (Roman infant), which appeared, seemingly out of nowhere.

Between them, Alexander and Cesare played politics as though it were a macabre game of Monopoly. When France invaded Italy in 1494, Alexander wasn't above appealing to the reviled, infidel Turks for help. The sultan responded by sending forty thousand ducats to raise an army, promising an additional thirty thousand if Alexander would dispense with his brother and rival, Djem, who happened to be a hostage in Rome at the time. Djem died of a mysterious illness within the month, and Alexander collected the entire seventy thousand. When

Cesare wanted to get rid of some allies whom he suspected of duplicity, he invited four of them to his camp and had them strangled after dinner. "Never was Rome so full of criminals," moaned Cardinal Ægidius, "never was the multitude of informers and robbers so audacious... Money, power, and lust governed everything."

But it was mealtime poisoning, not strangulation, that was the Borgia specialty, although their track record was spotty. Alexander died after ingesting some poison intended for his host. Cesare, younger and stronger, only got sick. Poisoning was so common that the English Victorian wit Max Beerbohm later observed, "No Roman ever was able to say, 'I dined last night with the Borgias.'"

By the time of Miguel Serveto's boyhood in Huesca, it had become common practice for not only the pope but also cardinals and bishops to live in splendor. Often a high Church official kept a large house for himself and another for his mistress (one pope kept his mistress in the Vatican). They dressed in expensive silks and jewels and ate often and well. Delicacies such as peacock tongue were frequently on the menu, and a certain Cardinal Cornaro gave sixty-five-course dinners with each course consisting of three different dishes. Nightingales flew out of pies and naked little boys jumped out of puddings.

That all this had been able to go on for as long as it did was due in no small part to the intellectual isolation of most of the Continent. There might be rumors of excess and even anecdotal information, but without hard evidence, or the promulgation of differing views, most people were inclined to accept the status quo as inevitable.

All of this now changed. Books criticizing the Church became instant bestsellers and their authors celebrities. And the biggest celebrity of all was Desiderius Erasmus.

Erasmus (who seems to have given himself the name Desiderius, which means "desired beloved") was without question the leading literary light of his time. Born poor and illegitimate in Holland in 1466, the son of a priest and his mistress, he went on, through his books and scholarship, to become a household name, sought after by every prince in Europe. Henry VIII wrote him a long, personal letter beseeching him to come to England ("We shall regard your presence among us as the most precious possession that we have"); Francis I offered him a highly prestigious position at his new college; Charles V solicited his services as advisor. He was painted by Holbein and entertained by cardinals; Pope Leo X was his intimate friend. His correspondence reads like a Who's Who of the sixteenth century: Sir Thomas More, Pope Adrian VI, Marguerite of Navarre, the king of Poland, Cardinal Wolsey, Martin Luther—the list goes on and on.

What Erasmus had that nobody else had, at least to that degree and in print, was wit. He was the Oscar Wilde of his time. One of his most hilarious and telling satires is a skit that finds the aggressive soldier-pope Julius II, whom Erasmus had met and couldn't stand, confronting Saint Peter at the pearly gates:

Julius: Open, I say!

St. Peter: You must show your merits first...

Julius: What do you mean by merits?...

St. Peter: What did you do?

Julius: I raised the revenue. I invented new offices and sold them... I recoined the money and made a great sum that way. Nothing can be done without money... I set all the princes of Europe by the ears. I tore up treaties, and kept great armies in the field. I covered Rome with palaces... I wanted the duchy of Ferrara for a son of my own...

St. Peter: What? Popes with wives and children?

Julius: Wives? No, not wives, but why not children?...

St. Peter: Is there no way to removing a wicked pope?... Not for murder?

Julius: No, not even if it were parricide.

St. Peter: Not for fornication?

Julius: Not for incest.

St. Peter: Not for poisoning?

Julius: No, nor for sacrilege...

St. Peter: You pretend to be a Christian, you are no better than
a Turk; you think like a Turk, you are as licentious as a
Turk. If there is any difference you are worse...

Julius: Then you won't open the gates?

As lacerating as Erasmus's wit could be, he knew how to hold himself short of an outright break with Rome. He never entered into the realm of serious theological debate, never questioned the fundamental tenets of the religion. Still, his work was read everywhere, and his pleas for reform and tolerance gained favor all over Europe. One prominent Oxford bookseller in 1520 said that one-third of his sales were of books by Erasmus.

Although he worked his entire life to promote reform within the Church, through one of his works he indirectly precipitated one of the

Desiderius Erasmus of
Rotterdam

great schisms in ecclesiastic history. In 1516, Erasmus completed a new edition of the New Testament, working solely from manuscripts, revising the Greek text and offering his own Latin translation. This translation included Erasmus's comments on errors, omissions, and, most significantly, unauthorized additions in Saint Jerome's fourth-century Vulgate. Erasmus's work cast doubt on the authenticity of some extremely key passages, including 1 John 5:7, which stated, "For there are three that bear witness in Heaven, the Father, the Word, and the Holy Spirit: And these three are One." This passage was generally cited as biblical justification for the Trinity, but the original Greek manuscripts from which Erasmus worked lacked this verse entirely and so he omitted it from his translation.

Although he had intended it as a scholarly reference, because of his immense reputation Erasmus's version of the New Testament was translated into almost all the vernacular languages and read throughout the Christian world.

‡

MIGUEL SERVETO QUICKLY outgrew the educational resources available to him in a small town. When he was thirteen, his father sent him to the university in Zaragossa, the capital of Aragon, about seventy miles southwest of Villanueva de Sijena. It wasn't long after he arrived that he came to the attention of the single most important member of the faculty: Juan de Quintana.

Quintana was a man whose experiences had led him far beyond the provincialism of a regional university in Spain. He had been educated at Paris and had survived the two-decade-long process required to earn a doctorate in theology. Quintana had also traveled across Europe, only recently returning to Spain from France, and his presence at Zaragossa was a major coup for the university. He was also appointed to be a member of the Cortes, the local ruling body, and was certainly the most educated man in the province. What Quintana did not bother to mention to the authorities in theologically conservative Zaragossa was that while he was out of the country studying, he had become a humanist and an admirer of Erasmus.

Quintana latched on to Miguel Serveto. He made him his personal secretary, effectively removing him from the student body for a private course of study and exposing him to source materials that were unavailable to the rest of the university. As a result, Miguel, now fourteen, began to study not only the assigned texts but, without fanfare, the classics and the humanists as well. And, of course, since he was being encouraged to absorb as much contemporary learning as he could, Miguel also read the books of a German monk named Luther.

✝

A MORE UNLIKELY CANDIDATE for revolutionary hero status than Martin Luther would be hard to imagine. The son of peasants, Luther showed no particular ability at learning while growing up. In fact, so ignorant, superstitious, and timid was he that when a lightning bolt struck a tree near him he took it as a sign from God and hotfooted it into a monastery.

Luther took his vows seriously. He worried whether he was saying his prayers properly. He worried whether he was learning enough. He worried whether he was worthy of being God's representative. This character trait was well suited to life at the monastery. Because he worried whether he was being a good monk, Luther outmonked everyone else, spending longer hours saying his prayers, doing penance, fasting, and, most importantly, reading Scripture. "I kept the rule of my order so strictly that I may say that if ever a monk got to heaven by his monkery, it was I," he said later.

In 1510, as a reward for all that monkery, Luther was given the opportunity to visit Rome on behalf of his monastery.

This was the Renaissance, and Pope Julius II, when he was not putting on his armor and conquering Italian cities like Bologna, was in the process of making Rome a monument to himself by sponsoring vast artistic and architectural projects. All of this campaigning and art, as well as the general upkeep of the Papal States and the replacement of older cathedrals, required financing, and for years that financing had come from the pockets of the common people of Europe.

At the time, the Church had perfected a sort of spiritual point system. If a person sinned, he or she could go to purgatory. It was possible, however, by visitation to relics (contribution required) or the purchase of indulgences, to buy back one's time in this undesirable location until assured a place in heaven. Still, it was impossible to know just how many years God had assigned to any individual sinner. Since Rome held more relics in one place than all other locations combined, a sinner making a pilgrimage there had the greatest chance of avoiding posthumous unpleasantness. In Rome they had a coin paid to Judas, the touching of which reduced a stay in purgatory by fourteen hundred years. Of course, you couldn't touch the coin for free.

When Luther arrived, he went, like any tourist, to visit the sites. He saw a piece of the burning bush, the chains of Saint Paul, and the white spots on the walls where the stones had turned to snowballs when thrown at Saint Peter. He saw the scissors used by the emperor Domitian to cut Saint John's hair, and the napkin of Saint Veronica on which was imprinted the likeness of Jesus. He touched the bones and dropped coins into the appropriate receptacles, but as he wandered around the city, he couldn't help but notice how *rich* Rome was, how magnificently the members of the Church lived.

He saw the grand houses, the expensive clothes, the wine, the women, and the art on the walls. He began to wonder if all the money Germany had given to Rome for crusades and other worthy projects wasn't actually going into the pockets of the pope and the other high Church officials. Even worse, he saw the bored and mechanical way in which the priests in Rome said Mass and administered the Sacraments, and he was shocked.

The high point of a visit to Rome was the Scala Sancta, a set of twenty-eight stairs. Whoever crawled up each stair on his or her hands and knees, faithfully reciting a prayer at each step, could release a soul from purgatory right then and there, no matter how many years that soul still had left. Luther went for his grandfather. He went all the way, but then, at the very top, something happened that would soon change the world.

He wondered whether any of this worked at all.

✝

LUTHER RETURNED TO Germany and studied. He read Scripture more intensely than ever before because he thought the answers to his dilemmas could only be found there. He read so diligently that the once fastidious but nondescript monk began to be known as something of a scholar.

Here another byproduct of the information revolution came into play—the development and rapid growth of universities. While the schools in France, particularly the University of Paris, were the acknowledged leaders, princes all over Europe rushed to establish schools in their provinces to increase their influence or as a measure of their importance.

All this created an enormous need for faculty. Almost anyone who could read Latin was pressed into service. All sorts of people who had never before given a thought to teaching suddenly found themselves behind the lectern. So it was that Martin Luther became a professor of Latin in 1515 at the newly established University of Wittenberg, just in time to witness one of the biggest deals the Church had ever attempted, one that would bring down the entire system of indulgences for profit.

In 1517, Albert of Brandenburg, a prominent member of the house of Hohenzollern (the family that four centuries later was to give the world Kaiser Wilhelm II and World War I), decided that he wanted to be archbishop of Mainz. Mainz, where Gutenberg's Bible had been printed some sixty years before, was extremely prosperous, and thus there were substantial revenues associated with the bishopric. Albert had political reasons for the move as well. He already held the sees at Magdeburg and Halberstadt, and adding Mainz would certainly make him the most powerful single churchman in all of Germany.

But Albert's path to theological and secular supremacy was by no means assured. As always, the Hohenzollerns were to be contested by their archrivals, the Hapsburgs, who, in Charles V, had a powerful patron in the wings.

The way to attain the position, Albert knew, was to buy it, and what made him sure that it would be for sale was Pope Leo X. Leo, who had succeeded Julius and who has been described as "as elegant and as indolent as a Persian cat," had expensive tastes even by papal standards and viewed his election as pope in 1513 as an excellent vehicle by which to gratify them. He delighted in spending vast sums of the Church's resources on carnivals, war, gambling, and the chase. He even altered the mode of papal dress by wearing long hunting boots, making it a good deal more difficult for the devout to kiss his toe.

Born Giovanni de' Medici, Leo also had the Medicis' great appreciation of the arts, and he further depleted Rome's treasury by spending large sums subsidizing great masters like Raphael. Although museum directors today may be thrilled by the resulting output, after only four years under Leo's administration, Rome was going broke.

At the moment that Albert of Brandenburg decided to become archbishop of Mainz, Leo was in even more dire need of funds than usual. To assure his legacy, he was very anxious to complete a huge project commenced by Julius, to whom he was always being unfavorably—and, he thought, unfairly—compared.

The old wooden basilica of Saint Peter's, constructed in the age of Constantine, was beyond repair, and Julius had cajoled and bullied the consistory into approving the construction of a dome as large as a football field over the remains of the apostles Peter and Paul. (Julius had cajoled and bullied Michelangelo into painting the ceiling of the Sistine Chapel just a year or two earlier.) Just when the piers had been laid, Julius's long-standing case of syphilis finally caught up with him. (For appearance's sake, it was let out that he died of fever, a catch-all illness that served to explain any number of fatalities. Pope Alexander VI, the one who had mistakenly ingested poison, was said to have died of a fever too.) With Julius dead, work on the new Saint Peter's had then lagged to the point where weeds had begun to sprout from the pillars. Unless the basilica could be completed, the site would be a constant reminder of Leo's financial, and perhaps spiritual, mismanagement to everyone who passed by.

Leo, Albert knew, would be ready to deal.

And so he did, the two coming to an arrangement worthy of a 1980s-vintage leveraged buyout. Leo, unable to resist the opportunity to solve his financial problems in one stroke, offered the archbishopric of Mainz to Albert for ten thousand ducats, under ordinary circumstances an outlandish sum. Albert, of course, agreed. But even he did not have that kind of cash on hand, and since Leo demanded the entire ten thousand up front, it was further agreed that Albert would seek to borrow the money from the great Fugger banking house in Augsburg. Given the quality of the participants, the Fuggers were happy to underwrite the deal. They put up the entire amount, which would be repaid by the new archbishop.

In order to give Albert the means with which to repay the Fuggers, the pope agreed to float an unprecedented public offering on Albert's behalf. Leo gave Albert the right to sell indulgences for eight years. One half of the proceeds would go toward retiring Albert's debt; the other half would be kicked back to Rome's capital budget, earmarked for the dormant construction site at Saint Peter's.

Indulgences were a sort of common stock investment in the afterworld, certificates signed by the pope and then sold to the faithful, guaranteeing remission of the sins of the purchasers. Even more than the visiting of relics, indulgences had become the principal fundraising tool of the Church. So many were sold that it became unwieldy for scribes to write them out by hand. In a great historical irony, among the first documents produced with movable type, predating Gutenberg's Bible by two years, was a stack of indulgences. The printed indulgences of 1453, the earliest known example of job printing, had blanks left where the name of the purchaser and the amount of his contribution could be filled in.

For Albert's deal, since there was a lot of money at stake and indulgences were obviously nothing new, Leo made this particular indulgence something really special. Purchasers of Albert's papal bull would enjoy a plenary and perfect remission of *all* their sins. They would be restored to the state of innocence that they enjoyed at baptism and would be relieved of the pains of purgatory. Not only did it cleanse a purchaser of past sins, it applied to the future as well. There was no set price, but it was understood that a sweeping indulgence of this sort shouldn't come cheap. Now, even peasants could return to innocence by giving over their meager life savings to the Church.

To further ensure the success of the offering, Leo dispatched his crack indulgence broker, a Dominican friar named Johann Tetzel, to Germany. Tetzel would arrive in each small town riding in a cart pulled by two horses, with a very large cross set right in the middle. The local dignitaries would meet him at the city gate and lead him through the streets. When the crowds had gathered, Tetzel made his pitch. According to William Robertson in his classic work, *The History of the Reign of the Emperor Charles V*, it went something like this:

> The souls confined in purgatory, for whose redemption indulgences are purchased, as soon as the money tinkles in the chest, instantly escape from that place of torment, and ascend into heaven ... even if one should violate (which was impossible) the Mother of God, the person [would] be freed both from punishment and guilt. This was the unspeakable gift of God, in order to reconcile men to himself. The cross erected by the preachers of indulgences, was as efficacious as the cross

of Christ itself. Lo! The heavens are open: if you enter not now, when will you enter? For twelve pence you may redeem the soul of your father out of purgatory; and are you so un-grateful, that you will not rescue your parent from torment? If you had but one coat, you ought to strip yourself instantly, and sell it, in order to purchase such benefits.

Tetzel conveniently left out the fact that half the money was going to bankers to pay off Albert's debt.

As Tetzel was making the rounds through Germany, he came to the outskirts of Wittenberg. He wasn't allowed into Wittenberg because the local prince, Frederick the Wise, would not allow it. Frederick had been persuaded by Luther that a piece of paper couldn't get you into heaven, and besides, he didn't particularly care for Albert. So Tetzel went right up to the border so that any of the citizens of the town, many of whom were members of Luther's flock, could cross over and buy from him, which they did, in droves.

Some then took their certificate and showed it to Luther.

Luther was appalled. He wrote up a placard in Latin, listing ninety-five objections to the current practices of the Church. As was the custom at the time, he nailed his placard to the door of the local church. "Indulgences are positively harmful to the recipient because they impede salvation by diverting charity and inducing a false sense of security," he wrote in the *Ninety-Five Theses.*

When it came to purgatory itself, Luther was even more persuasive:

Therefore I claim that the pope has no jurisdiction over pur-gatory...If the pope does have the power to release anyone from purgatory, why in the name of love does he not abolish purgatory by letting everyone out? If for the sake of miserable money he released uncounted souls, why should he not for the sake of most holy love empty the place?

Luther intended these remarks for an audience of scholars and as a basis for theologic debate only. They were never intended for general distribution. He did, however, send a copy to Albert (now Albert of Mainz), along with an explanatory letter, both of which Albert immediately forwarded to Rome. The genial Leo, in one of the great misreadings of events in history, is reputed to have said, "Luther is a drunken German. He will feel differently when he is sober."

From there, the whole affair might simply have blown over. But then something happened, something that would not have been possible fifty years earlier, or for any of the thousand years that the Church had held total sway over the spiritual life of Europe. A small Wittenberg press run by an insignificant printer named Hans Lufft took Luther's *Ninety-Five Theses* and had them printed, bound, and distributed. The book was even translated from Latin into German so that the common people could read and understand what Luther had written.

The books sold out and the public clamored for more. The Vatican, now taking "the drunken German" more seriously, issued a ban prohibiting Luther from preaching. Luther responded by writing out his sermons, including one that discussed what was wrong with the ban.

As Luther kept writing, Lufft kept printing. Riding the wave of his star author's popularity, Hans Lufft became one of the most important publishers in Germany. Other printers soon joined in. Johann Froben, Erasmus's printer in Basel, produced a single volume of Luther's work that contained the *Ninety-Five Theses, Resolutions, Answer to Prierias, Sermon on Penitence,* and *Sermon on the Eucharist* and wrote to the author that nothing he had ever printed had sold out so quickly. Six hundred were shipped to France and Spain, and others went to England. Ulrich Zwingli, who by now was running his own reform operation in Zurich, special-ordered several hundred copies and then sent out riders on horseback to distribute them throughout the countryside. Copies of Luther's writings made it to Italy, even to Rome itself.

Rome upped the stakes by excommunicating Luther, but it no

longer mattered. Once he had attained bestseller status, Luther's work was even more in demand. (That he publicly burned the bull that announced his excommunication did nothing to diminish his appeal.)

In 1520, this son of a peasant, a man who had been superstitious and illiterate into young adulthood, who had never been out of Germany except for one brief visit to Rome, stood at the Diet of Worms in front of Emperor Charles V, arguably the most powerful man in the world, and was told to recant. But by then Luther had with him his books, the power of the printed word, and, with it, the support of the people.

Martin Luther refused to recant. "Here I stand," he said.

It was the end of the papal bull market and the beginning of the Reformation. ‡

WHEN JUAN DE QUINTANA left Zaragossa for the larger,
more prestigious University of Barcelona, Miguel Serveto went
along with him. Soon afterward, however, in 1527 when Miguel
was sixteen, his father, now more convinced than ever that his
extraordinarily talented eldest son should have the best education possible, proposed that he be sent to study at the University of Toulouse,
one of the preeminent schools of law in Europe. Toulouse was close by,
as close as Barcelona to the east, only about one hundred miles north
of Huesca—although you did have to cross the Pyrenees. Here, the
elder Serveto felt, Miguel could not only acquire a prestigious degree
but also be safe from the forces of blasphemy that were now shaking
the Continent. Toulouse was known as a center of pious orthodoxy. The
city had even constructed a special iron cage attached to a wooden
platform at the river to be used for drowning those who deviated in
any way from canon law. A reformer later wrote:

> [Toulouse] was very superstitious, full of relics and other in-
> struments of idolatry, so that it was sufficient to be con-
> demned as a heretic if one did not take off his hat before an
> image or did not bend his knee at the sound of the bell call-
> ing for the Ave Maria, or if one tasted a single morsel of meat
> on a prohibited day. And there was no one who had delight
> in languages or letters who would not be watched and con-
> sidered suspected of heresy.

Wanting his protégé to get a more cosmopolitan view of the world, as well as the legal training that he himself lacked, Quintana granted Miguel two years' leave to study at the university.

What neither Anthon Serveto nor, evidently, Quintana knew was that unlike the city of Toulouse, the University of Toulouse had become a hotbed of radicalism. With ten thousand of the brightest students from across Europe and six hundred of the best lecturers, it was impossible for the university to be immune from the changes that Luther and his followers had precipitated. In many ways, the split at Toulouse between a conservative populace and insurgent professors epitomized the situation in France as a whole. Throughout the country, especially in Paris, the Church was tenaciously trying to maintain tradition—and the power of tradition—and the reformers were trying to break it down. In the middle, a balance of power unto himself, tilting sometimes this way and sometimes that, was the dashing, virile Francis I.

‡

FRANCIS HAD ASCENDED the throne of France in 1515 at the age of twenty-one. He enjoyed the hunt, outdoors and in, loved art, beauty, wine, riding, and, exhibiting a trait not uncommon in kings, having his own way. His defining moment had come in 1526, when, having fallen in battle in Italy against Charles V, he was taken prisoner and confined ignominiously in a tiny, marginally furnished, very un-Francislike room in an old castle in Madrid. Under this coercion he signed the Treaty of Madrid, agreeing to all of Charles's terms, including the surrender of Burgundy and Flanders. He was returned by barge to the French border, where he met his two sons, who, by the same treaty, had been consigned to Charles as hostages to ensure Francis's good faith. The boys, eight and seven, just over the measles, surrounded by military guard, about to be deprived of family, love, and schooling, were embraced by their father. Then Francis got off the boat, climbed onto his horse, yelled, "I am king again!" and proceeded to renege on the whole agreement. He rode off to his new château to meet his mother, sister, and mistress, leaving his two small sons to take his place in the tiny room in the old castle. It would be four years before the children were ransomed and returned to France.

Francis was not a deeply religious man himself, but he came to have an acute understanding of the manner in which religion could be manipulated to further political ends. With regard to the troublesome ideas of the new reformers, Francis was of two minds. On the one hand, Luther and his fellow reformers were causing the emperor a lot of trouble, and Francis was very much in favor of anything that caused Charles a lot of trouble. Accordingly, he made overtures to the German Lutheran princes and reformers and supported their efforts abroad whenever he felt it might needle Charles.

But reform had an uncomfortable way of spreading beyond borders, possibly even into France itself. As a result of an old agreement with Leo, Francis was in the unique position of being able to appoint the clergy in his own country. He had acquired this privilege in 1516

Francis I

after invading Milan and forcing the pope's hand militarily, much as Charles would force a later pope, Clement VII, to make him emperor. (Francis, ever the esthete, took both Leonardo da Vinci and the *Mona Lisa* home as spoils of war.)

The agreement with Leo made for an uneasy French alliance of church and state. While it was true that the clergy were now dependent upon their king and not their pope for their livelihood and advancement, it was also true that it would be this same clergy who would eventually loan Francis the 1,300,000 livres he needed to ransom his sons back from Charles. To the church in France, led by the theological faculty at the University of Paris, commonly known as the Sorbonne, the reform movement was heresy.

The reformers, however, were not without resources. They had their own champion in the person of Marguerite d'Angoulême, also known as Marguerite of Navarre, the king's older sister.

Marguerite d'Angoulême, sister of Francis I

Marguerite was a twentieth-century feminist trapped in the prejudice and sexual politics of the sixteenth. Intelligent, passionate, and yearning, she wrote poetry and a novel about sexual politics, studied Latin, Greek, Spanish, and Italian, and even mastered a smattering of Hebrew. She adored her brother and forgave all his transgressions. It was Marguerite who made the arduous journey to nurse Francis when he fell ill in Madrid, who played hostess to his vast, traveling court (when the king went hunting in Bordeaux, it took 22,500 horses and mules to move everybody in his entourage), who wrote him long, fervent letters in which she poured out all of her devotion whenever he was away.

But Marguerite's position as a member of the royal family sometimes made her a pawn in Francis's political machinations. Royal women existed to be married off for national gain, either to cement an alliance or to consolidate property. Only a very few were clever enough to get out of it.

Henry VIII's sister, Mary Tudor, was one of them. In 1514, when Henry double-crossed Ferdinand and made his deal with Francis's predecessor, Louis XII, he instructed Mary to marry Louis because Louis's wife had died without leaving him an heir. Louis was in his fifties, "bent over, sagging, thin and worn." He also had gout. Mary, on the other hand, was just eighteen, considered one of the most stunning women in Europe, and desperately in love with the manly Duke of Suffolk. She agreed to marry Louis if Henry would allow her then to marry whomever she wanted after Louis died, which promised to be shortly.

So Mary came to France and married the disgusting Louis. This was not merely a marriage of convenience. She was expected to provide an heir. After their first night together, Mary's legendary good looks seemed to have had some effect. Louis emerged from the nuptial bedchamber "very jovial and merry and in love," modestly proclaiming that "he had performed marvels." But the marvels didn't take, and soon Louis began to show signs of "wear and tear." He died a few months later, on New Year's Day, apparently still trying, but there was no heir.

But what to do with Mary? As Louis's widow she now had a claim on the French throne, or at least the French treasury. Francis, who had been the dauphin and was now the king, had been lusting after Mary since she had set foot in France. He graciously offered to solve this potential problem by divorcing his current wife, Claude, and marrying Mary instead. But Mary, having already sacrificed herself to one royal French marriage, had no intention of doing so again. To discourage Francis, she confessed her love for Suffolk, to the point of telling him the details of their secret love code. Once he realized that he could not procure her for himself, Francis was only too happy to help Mary marry Suffolk, since that would take her out of the marriage alliance business altogether and protect Francis's interests. So he arranged for Mary and Suffolk to marry secretly in Paris, promising to smooth things over with Henry.

But Henry would not be smoothed. As it turned out, he had been insincere. (Henry was often insincere.) He hadn't meant what he said about Mary marrying whomever she wanted after Louis. In fact, Henry wanted to *behead* Suffolk.

So Mary took matters into her own hands. She filched the famous "Mirror of Naples," a huge diamond on a pendant and one of the most prized heirlooms of France, out of her widow-of-Louis jewelry box, then smuggled it, along with some pearls and all of her Louis XII gold plate dining room service, to England by stuffing everything into donkey packs. Then she and Suffolk wrote a long apologetic note to Henry, telling him how sorry they were, and how they couldn't help it, and how they remained his loyal servants, and wouldn't he please forgive them, etc., etc., and, by the way, here was a little something to ease the pain.

When the theft was discovered, Francis was furious and demanded the return of the diamond, but it was too late. The Mirror of Naples appeased Henry enough that he allowed Mary and Suffolk to return to England with both of their heads still attached, although they were banished from London and forced to retire to an out-of-the-way spot in the countryside. The closest Mary would get to a throne again was the aborted nine-day rule of her granddaughter, Lady Jane Grey.

✣

MARGUERITE, IN MUCH THE same position as Mary, had a far closer relationship with her brother and was willing, albeit grudgingly, to marry anyone Francis thought would further his interests. Her first husband, the Duke of Alençon, had filed lawsuits against Francis; these were dropped with the marriage. In 1525, he fled the battle in which Francis was captured and died a coward. Her second husband, Henri d'Albret, king of Navarre, was eleven years her junior and not particularly happy about having been wed to someone he considered to be middle-aged.

Marguerite's spirit and intelligence only made the limitations of her marriages worse, but even so, she was unwilling to compromise her honor. She was pursued by a lover, Guillaume Gouffier, who went by the name of Bonnivet; he tried to coax her into adultery and, when that failed, sneaked into her bedroom one night to take advantage of her, but she fought him off, forcing him to retreat, scratched and bitten, to his own bedroom. She later had her revenge by writing down the whole incident, which was published as one of the stories in her roman à clef, the *Heptameron.*

Passionate and frustrated, she turned to the only outlet available to her—religion. Not the old, corrupt religion, but the new, more spiritual religion, sparked by the cultured French humanist Jacques Lefèvre d'Étaples and the revolutionary Martin Luther, and embodied by the reformist Cercle de Meaux.

Meaux was a diocese just east of Paris. In 1521, a year after Luther's pronouncement at Worms, the bishop of Meaux, Guillaume Briçonnet, a deeply devout, spiritual, yet practical man, became upset with the ignorance and superstition being heaped on his flock by the local Franciscans and invited a group of reform-minded evangelicals to the diocese to help sort the matter out. Lefèvre was one who came to lend a hand, as were Gérard Roussel and Guillaume Farel. They divided the countryside into sections and went around preaching a more enlightened Christianity. These men became known as the Cercle de Meaux.

Briçonnet was just what Marguerite was looking for, someone to give her life purpose and structure. She approved of his goal of gradual, gentle reform, and she struck up a correspondence with him. He, for his part, introduced her to the writings and ideas of Lefèvre and Luther and urged her to use her influence with her brother to further the cause. Marguerite became an immediate convert and, because of her celebrity, a leader and advocate of reform in France.

Marguerite was attracted to the intellectuals, and the intellectuals were attracted to Marguerite. The universities became the prime breeding ground of dissent in France. The University of Toulouse in particular was soon to receive an extra jolt. It was in January 1527 that Marguerite married Henri d'Albret, thus becoming queen of Navarre, at least that part of Navarre north of the Pyrenees. With the opportunity to set up a court of her own in order to provide a safe haven for those who shared her views, she chose Nérac, less than seventy miles west of Toulouse. The intellectual ferment quickly radiated into the surrounding French provinces.

A few months later, Miguel Serveto arrived at Toulouse.

‡

THE UNIVERSITY WAS structured according to the scholastic divisions of law, theology, medicine, and philosophy. Theology, as always, was dominant, and since civil law was to a great degree controlled by ecclesiastic doctrine, the law faculty was more an offshoot than a separate entity. The university was divided in another way as well—students were grouped by nationality, at least in their living arrangements. The Spaniards were all together, and it was the first time that Miguel Serveto felt the force of the prejudice against his country.

But it was also a period of great excitement at the university, and the lure of humanism and the revolution of reform crossed all national and ethnic boundaries. A student signaled his desire to be a part of this new movement by following the fashion of scholars and humanists and taking a Latin name. It was here, at Toulouse, that Miguel Serveto became Michael Servetus.

Although the students accepted the required curriculum, in many ways they created a curriculum of their own. From all over Europe they brought with them the new subversive literature, books like *Loci Communes*, by Luther protégé Philip Melanchthon, which passed the ideas of sin, gospel, and justification through a reformist filter and introduced the highly controversial notion of predestination. But the most subversive book that they read—a book that, if a student were caught with it, could lead to imprisonment or a terrible death—was the Bible.

Prohibiting access to the Bible had for more than a thousand years been the primary instrument of Church control. Only a select few were allowed to read the Scriptures and determine their meaning. The Church had used this power to further its own position with kings and commoners alike. Alternate interpretations might undermine Rome's iron grip.

But Erasmus's New Testament and the later, much more comprehensive *Biblia Polyglotta Compluti*, or Complutensian Polyglot Bible, changed all that. The Complutensian Polyglot was edited by the influential Spanish humanist Cardinal Ximenes and was published with the approval of the Vatican in 1522. It contained the entire Bible in the original Hebrew and Greek with the Latin Vulgate translation running in a parallel column throughout. Leo X so trusted Ximenes, was so confident that this new edition would support rather than undermine the authority of Rome, that he let Ximenes use the Vatican's own manuscripts. But Ximenes, who employed nine linguists, including three baptized Jews, to ensure authenticity, cared about scholarship, not politics.

Copies of both Erasmus's translation and the Complutensian Polyglot were passed secretly hand to hand, and reading the Bible became a constant and regular part of the students' lives. They ignored the threat of being burned at the stake or drowned in the river and did what university students always do—they stayed up late at night debating the philosophical and political implications of what they had read. And to many of them, including Servetus, the implications were that Rome had corrupted both the text of the Bible and the fundamental tenets of Christianity, and there could be no truth in Christianity until this corruption was eliminated.

Servetus was in a unique position because he read not only Greek but also Hebrew, which meant that he could read the full text of the Complutensian Polyglot in the original languages and see the differences between the ancient passages and the Vulgate translation. But Servetus's extraordinary scholarship took him one step further. He added Arabic to his repertoire so that he could read the Koran as well. He was still only seventeen years old.

From these studies, Servetus concluded that only a return to classic biblical scholarship could save the religion. While this was further than Luther had ever gone, it was not a unique point of view. Had Servetus stopped there, he might have blended in with other reformers and become an influential leader in the new movement. But Servetus, the minority student, always the outsider, would never be content to be a part of a greater whole.

‡

IN 1529, HIS TWO-YEAR LEAVE expired, Servetus left Toulouse to return to the service of Juan de Quintana. Quintana had had a very good two years. He was now confessor to Charles V and a member of the emperor's inner circle.

After a rocky beginning in Spain (the populace had not been pleased that Ferdinand had been succeeded by a short, pale, extremely homely nineteen-year-old Belgian who couldn't speak the language),

Charles was finally gaining acceptance. It hadn't hurt that Charles's troops had captured Francis in Italy—nobody was more surprised about that than Charles, who hadn't actually ordered his army to fight, the initiative, in this case, coming from one of his pluckier generals—but he'd made the most of it. He was now ready for the big prize.

For some years, Charles had wanted the official blessing of the pope for his election as emperor, thereby isolating Francis, consolidating his holdings, and ensuring the legal ascension of his line to the same title. Unfortunately, at that moment the somewhat fickle new pope, Clement VII, was more favorably disposed toward Francis, and it looked like Clement was going to need some convincing. When the pope entered into a military alliance with Francis, Charles, drawing on troops from Spain and Germany, invaded Italy and headed for Rome.

The wealth of the Catholic Church sat waiting in the largely undefended holy city, and the army, an unpaid and hungry rabble, itched

Charles V at sixteen, before his portraits began to be idealized

to get at it. When Charles tried to hold them back while negotiating terms with Clement, they mutinied and attacked against his orders.

On May 6, 1527, Charles's soldiers broke through Rome's tattered defenses, overran the city, and began an orgy of looting, rape, and murder. Members of the Church were singled out for particular brutality. Cardinals and other wealthy members of the Curia were tortured, held for ransom, then slaughtered. Nuns were violated in the streets or sold to brothels. The Tiber was choked with corpses. Anything the soldiers couldn't use, they burned. Every house in Rome was plundered, and the Vatican was used as a stable.

The imperial troops remained in Rome for nine months, leaving only when the food supply ran out and plague appeared. In their wake, they left over ten thousand dead and walked off with ransom payments many times larger than those that would have been demanded for a king.

The sack of Rome turned out to have far more significance than its military or even social consequences. It was an event that shook the Catholic Church to its moral foundations. Many of the most pious blamed the disaster not on Charles, but rather on the corruption that had overrun Catholicism. This was the wrath of God, Sodom and Gomorrah revisited.

Clement himself was spared the worst of it. He fled through a secret passage in Castel Sant'Angelo to safety outside the city but was eventually captured by Charles and held prisoner. Charles soon realized that an imprisoned, emasculated pope was not doing him much good, so he proposed a deal. After much harrumphing and six months in captivity, Clement saw his way to agreeing to a coronation. As Quintana's private secretary, Michael Servetus received one of the prized invitations to the event.

Rome being out of the question, the coronation was held in Bologna on February 24, 1530, the largest, grandest, most lavish affair of its time, a kind of inaugural ball, millennium party, and royal wed-

ding all rolled into one. There was a huge parade through the city.
Arches with golden inscriptions had been erected on every corner, and
marble statues of lions and eagles stood along the parade route. The
lions had red wine gushing from their mouths, the eagles white. One
hundred thousand people crowded the streets and rooftops, hung out
of windows, and stood on each other's shoulders, all to get a glimpse
of the pope and Charles. Before them came musicians, soldiers, princes,
cardinals, and dignitaries from across Europe, all dressed in flowing
finery. The pope, wearing a triple gold crown, was carried from his
palace to the Church of Saint Petronius in a golden chair under a

An 1875 representation of the crowd at the coronation
of Charles V at Bologna drinking white wine poured
from the statue of an eagle

VIL A INTER MEDIOS LEONES   INVALBV ETRVBRVM FVNDI

golden canopy. When the pope arrived at the church, Charles kissed his foot and begged to be received as his son.

Servetus, just eighteen, fresh from his reform-minded ivory tower, found this profligacy disgusting, epitomizing everything he had come to believe was the corruption that had overcome his Church. He wrote later:

> The Pope dares not touch his feet to the earth lest his holiness be defiled. He has himself borne upon the shoulders of men and adored as a God upon earth. Since the foundation of the world, no one has ever dared try anything more wicked. I have seen with my own eyes how the Pope was carried with pomp on the shoulders of princes, making threatening crosses with his hand, and adored in the open squares by people on bended knee. All those who managed to kiss his feet or his sandals deemed themselves happy beyond the others and pro-claimed to have obtained the greatest indulgences and that for this the punishments of hell had been remitted for many years. Oh, the most evil of the beasts, harlots most shameless.

This coronation was to be the turning point in Servetus's life. After witnessing this spectacle, he abruptly resigned from Quintana's service. But he'd seen too much to go tamely back to school and instead went off in search of the frontline of reform. Any remaining moderation he felt had been excised by the opulence and hypocrisy in Bologna, and his determination to lead a rebirth of Christianity would stay with him the rest of his life—and be the cause of his death. ‡

CHAPTER FOUR

THE REFORMATION, WHICH had begun slightly over a decade before with Luther's small act of defiance, had by this time spilled out of Wittenberg into nearly every corner of Europe. From Poland to Spain, the undercurrents of dissatisfaction with the established order coalesced around the new doctrine. The most receptive audience, however, located in a place where reform wasn't simply preached surreptitiously in isolated corners but actively—and sometimes violently—put into practice, turned out to be right next door, in Switzerland.

Then, as now, Switzerland was a confederacy of cantons (essentially city-states)—with German spoken in some and French in others—except that in the early sixteenth century their alliance was a good deal more tenuous than it is today. The Swiss confederation had been created in 1291 when three German-speaking communities near Lake Lucerne entered into an agreement—a "Perpetual Covenant," they called it—dedicated not so much to absolute independence as to resistance to absentee rule. By 1513, the confederacy had grown from three cantons to thirteen. Allied with but not exactly part of this arrangement were French-speaking Lausanne and Geneva.

These communities were still dedicated only to resisting Hapsburg or French domination, and whenever the threat from these two giants receded, the cantons amused themselves by creating flimsy alliances and then engaging in treachery or outright war with one another. The Swiss, as they soon discovered, were very good at war. Their merce-

naries—the sole national export, if it could be called that—found themselves in high demand for their stoicism, tenacity, and willingness to
fight with equal ferocity on either side of a conflict, depending on who
was willing to pay them more at any particular time. Pope Julius II used
them to great advantage in protecting Italy from the French; Francis
used them to equal advantage in fighting Julius's successor, Leo; and
Charles used them whenever he had a small problem anywhere in his
empire, which was just about all the time. "Their unity, and the glory
of their armies, have made famous the name of this so savage and barbarous nation," a contemporary observed. These Swiss were a far cry
from the bankers and watchmakers of the current day.

There was one exception, Basel, which had come into the group
late, about 1500. Basel took the rest of boorish, savage, and barbarous
Switzerland and gave it class. That was because Basel, rich and bour-
geois, had fallen early under the spell of humanism and had become
renowned throughout Europe as a great center of learning.

For more than a century, Basel had attracted the best scholars—Italians, Germans, and, after the fall of Constantinople, Greeks. One of
these wandering intellectuals, an Italian with a mouthful of a name,
Eneo Silvio Piccolomini, came for a visit in the 1430s and ended up
staying ten years. When he got a better job, he shortened his name to
the considerably more manageable Pope Pius II.

This was the same Pope Pius who had made Johannus Bessarion a
cardinal for bringing all of those manuscripts to Venice from Constantinople. Unlike many of the dilettante academics of the time, Pope Pius
was the real thing, a man who delighted in learning, and he retained
an affection for Basel even after he was ensconced in Rome. In 1459,
he authorized the foundation of a university in Basel that was openly
and unabashedly devoted to a humanist course of study.

Hundreds of Europe's most luminous scholars touched base at one
time or another at the University of Basel. Even that giant of giants,
Desiderius Erasmus, who had all the world to choose from, decided on

Basel as the place to research, write, and publish his groundbreaking translation of the New Testament. When he arrived, he was given as an assistant the chief preacher at the cathedral of Basel, a sallow, humorless but very able priest named Johann Hausschein.

The presence of the university had lured the printing business to Basel. The most prestigious printer in the world at the time, Johann Froben—a man who had had the foresight to publish both Erasmus and Luther—had set up shop in the city. Froben was the opposite of Aldus. Rather than turn out pages almost before a writer could finish them, he worked slowly, nurturing his authors and helping them over the rough spots. He even paid advances against royalties when it was clearly understood that sometimes there would be no royalties. Froben, Erasmus wrote, was someone "with whom you could throw dice in the dark."

From Basel's books and Basel's university the rest of the Swiss confederacy learned about humanism and reformation. The city was like a softly glowing star attracting energy and then sending it out again, gently but persistently until its warmth reached the uppermost reaches of the Alps.

It was to that Basel that Michael Servetus headed.

✢

THE BASEL AT WHICH he arrived, however, had changed considerably from the humanist paradise of the Erasmian days. The Reformation had not come gently to Switzerland, and even its most enlightened city had felt the sting. The biggest change was in Erasmus's old sour-faced assistant, Johann Hausschein.

Hausschein had undergone a complete transformation—he was not even Hausschein anymore. He had Latinized his name, which meant "house light," to the literally translated but significantly more impressive-sounding Johannes Oecolampadius. Emulating Luther, in

1528 he, also, had gotten married. (Erasmus, with great surprise, noted, "A few days ago Oecolampadius married a girl who is not bad looking.")

The new name and new wife were just the start. When the Basel town council passed an edict advocating freedom of worship, it was Oecolampadius, abandoning humanism for the very type of partisan zealotry that Erasmus abhorred, who led the protests. On February 8, 1529, a year before the coronation of Charles V in Bologna, eight hundred men, urged on by their new reform leader, rose before dawn and stood in the Basel marketplace demanding the end of Mass, the expulsion of Catholics from the government, and a general reworking of the town constitution. By evening, they had armed themselves and taken over the marketplace. The next day, the mob had grown to thousands and soon did what mobs will do. They ran through the streets, smashing every Catholic image they could find and laying waste to the city's churches.

"The smiths and workmen removed the pictures from the churches . . . not a statue was left either in the churches, or the vestibules, or the porches, or the monasteries," wrote Erasmus, describing the carnage. "The frescoes were obliterated by means of a coating of lime. Whatever would burn was thrown into the fire, and the rest was pounded into fragments. Nothing was spared for love or money."

By the end of the day, Basel was a Protestant city, and Oecolampadius was its most powerful citizen. Repulsed, Erasmus and nearly every other humanist professor at the university packed up and left town. A year later, to repressive, postrevolutionary Basel, now the intellectual center of Swiss Reformation, Michael Servetus came, eager to make a revolution of his own.

When he got to town, Servetus went straight to Oecolampadius's home, where he learned that Erasmus was gone but was himself invited to remain as a guest. While it was not at all uncommon for reform leaders to put up refugees personally, it is not hard to imagine Oecolampadius's reaction when the young, brilliant, highly charged scholar, fresh from a key assignment at Charles V's own court, appeared at his door. A more prized recruit would be hard to envision. He introduced Servetus to every important reform leader in the area and trumpeted the young man's virtues.

Rather than the acolyte Oecolampadius was expecting, however, someone who could be a strong right arm against the forces of reaction, here instead was a domineering, self-assured teenager who had no intention of being an appendage to anyone. He lectured his host on his shortcomings, insisting that Oecolampadius and the reformers had not gone nearly far enough. Without a willingness to attack the fundamental precepts of Catholic dogma, Servetus thundered, no meaningful reform was imaginable—there could be no possible restoration of the simpler, more generous Christianity propounded by Jesus himself. Servetus even came with his own battle plan for purging Christianity of Roman corruption. Everything, he insisted, came back to the Trinity.

‡

THE CONCEPT OF THE TRINITY arose out of the First Council of Nicaea, convened by Emperor Constantine the Great in 325 to deal with the divisiveness that had erupted from differences in interpretation as to the nature of God and the divinity of Christ. Constantine, the first Roman emperor to himself embrace Christianity, had just finished defeating his rival Licinius and uniting what was left of the Roman Empire, and now he wanted to unite the religion as well. There was a bishop named Arius, a Libyan, who was preaching that while God, the Father, was timeless, infinite, and divine, Jesus, the Son, was created by God and subordinate to the Father, and therefore not divine, or at least not as divine as the Father.

For the Church hierarchy the problem with this interpretation—one that was to plague Christianity for more than a millennium—was that if Jesus was concluded to be less than divine, he might have been simply a man made divine through faith and acts. And if *that* were true, might not that same potential be available to all men? And if *that* were so, how could the Church hold itself to be the irreplaceable intermediary between man and God, a position from which, even back in the fourth century, it derived its enormous political power?

Obviously, given these stakes, the teachings of Arius would not do. Constantine, as a recent convert, was all too amenable to the entreaties of Pope Sylvester I and other Church elders that he use his great might and prestige to help find a solution. So in late spring of 325, at Nicaea, Constantine convened the First Ecumenical Council of the Catholic Church.

The opening ceremonies were held in the central hall of the imperial palace. Constantine waited until all the bishops had entered, then, wearing a gold crown and a robe covered in jewels, strode in and took his place on a golden throne. Only after he was in his seat were the bishops allowed to sit as well. There were over three hundred of them, among them Arius himself, as well as thousands of priests, deacons, and acolytes.

The wrangling began almost immediately and went on for weeks. Constantine, way out of his depth with such esoteric ecclesiastical doctrine, didn't say much and soon stopped attending altogether. He continued, however, to provide palatial accommodations and sumptuous repasts for his guests.

The bishops wrestled with the problem of finding a means to reconcile what seemed to be three separate and distinct definitions. From the Hebrew Scriptures and the teachings of Jesus, God was one, the omnipotent and omnipresent Father, limitless, timeless, and immutable. Christ, on the other hand, seemed to be both God and man, both Son of God and God himself. Then there was God who was present in all men.

The debate raged on until, finally, the council came up with this:

We believe in one God the Father Almighty, Maker of all things visible and invisible; and in one Lord Jesus Christ, the only begotten of the Father, that is, of the substance of the Father, God of God, light of light, true God of true God, begotten not made, of the same substance with the Father, through whom all things were made both in heaven and on earth; who for us men and our salvation descended, was incarnate, and was made man, suffered and rose again the third day, ascended into heaven and cometh to judge the living and the dead. And in the Holy Ghost.

Those who say: There was a time when He was not, and He was not before He was begotten; and that He was made out of nothing; or who maintain that He is of another hypostasis or another substance [than the Father], or that the Son of God is created, or mutable, or subject to change, [them] the Catholic Church anathematizes.

From that day forward, then, God was to be a unity of three entities: Father, Son, and Holy Spirit. All were equally God, and each shared in the divine attributes of ultimacy, eternity, and changelessness; yet they were distinguishable in their relation to one another and in their roles within earthly life and destiny. The Father (God as both the Christian and Semitic religions knew Him) remained largely the same. Jesus, however, became more than a prophet adopted by God—he became the Son of God in a unique sense. He was God's Word (*Logos*) made flesh, divinity incarnate in a human. Then there was the third aspect, the Holy Spirit, from which believers received their faith, their confidence in the truth of that faith, and their holiness, and without which the sacraments of baptism and the Eucharist had no meaning.

In the end, only two bishops refused to go along with the new definition. They were anathematized and banished. Arius's works were then burned, and he was exiled to Illyria, site of present-day Albania, as lacking in charm then as it is now. To close the council, Constantine celebrated the twentieth anniversary of his rule and invited the bishops to a huge feast, at the end of which he bestowed opulent parting gifts on each of them.

Despite the council's edict, designated as the Nicene Creed, it remained difficult for the Church, even on pain of heresy, to convince the faithful to embrace the new doctrine, which many found incomprehensible. Saint Jerome's inclusion of the Trinitarian passage in 1 John of the Vulgate Bible did not wipe away the doubts. The Trinity continued to be a hard theological sell until, in his great work *De trinitatis* (*On the Trinity*), Saint Augustine provided an effective logical underpinning to the concept by lucid analogies to human experience, using such tripartite combinations as memory, understanding, and will. From there, the Trinity became accepted as the absolute cornerstone of the Christian experience. Antitrinitarian movements continued to spring up periodically over the centuries, but each was brutally suppressed, its proponents usually tortured and then executed as heretics.

Servetus, whose biblical scholarship even at nineteen was colossal, knew that nothing of the Nicene Creed was stated or even hinted at in the Scriptures, which he had read in the original Hebrew and Greek. While studying the Bible at Toulouse he had found "not one word about the Trinity, nor about its Persons, nor about Essence, nor about a unity of the Substance." The Trinity was a contrivance—sheer mysticism—and Christianity could never be purified until it was stripped away. Servetus, from his study of the Old Testament and the Koran, was convinced that the old competing Arian belief that Christ was a man who became divine as a result of God's word was, in fact, the correct interpretation.

As a result, Servetus argued at Oecolampadius's dinner table, God was in all of us, and man did not need a mediator. "I say, therefore," he was to write only one year later, "that God himself is our spirit dwelling in us and this is the Holy Spirit within us. In this we testify that there is in our spirit a certain working latent energy, a certain heavenly sense, a latent divinity and it bloweth where it listeth and I hear its voice and

I know not whence it comes nor whither it goes. So is everyone that is born of the spirit of God."

Servetus insisted to Oecolampadius that he personally could disprove the notion of the Trinity and therefore undermine the entire rotten structure on which stood the power of Rome.

✝

WHAT SERVETUS HAD NOT taken into account was that it does not take very long for revolutions to turn reactionary. In fact, it is usually one of the first byproducts of success, when the erstwhile revolutionaries discover, often to their surprise, that they themselves now have some substantial stake in a new status quo. Now that he had established himself in power, Oecolampadius was no longer all that interested in undermining Rome. He was far more interested in consolidating Basel. Also, like many of the other reformers, including Luther, Oecolampadius was not optimistic about the nature of man. He feared a religion with no Son of God as an intermediary.

Still, a convert of Michael Servetus's energy and intellect was not to be let go lightly, so Oecolampadius let him stay at his house for ten months, trying to sway him from his dangerous and radical views. Servetus would not budge, however, and relations between the two became increasingly tense. After a while, they ceased speaking altogether, and Oecolampadius took to writing letters to Servetus even though they were living in the same house. "To Servetus the Spaniard who denies that Christ is the consubstantial Son of God from Johannes Oecolampadius," he addressed one. In another, he wrote, "By denying that the Son is eternal you deny of necessity also that the Father is eternal," a statement that betrays a far lesser grasp of logic and the nuances of the Scriptures than was possessed by his barely postadolescent guest.

Finally, when it became clear that his arguments were futile, Oecolampadius turned on Servetus altogether. At a summit meeting of Swiss reform leaders, he made a point of telling everyone that there was a Spaniard named Servetus living under his roof who was spouting abominations.

Soon afterward, Servetus found out that he was about to be denounced. Since a man in Basel had just been executed for a much less significant deviation from the new reforms, it was clear, even to someone with Servetus's massive social naiveté, that it was time to leave. He fled the city in May of 1531 and headed for Strasbourg, where the reform leaders Martin Bucer and Wolfgang Capito were much more tolerant and liked him personally.

In Strasbourg, where he felt safer, Servetus realized that he didn't need the approval of Oecolampadius or anyone else to make his ideas heard. It was now possible to fight the Church, any Church, orthodox or reformed. With the new technology, he could take his case directly to the people.

Michael Servetus began to look around for a printer.

‡

THROUGH A SUPPORTER, he was put in touch with Johann Setzer, who agreed to publish his book. This was a big coup for a new young author. Setzer had almost as prestigious a name as Froben and was even more prolific. In nine years, he had issued about 150 titles. Setzer was based in Haganau, about fifteen miles from Strasbourg, in Alsace. Servetus moved there to help supervise the printing.

He decided to call his work *De Trinitatis Erroribus* (*On the Errors of the Trinity*), a direct slap at Saint Augustine. The book itself was 120 pages, octavo, of course—mini-octavo, actually, called a duodecimo, with pages only 3¼ inches by 6 inches, making it that much easier to stash away on short notice. It was divided into seven sections, each headed by an "argument" (a thesis Servetus intended to demonstrate), followed by a synopsis of the points that constituted his proof, then a series of numbered paragraphs elaborating on each point.

As even Servetus later acknowledged, the writing itself was often crude and rushed, betraying both the author's youth and his sense of urgency about getting it to press. Still, even his fiercest detractors acknowledged that *Errors of the Trinity* was a prodigious piece of scholarship. Servetus cited over thirty sources in Latin, Greek, Hebrew, and Arabic and quoted or alluded to fifty-two of the sixty-six books of the Bible, and six books of the Apocrypha.

Beyond that, however, the only other thing many of them acknowledged was their fury. It was not simply that this teenager was attacking what was now just about the holiest concept in Christianity, Catholic or reformed, but that he had done so in language that in the most generous terms would be described as immoderate. Through much of the book, particularly in the early stages, Servetus wrote as if addressing an unnamed opponent—it is not difficult to imagine who that might have been—and he often treated the opponent's positions with outright ridicule. About viewing the Holy Spirit as "a separate being," Servetus wrote that it was "practical tritheism, no better than atheism." He added that the doctrine of the Trinity itself was "inconceivable, worst of all [it] incurs the ridicule of the Mohammedans and the Jews." Finally, he observed, "I know not what madness it is in men that does not see that in the Scriptures every sort of unity of God is always referred to as the Father."

While it is possible that this was a conscious attempt to be inflammatory, it is more likely, judging from the rest of the work, that Servetus simply had become so frustrated with what he perceived to be the unwillingness of those around him to see the obvious that he was unable to stop himself from shaking them by the lapels. Servetus was *so* smart that it never seemed to occur to him that his arguments would be more effective if he didn't imply that anyone holding an opposing view was an idiot.

Language aside, the book was hardly heretical in intent. A preeminent Unitarian scholar, Earl Morse Wilbur, wrote that *Errors* "is suffused with passionate earnestness, warm piety, an ardent reverence for

Scripture, and a love for Christ so mystical and overpowering that [he] can hardly find words to express it." Nor, surprisingly, does the work attempt to throw out the concept of the Trinity entirely but only the manner in which it had been imposed on Christianity. Servetus asserted that the Father, the Son, and the Holy Spirit were *dispositions* of God, not separate and distinct beings. That latter definition, he said, was purely an invention—even Saint Augustine admitted that the concept was merely implicit in the Scriptures and could be discovered only through revelation. It was the philosophical contrivances used to prove the Trinity that were the cornerstone of Church corruption.

His own point of view can be summed up in his introduction to Book VII:

The incomprehensible God is known through Christ, by Faith, rather than by philosophical speculations. He manifests God to us, being the expression of His very being; and through Him alone God can be known. The Scriptures reveal Him to those who have Faith; and thus we come to know the Holy Spirit as the Divine impulse within us.

‡

WHEN SETZER SAW SERVETUS'S manuscript, he knew he had a problem. Just the title alone could get him burned. He still wanted to publish it—heretical books sold extremely well—but he did not want to be identified with it, just in case this one was a little *too* heretical. Any risk, Setzer felt, should be borne by the author alone, so he put out the book without a publisher's imprint.

On the Errors of the Trinity justified Setzer's faith in the commercial potential of heresy. The entire first printing, probably around one thousand copies, sold out almost immediately, and soon both book and author were being discussed everywhere. More than a few found his arguments cogent and persuasive, among them a number of senior reform theologians. Capito wrote to Oecolampadius that "the book be-came remarkably popular." Sebastian Franck, a liberal Catholic priest, wrote from Strasbourg to a friend, "The Spaniard, Servetus, contends in his tract that there is but one person in God. The Roman Church holds that there are three persons in one essence. I agree rather with the Spaniard."

In fact, the Trinity had already been causing problems for the re-formers, independent of anything Servetus had written. Luther left it out of his catechisms, and others had tried to avoid the subject entirely. Nonetheless, they were hesitant about eliminating the Trinitarian doc-trine entirely and casting such an obvious insult at the Catholic Church. Servetus, it has been argued, by the directness of his attack, brought the issue prematurely into the open and forced the reform move-ment to decide whether it would support the Trinity or not. Without Servetus's book, the Protestant churches might well have later rejected the Nicene Creed and adopted Servetus's view of the Trinity as three dispositions of God.

As it was, however, they jumped the other way. In 1533, Me-lanchthon wrote that he was "always afraid disputes about the Trinity would break out some time or other." He added, "Good God! What tragedies will this question . . . raise among posterity?"

Not yet understanding the degree of animosity he had evoked, but seeing only how his book was on everyone's lips, Servetus, like any new author buoyed by success, began sending out review copies. He tried to get quotes from Erasmus and Luther. He even sent copies to Catholic bishops in Spain, especially to Zaragossa, in his home province.

But much as Salman Rushdie was to discover four and a half cen-turies later, underestimating the zeal of one's religious opponents can be dangerous. Not only was Servetus's book instantly banned, but he himself was sentenced to death in absentia by the Inquisition in Spain.

But in absentia wasn't nearly enough for the inquisitors. They wanted him back, they wanted him dead, and they were willing to do almost anything to make it happen. They sent out spies to Servetus's hometown. They interrogated his friends and family. They intercepted his mail and read his letters.

The inquisitors in Spain soon discovered that they were not the only ones after him. Reform leaders were now equally furious. Oecolampadius took the lead in denouncing his former houseguest and used all his influence to stem the growing support for Servetus's ideas. He put pressure on Bucer and Capito, the reform leaders of Strasbourg, to denounce him as well, hoping to deny Servetus any safe haven. In a letter to Bucer, Oecolampadius wrote, "Our friends at Berne... are very much offended with the book... I desire you would acquaint Luther, that this book was printed out of this country, and without our knowledge... but that [Servetus] thinks he knows more than everybody else. Our church will be very ill spoken of, unless our divines make it their business to cry him down... we know not how that beast came to creep among us." Bucer, Servetus's erstwhile champion in Strasbourg, who had previously referred to him as "Michael *dilecte*" (delicious), now declared in a public sermon that "Servetus deserved to be cut in pieces, and to have his bowels torn out of him."

Still, the book's support did not flag, and its influence even began to spread. Indeed, it was the very acclaim that Servetus's book received in important centers of learning like Venice that caused such consternation among the Protestant leadership. So pronounced was Servetus's impact on Italian humanism that no less a figure than Melanchthon, as late as 1539, personally wrote a letter to the extremely Catholic senate of Venice beseeching the senators to "use their utmost endeavors, that the impious errors of that man might be avoided, rejected, and abhorred."

Back in Spain, the inquisitors learned that Servetus was shuttling back and forth between Switzerland and Germany, trying to soften Oecolampadius's opposition through direct appeal. Servetus had even published a second, less strident book, again with Setzer, called *Dialogorum De Trinitate Libri Duo* (*Two Dialogues on the Trinity*) to placate his Swiss critics. But by that time it didn't matter. Both *On the Errors of the*

Trinity and *Dialogues* were banned in most of Switzerland, including Basel, and in Strasbourg.

With the competition intensifying to grab him first, the inquisitors in Spain, hoping to coax Servetus back, went to great lengths to hide the fact that they had already condemned him. By law they were required to post the order of his condemnation on the door of the cathedral of Zaragossa on a holy day. Instead, these instructions were issued:

> We deem it expedient to try every possible means to lure the said "Miguel Reves" [Servetus] back to Spain, enticing him by promises of favors or other offers, and if this fail then exert pressure. A few suggestions to that end are appended... For this purpose it is not wise to publish the edict so ceremoniously as we said. Rather it should be read with dissimulation so that no one may suppose or understand that the said Reves is summoned by the Inquisition, for that would be to notify his relatives and friends and they would alert him to accept no offer that might be made. And never mind about affixing the edict to the church doors, or if you do, let it be done at an hour when no one can read, and take it down at once before any one has read it.

Then they sent his youngest brother Juan, the priest, to Germany to transmit to Servetus an offer of protection from the Protestants, as well as a high position and honors and the wish of his family to see him again. As Juan went to seek out his brother, the reformers in Switzerland stepped up their efforts to arrest him.

But both sides were too late. Michael Servetus had disappeared. ‡

WHILE SERVETUS'S BROTHER and the reformers searched throughout Switzerland and Germany, a dark, highly educated twenty-two-year-old named Michel de Villeneuve enrolled at the University of Paris to study mathematics.

Even back in 1533, Paris was Paris: chic, sophisticated, the envy of its less fashionable neighbors. With a population of 300,000, it was the largest city in Europe after Constantinople. While it was true that the streets were impossibly narrow and the low-storied houses so jammed together that the stench of refuse, both human and otherwise, wafted in the gentle breeze, what sixteenth-century city did not have its share of inconveniences? Paris also had the most skilled goldsmiths, the most opulent jewelers, the best food, the most cultured manners, and the most elegantly adorned women in the civilized world.

Dominating the intellectual life of the city was the University of Paris, the single most powerful and influential institution of learning in Europe. There were the usual four faculties, of which, also as usual, theology, known as the Sorbonne, was preeminent. For admission to the doctoral program in theology, a student had first to complete a prerequisite five-year arts course. Of the top graduates, only those considered sufficiently industrious to endure the rigors of an additional fifteen-year course of study were allowed the opportunity to earn a degree. A doctorate in theology from the University of Paris entitled the bearer to join the faculty, teach at the college, and help make religious policy—and therefore political policy—not only for France, but for the rest of Catholic Europe.

To head theology during this time of turmoil the faculty chose Noël Béda, a hard, cold, narrow-minded, suspicious man who embodied the spirit of orthodoxy. He held the position of syndic to the faculty and was responsible for setting the agenda for meetings and seeing that decisions were enforced. It was originally conceived as an annual post, but Béda was first appointed in 1520 and held the position for thirteen pivotal years. A teacher as well, he beat Latin syllogisms into his students and by the force of his own will tried single-handedly to hold back the encroachment of humanists and reformers alike.

Béda was one of the few among his peers to recognize the power of books—and thus the necessity of suppressing them. In 1521, he had convinced Francis and the Parlement of Paris to make it a criminal offense to print or sell any book that dealt with or touched on religion—which meant just about every conceivable book—without prior permission of the faculty. When that proved insufficient, he put out a second proclamation two months later requiring anyone who owned a work by or about Luther to turn it over to the Parlement within a week or face a hefty fine and jail sentence.

But then as now, there was nothing like a little controversy to improve the commercial prospects of an author's work. Béda's attempt at suppression only served to bring Luther to the attention of the public, thereby making him even more popular than before. And when Luther's disciple, Melanchthon, weighed in with *Loci Communes*, the University of Paris's arts faculty made it a point to tweak the Sorbonne and openly pass copies of the book around to staff and students.

Béda's next target was the Cercle de Meaux, the humanist reform group that had come under the protection of Marguerite of Navarre. In 1523, he condemned the sermons of two of its members and forced them to recant. He also had the Sorbonne pass a resolution condemning translations of the Scriptures into Greek, Hebrew, or French, a direct attack on Jacques Lefèvre, one of Marguerite's favorites, who had just published a French version of the New Testament. He went after others in Marguerite's set, including Louis de Berquin, a young nobleman who was responsible for translating Luther's books into French, and was about to have him tried for heresy when Marguerite intervened. Francis saved Berquin, but all of his books were confiscated from his library and burned just outside of Notre-Dame. Marguerite later saved him again, but Béda won out in the end. The Inquisition waited until Francis was out of Paris before hurriedly arresting Berquin, then even more hurriedly passing sentence and carrying it out. Berquin was burned at the stake in 1529.

Between 1529 and 1533, the forces of orthodoxy and the forces of humanist reform battled in France, with neither side able to establish a clear victory. Francis, ever the pragmatist, favored Béda and the Inquisition as a means of keeping order but was often swayed equally by the passion of his sister. No one knew which side would be in ascendancy from one day to the next.

It was into this incendiary environment that Michel de Villenueve came to begin his course of study at the University of Paris. Also at the university at this time was another student, two years older, a brilliant, ambitious, driven man whose life and work would haunt Michael Servetus's own like a deadly shadow.

That student, born Jean Chauvin, had Latinized his name in Paris to Johannus Calvinus, before later shortening it to John Calvin.

✝

AMBITION BEGETS IDEOLOGY, not the other way around.

Jean Chauvin was born on July 10, 1509, in the cathedral town of Noyon, in Picardy, about fifty miles northeast of Paris. The fourth of five sons, Jean's mother died when he was three. His father, Gérard, was a notary in the service of Charles de Hangest, the bishop of Noyon. The de Hangests belonged to the first order of French aristocracy.

Charles was one of the twelve peers of France, and the family had held the bishopric for as long as anyone could remember. All ecclesiastic and political affairs in Noyon revolved around them, and the economy of the town depended on them.

The Chauvin family, by contrast, was only one small step removed from the laboring class. Gérard was the first not to work with his hands. His position in the service of Bishop de Hangest represented a great leap forward in the family fortunes. It gave him access to the town's leading citizens and to favors from the Church. Most importantly, it allowed Jean, an obviously bright boy, to mingle socially with the three de Hangest sons.

And so Jean Chauvin grew up in the company of noblemen. He ran in and out of the de Hangest home like one of the family. He went to the local private school with them, played games with them, had meals with them. When the de Hangest boys got a special tutor, their friend Jean sat in with them and received the lessons as well. He was like the one scholarship student at an elite boarding school, better at his lessons by virtue of his sharp intelligence but always aware of the chasm between himself and these golden boys. In this chasm lay the seeds of John Calvin's burning ambition.

When it came time to go to college, the three de Hangest boys naturally chose the University of Paris. Jean wanted to go as well, but it was expensive to go to the University of Paris. The Chauvins didn't have that kind of money. So Gérard asked the de Hangest family to help his son. Through their influence, Jean was appointed a chaplain of the local church. The post came with a salary. The boy, only twelve and obviously in no position to fulfill the duties associated with the job, paid a small percentage of the money to someone else to be the real chaplain, then used the rest to meet his expenses. Although he would not return to Noyon again except for an occasional visit, and once to bury his father, Jean would nonetheless hold two more of these honorary positions over the course of the next ten years, thus subsidizing his entire schooling.

That taken care of, Jean Chauvin went off to the University of Paris with his aristocratic friends. He spent his first three months at the Collège de la Marche, where he Latinized his name and studied with an excellent teacher, Mathurin Cordier, a humane, civilized man who is credited with polishing Calvin's Latin and French. Soon, however, Calvin transferred to the infamous Collège de Montaigu, seat of orthodoxy, headed by Noël Béda.

It would be difficult to be farther removed from the modern vision of higher education—ivy-covered buildings, green commons, coed dormitories—than the Collège de Montaigu. Students at the University of Paris were boarded in slums, fed rotten food, beaten in class, and generally deprived of sleep and exercise. And of all the colleges at the University of Paris, Montaigu was the worst offender. Erasmus himself had attended Montaigu but left after a year. He couldn't stand it, and once again food played a part, as Francis Hackett noted in his biography of Francis I:

> Erasmus so piteously described [Montaigu as] a barrack, filthy, bleak, inhospitable, reeking with the foullest smells, clotted with dirt, brayed with noises, where the dinner would be stale bread and half a herring. Here, at four in the morning, a small wretch of fourteen would begin his lessons. With short breaks they would go on to seven in the evening, larded with mass, with religious exercises and with floggings.

Some students turned to drink and others died. Rabelais called it "Collège de pouillerie [filth]," saying, "If I were king of Paris, the devil take me if I should not set fire to it, and burn the principal and regents who endure such inhumanity before their very eyes." According to Erasmus biographer George Faludy, the Parisians themselves called it "the very cleft between the buttocks of Mother Theology."

And people wonder where Calvin got his austerity.

Nothing affords a more precise picture of the conditions under

A doodle of John Calvin by one of his students

which an enterprising young sixteenth-century scholar acquired an education than the dispute that was raging in 1523, when Calvin first arrived, between the Collège de Montaigu and the Collège de Sainte-Barbe, another elite part of the university, located directly across the street.

The street was the rue Saint-Symphorien, also known as the rue des Chiens, or the Street of Dogs. The rue des Chiens was more sewer than boulevard, owing to the fact that Montaigu drained its wastes into it. When Sainte-Barbe complained, the city council ordered the street paved, with both colleges bearing the cost. The result of the paving was that Montaigu's sewage no longer settled in the street but instead slid down the pavement, which sloped downhill and onto Sainte-Barbe's front doorstep. The college complained again, this time in vain. Sainte-Barbe tried to remedy the situation by covertly breaking up the pavement and reversing the slope of the street back toward Montaigu. It was conceived as a night operation, and the students were recruited for the work. But it was too big a job for a single evening, and Montaigu discovered the ruse in the morning. The next evening, when the Sainte-Barbe students took up their picks and shovels, they were pelted with stones from the upper-story windows of Montaigu. The Sainte-Barbe students returned fire, and everybody poured into the street; there were many casualties and much property damage, including broken windows and a damaged chapel crucifix. In the morning both colleges agreed to put in a drain.

$$\maltese$$

AS A RESULT OF THE proceeds from his absentee chaplaincy, Calvin had enough money to live like one of the richer students and had things a little bit better. He boarded out, which gave him slightly more freedom (and fewer offensive sensory assaults), and, most importantly, his relative wealth enabled him to strike up a friendship with Nicholas Cop, son of Guillaume Cop, a professor of medicine at the university.

Guillaume Cop was a scholar, a man of letters, and Francis's chief physician, which gave him considerable clout and some celebrity. He was also a humanist, and Béda's leading opponent at the university. It was Cop who had circulated Melanchthon's work in direct violation of the Sorbonne's edicts. He was friends with Guillaume Budé, the preeminent French literary humanist, and he also corresponded with Erasmus. Although the Cops were certainly more educated and accomplished than the de Hangests, Calvin's relationship with this family became very similar to his relationship with his first benefactors. The Cops were upper class and genteel; they lived nicely. Because Calvin had the manners of an aristocrat he was often invited to their home. There he met the great Budé himself. Budé was a man who did not get his hands dirty, who moved back and forth between the court and the great minds of France, a gentleman scholar who nonetheless wielded influence—the French Erasmus.

Everything, in short, that Calvin had decided he wanted to be.

But before he could become Erasmus, Calvin had to contend with his father, Gérard. By 1528, when John Calvin completed that prerequisite five-year arts course, a rising star with every intention of staying on in Paris and fulfilling his dream, Gérard had run into some problems back in Noyon. It seems there had been some misunderstanding about the old bishop's accounts, and the bishop had wanted to see the books. Gérard took offense at this and refused. Perhaps he felt his honor was at stake. Then again, he kept refusing to show the books until the Noyon clergy felt the need to excommunicate him. Given the severity of the punishment, this would seem to be carrying honor a little too far. Perhaps there was something in the books that Gérard did not want the bishop to see after all.

Anyway, the entire experience rather soured Gérard on the Church. He decided to pull his son out of it and get the boy into something sensible, like law, which even back in the sixteenth century was an extremely lucrative profession and could be counted upon to provide the sort of living that would support not only a young man but his excommunicated father, and his father's second family as well. Therefore, as soon as Jean had taken his degree, Gérard instructed his son to leave Paris to go study law at Orléans. This Calvin, as a dutiful son, agreed to do, although he was not happy about it.

The University of Orléans offered a much more relaxed atmosphere. Students had more freedom and weren't beaten by their professors. Calvin studied law and made the acquaintance of a new circle of humanists and moderate reformers. Rabelais was around, and they might have been thrown together through friends. Once again, Calvin distinguished himself as a student, working long hours, mastering the finer points of his law studies. But still, he didn't have his heart in it. His passion was the classics.

Soon, he had an opportunity to exercise that passion. Marguerite had been given the Duchy of Berry by her brother in 1517. There was a school there, the University of Bourges, and Marguerite made it a pet project, inviting outstanding professors who could be expected to teach along the new reformed lines. In 1529, she secured a real plum, Andreas Alciati, an Italian legal scholar who had written his first book at fifteen and was the leading humanist lawyer in Italy. Calvin and some of his friends spent eighteen months in Bourges to attend Alciati's lectures.

Alciati, however, turned out to be a disappointment—as an Italian he was apparently too much of a hedonist for Calvin's taste. But at Bourges, Calvin did learn Greek from Melior Wolmar, another humanist Marguerite had lured to her school. Now he could read the classics and Erasmus's latest edition of the New Testament. He returned to Or-léans and was licensed for his law degree. But instead of becoming a doctor of law and setting up a practice right away, he went to Paris. Francis, in one of his liberal moods, had been persuaded by Cop and Budé to establish a new school called the *Lecteurs Royaux* (Royal Readers), dedicated to teaching Latin, Greek, and Hebrew. The center of French humanist study immediately shifted there, and Calvin simply could not resist going too.

Then, in 1531, Gérard died, and Calvin was free to give up any pretense of establishing a law practice. He was twenty-two, learned, ambitious, and prepared. He had a large circle of influential, aristocratic friends in Paris, Orléans, and Bourges. He knew the Cops, he knew Budé, and it is possible that he had been introduced to Marguerite herself. The time had come for him to make a name for himself.

So he wrote a book.

The book was called *Commentary on Lucius Anneas Seneca's Two Books on Clemency.* Seneca, the Roman playwright who is best known for adaptations of *Oedipus, The Trojan Women,* and *Medea,* was also tutor and advisor to the emperor Nero. Such a man might seem at first blush an unlikely subject for a humanist treatise, but Seneca was a philosopher as well and known to have exerted a calming influence on his mentally unbalanced young charge.

Calvin intended the book as the kind of gentle call for reform and tolerance that had gained Erasmus his great reputation. (Erasmus had, in fact, already translated some of Seneca's works some years before.) It was written in polished Latin and used suggested parallels rather than outright argument to make its points. In his preface, Calvin adopted a tone of fawning modesty that belied the self-confidence of a man who had been assured by his influential friends of an interested and sizable audience:

> Whoever in this day has been born with more than average ability ... generally rushes out with it into the world, fired with the ambition of getting fame, so that posterity may venerate his memory with monuments to his genius ... Hence the insane passion to write something ... Publishing inchoate books the writers often plead the inexperience of youth, or the wanton entreaties of their friends, and chatter I know not what trifles to escape the imputation of having committed a mistake. As for me, I should want to bring forth no embryos at all if I could produce only premature ones; in fact, I should rather abandon them as abortions than bring them forth before their time. My purpose is not so much to commend myself to the benevolent reader as to the critical one, the more so since I come from the common class of people and even if I should be gifted in erudition to a moderate degree, I have nothing that could excite any hope of fame.

Calvin was extremely displeased when he was told that in order to get his book published, he was going to have to pay for it himself. But no matter—he dug into those Noyon benefices and forged ahead. He put out his book, held his breath, and waited to be discovered.

Soon after publication, Calvin decided to help discovery along a bit. In a letter dated April 22, 1532, he wrote to his friend François Daniel:

The die is cast. My Commentaries on the books of Seneca De Clementia have been printed, but at my own expense, and have drawn from me more money than you can well suppose. At present I am using every endeavour to get some of it back. I have stirred up some of the professors in this city to make use of them in lecturing. In the University of Bourges I have induced a friend to do this from the pulpit in a public lecture. You also can help me, if you will not take it amiss. You will do so on the score of old friendship, especially as without doing any damage to your reputation you may do me this service, which will also tend perhaps to the public good. If you are willing to oblige me I will send you a hundred copies or as many as you please. Meanwhile accept this copy for yourself, and do not suppose by accepting it that I hold you bound to do what I ask.

But Calvin had miscalculated. He missed the market. By the time he published *Commentaries*, the public had tired of discreet gentlemen's analyses and moved on. In 1532, people wanted more exciting stuff, like that hot new down-with-the-pope, get-rid-of-the-Mass, let-priests-marry Protestant genre coming out of Germany. Many were reading that fiery attack on the Trinity that had been published in Haganau by a brilliant young Spanish heretic.

So John Calvin, in his first effort, experienced what many new authors with bad timing and equally bad luck experience: his book bombed. Nobody bought it. Nobody talked about it. Nobody clamored for a sequel. It was, for all intents and purposes, as if the book had never existed.

Later, Calvin scholars and even Calvin himself would pinpoint the time of his conversion to Protestantism as the period just *before* this book came out. In his *Commentary on the Psalms,* published much later, in 1557, he wrote:

> Since I was more stubbornly addicted to the superstitions of the Papacy than to be easily drawn out of that so deep mire, by a sudden conversion, He subdued my heart (too hardened for my age) to docility. Thus, having acquired some taste of true piety, I burned with such great zeal to go forward that although I did not desist from other studies I yet pursued them more indifferently, nor had a year gone by when all who were desirous of this purer doctrine thronged to me, novice and beginner that I was, in order to learn it.

The Seneca book, it is therefore argued, was an afterthought, a trifle of no real importance, particularly to Calvin. Still, it seems unlikely that a man who wrote a letter fervently pressing a hundred copies of his book on his friend was not passionate and desperate for that book to succeed.

Failure was something Calvin had not experienced before. He had not foreseen it. He was not prepared for it. And this failure was even more ignominious because he had *paid* for it. It was a good thing his father was dead. Gerard Chauvin would have had a few choice words to say about *that.*

John Calvin realized that he was not going to be the new Erasmus. So he gritted his teeth and decided to be something else.

‡

SOON AFTERWARD, IN 1533, Calvin returned to the University of Paris, where his friend Nicholas Cop had just been made the new rector.

In contrast to Calvin, Cop's star was definitely ascending. He was by this time a doctor of medicine like his prestigious father and, through his father, knew many influential people, including Marguerite herself. As rector, he was now a person of even greater standing at the university, and therefore within the reform movement as well. And in Paris in early 1533, it seemed, for the first time, that the reformers might have the upper hand.

Francis was gone, off on one of his big hunting expeditions, and he had left Marguerite and her husband, Henri of Navarre, in charge of the city of Paris. Marguerite had promptly taken advantage of this situation by inviting Gérard Roussel, a member of the Cercle de Meaux, to Paris under her protection. Roussel was a fiery speaker, and everywhere he went, controversy followed. Marguerite invited him to preach at the Louvre before an audience of some five thousand Parisians during Lent.

Béda was, to say the least, displeased and began accusing everyone in sight, including Henri, of heresy. Marguerite complained in a letter to Francis. Francis didn't like having his brother-in-law called a heretic—it was bad for family relations, and he needed Henri's support. He had Béda kicked out of Paris. One Béda supporter moaned that "the theologians had suffered such a defeat that their only hope was for Marguerite, who was pregnant, to die soon."

The Sorbonne wasn't through fighting, however. In October some of the students put on a play ridiculing Marguerite, depicting her as a puppet of Roussel and an overbearing shrew who went around spouting heresy and making everyone miserable. At the same time, the theological faculty censured Marguerite for publishing *Mirror of the Sinful Soul,* a long religious poem with Lutheran overtones. The faculty went so far as to raid the Parisian bookshops in an effort to suppress it.

Again, Marguerite complained to Francis (who was now in the south of France). Francis wrote to the Sorbonne and told the faculty that if they were going to treat his sister like that, they had better list their reasons, and the reasons had better be good ones.

At this point Nicholas Cop stepped in. He had strong positive feelings about *Mirror of the Sinful Soul*—Marguerite had sent him an inscribed advance reader's copy. As rector, he called a meeting of all the faculties and forced the Sorbonne to back down. Cop's victory was complete: on October 8, fifty-eight members of the Sorbonne had to sign a statement that they had never even read *Mirror of the Sinful Soul*, and so obviously could not pass judgment on it.

For the first time it seemed possible that the reformers could win in France, and the leader of the movement might well be Nicholas Cop. And right behind Cop was his friend, supporter, intimate, and new number two man, John Calvin.

But there was now someone else to consider. It had not taken long for Michel de Villenueve to seek out and join the most radical faction he could find at the university. Eventually he felt sufficiently comfortable to reveal to some of the key members of this French reform underground that he was, in fact, Michael Servetus, author of the celebrated *On the Errors of the Trinity*, a book that Calvin could not have helped but known. Servetus, two years younger, was already a famous scholar and a wanted man, someone who had traveled extensively, held a senior position at the emperor's court, been on the frontlines of the revolution in both Switzerland and Germany, and was now an up-and-coming member of the movement in Paris at just the right time.

Calvin hated him.

‡

THE REFORMERS, FRESH FROM backing down the Sorbonne on *Mirror of the Sinful Soul*, realized that this was the moment to press their advantage and decided to use the occasion of Cop's inaugural speech to the university, All Saints' Day, 1533, to make their statement. Calvin, bristling with ambition and desperate to make his mark, helped Nicholas Cop compose a speech with mild but unmistakable Erasmian and Lutheran overtones. Although the rhetoric was nothing compared to *On the Errors of the Trinity*, it was nonetheless sufficient to prompt the Sorbonne to label it heretical and call for a purge at the university. This time the reformers had overplayed their hand. Francis, fickle as ever, did not intervene, and arrest warrants were issued for those thought to be responsible.

When the police came for Cop, he had already fled, later to resurface in Basel. When they came for Calvin, they found only a rope made of twisted bedsheets hanging out the window. From Paris, he walked all the way to Noyon dressed as a vineyard worker.

As for Michael Servetus—he had disappeared once more. ‡

ᴀFTER COP'S INAUGURAL, reform in France was once again forced underground. Many of the leaders fled and others went into hiding, but for once in his life, circumstances favored Servetus. Had he arrived in Paris earlier, with more time to establish himself, his name, along with Calvin's and Cop's, would surely have been on the Inquisition's wanted list. As it was, however, Michel de Villeneuve (or Villanovanus as he Latinized the alias) was still largely unknown outside the movement itself, and no warrant had been issued for his arrest. As long as he did nothing to publicly call attention to himself, he could remain in Paris with his new identity intact.

Calvin, who could only come back to the capital at great personal risk, kept in touch with other members of the movement from Noyon. But when he learned in January 1534 that Marguerite was again attempting to intercede with Francis, he took the chance and slipped quietly back into Paris. He was now of sufficient stature to obtain a private audience, but she told him that it was still too dangerous for him to remain, so Calvin accepted the invitation of a friend at Angoulême, a Marguerite stronghold in the south.

It was at Angoulême that Calvin began a project that was to change the course of Christianity. It started simply enough: his host, Louis du Tillet, a canon of the local cathedral, knew all of the reformed ministers in the area and naturally invited them over to meet his friend, John Calvin, recently of Paris. Calvin became a minor celebrity, studying with them, exchanging ideas, and touring the countryside. Eventually, some of the rural pastors, impressed by his scholarship and erudition, asked if he wouldn't write them a sermon or two.

Calvin complied, and even did a little preaching on his own. It was his first experience in a country parish, a hands-on opportunity to mingle with the laity and observe the shortcomings in their spiritual education. He began jotting down his thoughts on the nature of religion, organizing the primary principles so as to make them accessible to a general audience.

The notes grew, and Calvin began to realize that the reform movement as a whole lacked a clear and practical explanation of its philosophy. As a result, the common people were having trouble accepting its positions. He decided to write a little manual, a sort of spiritual how-to, laying everything out simply and easily. Calvin was later to write in his preface:

> All I had in mind was to hand on some rudiments by which anyone who was touched with an interest in religion might be formed to true godliness. I labored at the task for our own Frenchmen in particular, for I saw that many were hungering and thirsting after Christ and yet that only a very few had even the slightest knowledge of him. The book itself betrays that this was my purpose by its simple and primitive form of teaching.

Calvin began by laying out his own religious philosophy. It was passionate, heartfelt, reasoned, and bleak. Over and over throughout the pages ran the message: Man is nothing; God is everything. Man is small, corrupt, weak. Free will is an illusion. God alone decides who will be saved. An individual cannot alter that decision by good works or other exertions. It is made before that person is born.

Through Christ, Calvin continued, man as a species participates in salvation. To understand God, people must turn to the pastors and teachers of the true Church, for which he, Calvin, was prepared to provide a definition.

In the writing of his book, Calvin brought to bear the full force of his superior legal training and intensely analytic mind. The result was a volume that reconciled religious practice with almost every aspect of daily life. It proceeded with relentless logic, like arguments in some divine legal brief. One by one he defined the terms of the Church: faith, Christ, penitence, redemption, Scripture, the soul, the Trinity, righteousness:

> Original sin ... may be defined as a hereditary corruption and depravity of our nature, extending to all the parts of the soul ... Because our weakness cannot reach his height, any description which we receive of [God] must be lowered to our capacity in order to be intelligible ... We thus see that the impurity of parents is transmitted to their children, so that all, without exception, are originally depraved.

Calvin's book would become known as *Christianae Religionis Institutio* (*Institutes of the Christian Religion*). More than any other single act, the writing of this book is responsible for Calvin's enduring legacy. It has been called by Will Durant "the most eloquent, fervent, lucid, logical, influential, and terrible work in all the literature of the religious revolution."

Calvin would spend the rest of his life expanding and revising the *Institutes*, and it would eventually run to 1,118 pages. From the moment it appeared in print for the first time in 1536, it caused a sensation. It was to do everything that its author had hoped for with his first book, and more.

But 1536 was still two years away.

‡

DURING HIS STAY AT ANGOULÊME Calvin became increasingly aware that the time had come for him to choose between two paths. He now knew what he believed in: the question was, how best to work toward this vision? Despite his fugitive status, it might still be possible to make peace with the established Church and work for reform from within. This alternative had much to offer. It was the way of Erasmus and Lefèvre, the humanist way of moderation, the way in which Calvin had been conditioned to believe since he first began his studies and embraced the classics. It was the conservative, practical way to proceed. Not insignificantly, this choice would allow him to stay in France.

The second path was much more risky—he could break with the Church completely and secure his place at the forefront of the reform movement. But the movement was currently in tatters, its leaders spread out, their authority weakened. Who knew if they would regroup and become a real force for change? This path could also easily mean permanent exile. What if he made the break and found himself not a power in the world, but a refugee allied to a fringe group, helpless to do anything but natter from the sidelines?

In an act that demonstrated both his courage and the purity of his beliefs, in March 1534, Calvin left the relative safety of southern France, returned to Noyon, and abruptly resigned his phony chaplaincy. He not only gave up the benefices of an office he had held since he was twelve, which still accounted for the lion's share of his small income, he announced that at twenty-four, he now considered himself as officially and publicly cut off from the Catholic Church.

He spent the next months wandering, planning, working. He was intent on completing his book and his mission. "Calvin," wrote Francis Hackett, "with his metallic voice, his consuming gravity, his fierce appetite for abstraction and his cold appetite for power—he built on a book, not *Das Kapital*, only the Bible. He was molding his absolute system . . . carried from secret lodgings to secret lodgings, the body a black lantern for the burning brain." Although he avoided Paris where possible, on one occasion, in late summer of 1534, he felt compelled to venture in despite the danger.

With Cop in exile and many of Marguerite's older allies afraid to show themselves, a vaccum had formed in the leadership in Paris. One of the more radical reformers who had remained in the capital had been spreading ideas that Calvin found repugnant but that were nonetheless gathering support. Calvin had met this man before and knew him to be brilliant, charismatic, and persuasive.

The man was Michel de Villeneuve—Michael Servetus.

Calvin knew he must act quickly to oppose the threat from the Spaniard. His vision of a united church based upon the precepts that he was just now committing to paper could be lost forever if Servetus's alternative of a simpler and more compassionate Christianity gained acceptance. In Calvin's view, this optimistic construction of man and his relation to God was intensely corrupt. He challenged Servetus to a secret debate.

The confrontation was to take place in the rue Saint-Antoine, which ran through a grimy section of Paris across the river from the university, in the very shadow of the Bastille. Three centuries later, Charles Dickens would have Madame Defarge ply her knitting needles and malice here in *A Tale of Two Cities*. The exact location for the debate was known only to the participants and those deemed sufficiently trustworthy to be allowed to observe. Everyone involved understood the danger. Calvin was to say later of this meeting that he had risked his life to try to convert Servetus.

Two brilliant minds—Calvin the coldly logical reformer against Servetus the mystic revolutionary. It might have been one of the great intellectual confrontations in history.

Except that it never happened. Servetus did not come.

The reasons for Servetus's failure to appear at the debate with Calvin have been guessed at ever since. He never spoke of it himself or mentioned it in his writings. Some speculated that he was detained and couldn't make the appointment. Others thought that he feared for his safety, still others that he had been tipped off that the meeting was a trap. Certainly, he had more to lose than Calvin. If he had been caught and his real identity revealed to the Inquisition, there was virtually no chance that he could have come out of it alive.

There is another possibility. Calvin needed this debate and Servetus did not. Calvin had just made a momentous decision and was desperate to prove that he had made the right choice. He needed the recognition, the celebrity. Servetus's obsession lay solely in the acceptance of his ideas. At no time in his life did he demonstrate ambition for personal or political power. In fact, he often shunned it. Both traveling with Quintana and at Oecolampadius's dinner table, all Servetus needed to do was temper his opinions, and a powerful position would have been sure to follow. But temperamentally, Servetus proved to be much like Isaac Newton—a pure intellect, ignorant, even dismissive of social necessities. He could be rude, intolerant, and domineering—unwilling and probably unable to moderate his passion or his views in order to achieve a larger goal. A less politic person is hard to imagine.

Whatever the reason, Calvin was left standing in front of a meeting with no one to debate, ignored and dismissed by an adversary, intentionally made, he felt certain, to look ridiculous.

He never forgot it.

✝

UNKNOWN TO EITHER MAN, however, the question of who would lead reform in France was about to become moot.

On October 18, 1534, the citizens of Paris, and of five provincial cities in France as well, woke up to find a one-page broadside posted on church walls, doorways, and public buildings. It had been taken from a pamphlet written by a reformer, Antoine Marcourt, who had been exiled to Switzerland from Lyon and was then first pastor of Neuchâtel. Hundreds of copies had been smuggled into France by a servant of the king's apothecary. The broadside, a four-point paper decrying the Mass and calling for its abolition, was entitled *Articles véritables sur les horribles, grandz & importables abuz de la Messe papalle* (*True Articles on the Horrible, Great and Insufferable Abuses of the Papal Mass*).

This paper represented the most radical segment of the reform movement, not so much in the arguments it made as in the language in which it was expressed and, most importantly, in the manner in which it was delivered. One of the provincial towns where *Articles véritables* appeared was Amboise, where Francis had a château. Francis, who happened to be staying at the château on October 18, woke up to find a copy pasted on the door of his bedchamber.

Francis was livid. It wasn't so much the content—although that was bad enough—as the idea that anyone would be sufficiently brazen to violate the sanctity of the royal apartments—*his* royal apartments. At that moment, the king abandoned all pretense of religious evenhandedness, which had only been prompted by diplomatic necessity anyway, and threw his full and enthusiastic support to the conservatives.

Reformers were pursued mercilessly. An attractive reward was offered for information leading to the discovery of any "Lutheran." There were hundreds of arrests. Within a month, the executions began. The victims were simple people—a shoemaker's son, a printer, a weaver, a draper.

For this insult, ordinary burnings weren't enough. On January 21, 1535, an immense Francis-size royal procession wound its way from the Louvre to Notre-Dame, with the king himself at its head. Along with him came all the trappings of orthodoxy. The nation's most precious relics—the Shrine of Saint Genevieve, the True Cross, the Crown of Thorns, the Robe of Purple—all these were taken from the vaults and carried aloft in the streets. The city officials, the nobility, the university faculties, the Swiss guard, the musicians, the heralds—everyone, including Francis, dressed for a funeral, bareheaded and carrying a candle. High mass was held at Notre-Dame, and afterward Francis spoke.

What had happened with the placards, he said, this wasn't France.

These were low people, vile people, heretics. They must be removed, like a disease. If his own arm were infected with such corruption, Francis told the crowd, he would not hesitate to cut it off. If his own children had done this, said the man who had sentenced his sons to four years in a Spanish prison, the punishment would be the same.

Then began the burnings. Before the Affair of the Placards, as it came to be called, victims had had their necks broken prior to being tied to the stake. Now heretics were to be burned alive. Special machines were even devised so that the condemned could be lowered into the flames, then raised up and lowered again and again to prolong the agony. Six people burned to the jeers of the crowds on the day of the procession while Francis and his court ate dinner.

The burnings continued. Calvin's friend and landlord was among the condemned. More and more were consigned to the flames until finally the pope himself ordered Francis to stop.

Religious tolerance in France was over. Even Marguerite was now helpless. Despite political overtures to the German reformers later in 1535, Francis remained orthodox at home, becoming increasingly so as he aged. In 1539, the Inquisition would be reintroduced all across the country, and ecclesiastical courts granted ultimate authority under the king. Entire villages would be destroyed and their occupants slaughtered on the altar of piety.

As for those reformers still in France in the aftermath of the placards... no one had to tell them twice what to do. Protestants poured across the French border into Switzerland and Germany, and once again, Basel was the destination of choice. Oecolampadius was dead (another middle-aged man who succumbed shortly after marriage), and the city had recovered something of its past reputation. Erasmus, now frail and housebound, had come there to die. Cop was there, as were Capito and Guillaume Farel. There were enough scholars to effectively staff a university in exile. It was the obvious choice for Calvin as well.

He almost didn't make it. On the way, Calvin and his traveling companion, Louis du Tillet, the friend who had put him up at Angoulême, were robbed of all of their money and a horse by one their servants. It was only by borrowing from another servant that they were able to make it across the border.

But Servetus—Servetus could not go back to Basel or Strasbourg, or to any of the other reform-minded cities in Switzerland even if he wanted to. He was too well known there. He would be discovered and punished for his former heresy. Spain, too, was out of the question.

But France, oddly enough, was not. There were large parts of France where the name Michel de Villeneuve meant nothing. Even more in his favor was the rumor going around that the heretic Michael Servetus had starved to death in a castle dungeon. If he could just find someplace far enough from Paris for safety yet sophisticated enough to provide work for a scholar, and then keep his head down, he might be safe. ‡

CHAPTER SEVEN

IN THE SPRING of 1535, Michel de Villeneuve arrived in Lyon.

Over two hundred miles to the south of Paris, Lyon, the second-largest city in France, was a boomtown. It was the country's textile and silk center, dating from a monopoly granted by Louis XI, as well as France's banking and financial hub. When Francis needed to borrow (which was regularly), it was to Lyon that he came for letters of credit. Commerce was fed both by traffic coming up the Rhône from the Mediterranean and down from the Alps through Geneva, which lay just to the east. There were four major trade fairs held in the city each year, and hordes of foreigners flooded in to transact business.

Like every other boomtown, Lyon was a freewheeling city. People were coming and going all the time. Fortunes were made, and the poor slept in the streets. There were no guilds, no impediments to starting a business. All it took was capital.

The intellectual life in Lyon was vibrant and, by Parisian standards, unconstrained. The repression that had effectively closed down the capital was largely ignored here in the frenzy to make money. A number of the most important French poets came to Lyon to write. The city had more than its share of intellectuals sympathetic to both humanism and reform, but they didn't make a fuss about it and nobody bothered them.

For a scholar on the run under an assumed name, looking to establish a new identity, Lyon had the further advantage of being the only city in France outside of Paris that had its own independent printing and publishing industry. Rabelais himself worked as a physician there and had his major works published by Lyonnaise printers. By the time Servetus arrived, Lyon was home to over one hundred different publishing houses, some of which were among the most respected and famous in Europe.

One of these was the house of Trechsel, owned by the brothers Melchior and Gaspard Trechsel, who had inherited the business from their father. The Trechsels had been looking for some time for a scholar of sufficient ability to oversee a major project, a book that would cost a good deal of money to produce but, if done properly, could be relied upon to generate hefty sales and profits. It was to be in folio, one of those books that could only be read on a lectern, and was to take advantage of the explosion of curiosity about empirical science.

When Michel de Villeneuve walked in the door, the Trechsels realized that they might have their man. Villeneuve, twenty-three years old, fluent in at least five languages, Paris-trained in mathematics, Toulouse-trained in law, with an ego to match and no money, was hired instantly. They tried him out at first as a proofreader, but soon he was assigned to the big one—editing and updating the definitive version of Ptolemy's *Geography*.

‡

PTOLEMY, BORN CLAUDIUS PTOLEMEIUS, was one of history's most shadowy scientific geniuses. He was probably a Greek who was born in Egypt at the end of the first century A.D., although it is also possible that he was an Egyptian who was born in Greece. As an adult, he lived and worked in Alexandria. While Ptolemy was not the greatest original thinker in history, he was arguably the most brilliant extrapolator. His ability to build on existing knowledge and take theory to a far more advanced and sophisticated level was astounding, all the more so because although he was primarily a mathematician, he applied his skills to a number of diverse scientific disciplines.

Ptolemy is also history's most ill-starred scientific theorist. He is best known for the creation of two major theoretic models, but in each, he made one grand incorrect assumption, and he is now better remembered for his mistakes than for the huge leap forward that each model represented in its own field. What was worse, in each case Ptolemy had a choice of two competing theories on which to base his model and both times chose the wrong one. All was not lost, however. In one case, Ptolemy's erroneous model turned out to be mathematically cleaner in calculating the very thing it was wrong about, and in the other, it was inadvertently responsible for one of history's greatest discoveries.

For his first construct, astronomy, Ptolemy had to choose, as a starting point, between the theories of two Greek astronomers—Aristarchus, who in the third century B.C. asserted that the earth revolved around the sun, or Hipparchus, who a century later postulated that the sun revolved around the earth. Ptolemy chose Hipparchus. In his historic work the *Almagest*, he devoted each of thirteen sections to a different astronomical concept. He developed his model with the earth as the center, followed outward in succession by the moon, Mercury, Venus, the sun, Mars, Jupiter, Saturn, and the stars. Despite the blunder, Ptolemy's model achieved an incredible degree of accuracy through the brilliant use of epicycles, or circles upon circles. It compared the motions of the planets and could be used to predict their future positions. In addition, using his geocentric model, Ptolemy formulated the mathematics necessary to explain aberrations of planetary orbits and correctly measured the moon's distance from earth at fifty-nine times the earth's radius.

The mathematics of the geocentric model were so elegant that the *Almagest* is still in use today, and Ptolemaic astronomy allowed scientists to compute the position of the stars and planets more accurately than did the Copernican model. For his accomplishments, Ptolemy has both a Mars crater and a lunar crater named for him.

Ptolemy's geographic model was even more groundbreaking. He was the first to project the spherical surface of the earth onto a flat plane (contrary to schoolchild fantasy, the idea that the world was round had been put forth about five hundred years before), and the first to standardize measurements so that the coordinates of every map, no matter the scale, bore the same relationship to one another.

When Ptolemy decided to take on geography, the concept of dividing the globe into latitudinal segments had already been widely accepted by those trying to make some sense of the lay of the land (and the water). Ptolemy, as always, took the concept exponentially further. He divided the earth's surface into a grid composed of latitude and longitude, then, taking Hipparchus's division of the earth into 360 equal parts, or "degrees," he broke down each degree into *partes minutae primae* ("minutes") and *partes minutae secundae* ("seconds"). Ptolemy further enhanced his claim to the title of father of modern geography by calling the lines of latitude parallels and the lines of longitude meridians. In his *Geography*, Ptolemy provided the latitude and longitude of over eight thousand cities, rivers, mountains, and seacoasts. He changed the scale of his maps to provide greater detail for highly populated areas without changing the relative distance of one place from another. He oriented maps with north at the top.

All that remained to cement Ptolemy's immortality was to settle on the circumference of the earth so that all of these wonderful measurements would be correct. Again, there were two choices. The Greek mathematician Eratosthenes, also chief librarian of the stupendous library at Alexandria, had calculated that the earth was about 28,000 miles in circumference. Two other Greek mathematicians, Posidonius and Strabo, had decided some years later that the earth was only 18,000 miles around. Eratosthenes, as we now know, was a little high but pretty close. Posidonius and Strabo, on the other hand, were *much* too low, with an estimate that would shrink the distance a mariner must travel across the oceans to the west to reach the Indies by thousands of miles.

Ptolemy, of course, chose the second estimate. He also believed that Asia stretched a good deal farther to the east than it actually did. The combination of a shrunken circumference and an elongated Asia left the impression that the distance a ship going west must traverse to reach the Orient was only about 5,000 miles, less than half of what it actually turned out to be. That misapprehension did not cause much of a stir at the time, but about fourteen hundred years later it did spark the interest of an obscure Genoese navigator named Christopher Columbus.

A couple of centuries after Ptolemy wrote it, the *Geography* disappeared and lay dormant, at least in Europe, for over a thousand years. Then, in the fourteenth century, ship captains began to chart their voyages, particularly shorelines and places where submerged rocks or other marine hazards might lie. These charts were called *portolanos*, which meant harbor guides. As ships ventured farther and farther afield, the resulting charts began to create a fuller geographical representation of the world on a larger scale. The picture that emerged was far different from the Church-approved geography drawn, at least in theory, directly from the Scriptures. Given a choice of adhering to theology and piling up on a shoal or believing in heresy and sailing about safely, the captains quickly—and quietly—chose the latter. Thus geography became the first scientific discipline where empiricism overwhelmed theology.

As for Ptolemy himself, he was rediscovered in the 1400s, and Latin translations of the *Geography*, varying widely in accuracy, began to appear. In addition, the translators took to supplementing second-century information with more contemporary ideas. By 1524, when a German humanist, Bilabald Pirkheimer, completed a translation that was published in Strasbourg the following year, its relationship to the original work was vague at best and riddled with inaccuracies. A Greek edition published in 1533 with a foreword by Erasmus, one of the last works the great humanist would produce before his death three years later, was not much better.

At a time of growing interest in empiricism, Ptolemy's popularity was increasing, and the newest member of the Trechsel editorial team was given the task of creating a better Ptolemy. This meant that Servetus (writing as Michael Villanovanus) was responsible not only for translating and correcting the text but also for composing entirely new sections to update the work.

Servetus chose to use the Pirkheimer edition as his base but compared it to the oldest Latin and Greek editions he could find in order create a more authentic book. He entitled his edition *The Eight Books of the Account of Geography by Claudius Ptolemy of Alexandria, now for the first time edited according to the translation of Bilabald Pirkheimer, but compared to the Greek and early editions by Michael Villanovanus.* This version was so extensive, so much of an improvement on what had gone before, that there are some who have claimed that Servetus was the father of comparative geography. Although this is probably an overstatement, the 1536 edition was both the most careful rendition available of Ptolemy's original conception and as exhaustive an ethnological treatise as had been done anywhere.

It was an enormous job, taking over two years. The book included fifty maps, all of which were accompanied by a statistical abstract and a commentary on the populace, climate, and industry of the area. Servetus carried over Pirkheimer's notations if he felt they were appropriate, but overwhelmingly the notes that made up the commentaries were his.

Servetus being Servetus (or Villanovanus), he could not resist expressing himself pointedly, provocatively, and with wit. The English, he noted, were brave, the Scots fearless, the Italians vulgar, and the Irish "rude, inhospitable, barbarous and cruel." Opposite the map of Germany, he wrote, "Hungary produces cattle, Bavaria hogs, Franconia onions, turnips and licorice, Swabia harlots, Bohemia heretics, Bavaria again thieves, Helvetia hangmen and herdsmen, Westphalia liars and all Germany gluttons and drunkards." He was a good deal more kind

Tabula nouatotius orbis.

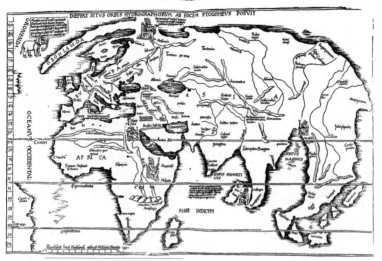

A map of the world from the 1541 edition of Ptolemy's Geography, *edited by Servetus as Villanovanus*

to France, except that he noted that "I have myself seen the King [Francis] touching many laboring under [scrofula, a particularly disgusting condition that causes tumors and ulcers to break out on the victim's neck], but I did not see that they were cured." (Francis, who claimed to be able to cure scrofula by touch, was said to be miffed, and the comment was altered in the second edition.) Servetus was dismissive of his native Spain, where, of course, under his real name he was a wanted man.

About Palestine, the legendary land of milk and honey, Servetus retained Pirkheimer's general description but added a joke:

> Know, however, most worthy reader, that it is mere boasting and untruth when so much excellence is ascribed to this land; the experience of merchants and others, travelers who have visited it, proving it to be inhospitable, barren, and altogether

without amenity. Wherefore you may say that the land is *promised*, indeed, but it is of *little promise* when spoken of in everyday terms.

This passage, which he did not even really write, was to come back and haunt him later because, unfortunately, one of those who ascribed excellence to the Holy Land had been Moses.

‡

THE *GEOGRAPHY*, AS EXTENSIVE as it was, was not Servetus's only project for the Trechsels. With his fluency in Latin and Greek, he was often called upon to read and correct medical texts. Among these was a French pharmaceutical guide entitled *Pentapharmacuum Gallicum*, written by Symphorien Champier, a physician of international renown and the founder of the medical faculty at Lyon.

Champier was an eccentric, made up of equal parts bravery, generosity, curiosity, humbuggery, and shameless self-promotion. He was chief medical officer to the duke of Lorraine, and in that capacity attended the wounded on the battlefield. Champier was the physician of choice among the local aristocracy, but he also visited the slums regularly to treat plague victims.

He was known by everyone in the city, and no major social function was complete without him. He was free with his opinions. When the town council proposed a tax on wheat, Champier, a humanist, quoted the classics and persuaded the officials to switch the tax to wine. Soon afterward, his home was ransacked by an outraged mob.

Medicine was another area of science where empiricism was beginning to undermine theology, but there remained a large number of doctors who continued to believe that God, medicine, and the stars were intertwined in a grand, holistic, astrological design. Champier, never shy, was one of the most forceful and prolific advocates of this position. His defense of Church-approved medicine against the advance of empiricism, including his *Prognosticon perpetuum Astrologorum, Medicorum et Prophetarum (The Guide of the Astrologer, Physician and Prophet in their Prognostications or Forecasts)*, was extremely popular with high Church officials. Among his closest friends was Cardinal François de Tournon, one of the heads of the French Inquisition, to whom Champier dedicated a number of books.

Champier became another in the long line of older, celebrated men who found Servetus irresistible. He more or less adopted his new young editor (thirty-nine years his junior), appointing Servetus his personal secretary, and proceeding to introduce him to every important physician-astrologer, intellectual, and high Church official in Lyon. More than once, Tournon, a ferocious pursuer of heretics, sat across the table from Michel de Villeneuve and engaged in dinner conversation with one of the most notorious heretics of the decade.

Servetus's transformation was complete. There wasn't a whisper of heresy about him. Everyone who knew that Michel de Villeneuve was actually the arch-heretic Servetus had fled the country. He went to Mass and avoided ecclesiastical debate. For the first time, he had money in his pocket and the promise of success in a respected field outside of theology.

Servetus's gratitude for Champier's patronage went beyond the reinforcement of his alias. A genuine mutual respect and affection seems to have grown up between them. Through Champier, Servetus not only gained acceptance by a stratum of society to which he had not previously had access, but also was exposed to an area of learning outside theology in which his immense curiosity and thirst for knowledge might be satisfied.

France, too, had calmed down. With most of the key reformers now in exile, the Protestant threat had largely receded, and for the most part, the Inquisition went back to burning books rather than people. With France safely Catholic once again, Francis turned his attention back to his old nemesis, Charles. He began to mobilize for war, which came in 1536, when he provoked Charles by invading Savoy, to which Charles responded by invading Provence.

With the king facing south, Servetus felt safe enough, on Champier's recommendation, to return to Paris. In 1536, Michael Servetus, once again under the name of Michel de Villenueve, registered at the University of Paris, this time as a medical student. ‡

CHAPTER EIGHT

THE MEDICAL SCHOOL at the University of Paris was located in the rue de la Bûcherie, one short block from the Seine
in the Quartier Latin. (The Latin Quarter got its name from
language, not ethnicity. In the university district, everyone
spoke Latin, not French.) In order to apply for a baccalaureate in medicine, a student generally needed the same prerequisite five-year arts
course that the Sorbonne demanded of its theology students. This requirement was waived for Michael Villanovanus who, with an impressive and demonstrable record of scholarship and publication, was
deemed qualified to undertake the course of studies.

At the moment Servetus arrived for the fall 1536 term, the study of
medicine was poised, after over a thousand years of intellectual tyranny,
at the brink of the modern age. For more than a millennium, any information regarding the structure, function, or medical treatment of the
human body had been strictly limited by the Church to the teachings
of one man—the great second-century Roman physician Galen.

✝

IN THE HISTORY OF SCIENCE, there has never been a single individual who did as much to both move his discipline forward and hold
it back as did Galen. He was born in 130 A.D. in Pergamum, in what is
now Turkey, the son of an architect who named him "quiet and peaceful" so he wouldn't be like his mother. Galen was first trained as a

philosopher but at seventeen switched to botany and medicine, and then went off to study in Alexandria, the preeminent center of medical learning at the time. After he finished school, he returned home and got his first break when he was assigned as head of sports medicine at the local gladiatorial school.

Medical knowledge in the second century was primarily reliant upon the teachings of Hippocrates and Aristotle and suffered from several enormous disadvantages, none so great as the absolute prohibition against human autopsy. Although a few hardy Greeks had taken a peek inside a dead person as early as 500 B.C., by Galen's day the Romans were sure that if you cut a person up after he or she was dead, the spirit would come back and get even. Also, the revenge would not necessarily be restricted to the person who did the cutting. Thus a physician was forced to conduct his business lacking the fundamental blueprint of the trade. It was like a mechanic trying to figure out what was wrong with your car without being allowed to open the hood.

But Galen was at gladiatorial school, where there was no shortage of grisly and extensive wounds that a curious and enterprising young physician could peer into. It was an effective way to learn a lot about muscles and bones, and at least see a lot of blood. Galen also observed that in those fallen warriors who received spinal injuries, the exact location of the trauma on the spine determined which areas of the body lost muscle function. An injury just above the waist meant that only the legs would be paralyzed, while one above the shoulders meant that use of the arms was lost as well. With the most serious spinal injuries, the victim lost the ability to breathe and died altogether. From these observations, Galen developed a hypothesis about nerve and spinal cord function.

Not only was Galen unusually successful in patching up the gladiators, but he also began to apply his extensive knowledge of botany to curing illness and disease. Depending on the condition, he variously prescribed opium, wine, turpentine, honey, grape juice, and barley water, as well as plant extracts and the occasional cold compress. He became an expert pharmacologist and traveled widely to obtain unusual herbs, plants, or flowers.

He did so well in Pergamum that he took himself and his growing reputation to Rome to become a celebrity physician, a venture at which he was almost immediately successful. "[I] called on the mighty in the morning and dined with them in the evening," he wrote. He was soon lecturing, and his fame spread to the point where the sick wrote to him from all across the empire. So confident was Galen in his healing ability that he had no qualms about prescribing by mail. Here, too, he was often successful, and it was said that Galen "left no clinical studies, only miraculous cures." He became sufficiently renowned that he was summoned by the emperor, Marcus Aurelius, and appointed as personal physician to his son Commodus.

(Commodus, who has since been immortalized by Hollywood in the movie *Gladiator*, was not killed in the arena by Russell Crowe but rather strangled in his bathtub by a wrestler named Narcissus after being insufficiently poisoned by his mistress. The real Commodus could not have been farther from the preening coward of the film. He was the only emperor to actually enter the arena as a combatant. He personally fought tigers, panthers, and elephants, and was said to have once killed one hundred tigers using only one hundred arrows before breakfast.)

Galen did as much as he could to learn about human anatomy. With human corpses forbidden, he procured goats, pigs, and monkeys and cut them open. (Monkeys were best, of course, but you couldn't always get a monkey.) From these dissections, called anatomies, Galen went on to correctly theorize about human kidney and bladder function, as well as describing the role of the brain in controlling such functions as sight and speech. But observing only dead animals had its shortcomings. There is not necessarily a strict congruence between the innards of people and animals. Even primates have a substantially different physiology from humans. As a result, many of Galen's extrapolations, like that of a lobed liver and a two-boned lower jaw, were simply wrong.

Another drawback to Galenic anatomy was the inability to examine bodily processes, most of which ceased after death. Nowhere did this cause more problems than in the description of the circulatory system. While Galen did demonstrate that arteries carry blood, not air—a major step forward in the second century—and described the structural differences between arteries and veins, as well as mapping out heart valves, he also believed that the liver, not the heart, was the system's main organ and that blood moved from the liver to the outer portions of the body to create flesh. In addition, Galen taught that the arterial and venous systems were separate and that blood moved from the left side of the heart to the right through pores in the septum, or dividing wall. The heart was the spiritual rather than the mechanical hub of the system and, according to Galen, was the hottest part of the body. The lungs filled with air only to cool the heart and keep it from exploding.

As to disease, Galen drew on Aristotle and postulated that all bodily disorders were caused by an imbalance in the four "humors" present in each person—blood, phlegm, yellow bile (choler), and black bile (melancholy). Each person had his or her own distinctive balance of these four humors, and too much or too little of one or more of them caused illness. (It also meant that each person had his or her own unique body temperature.) A proper rebalancing of the humors would provide a cure, so recommended treatments were often limited to inducing a patient to bleed, sweat, vomit, urinate, or have diarrhea. It was no picnic to be ill in the second century.

While there is no doubt that Galen produced a remarkable and persuasive portrait of the body and its functions, what caused him to evolve into the figure of omniscient authority that he eventually became was that he wrote *everything* down. Galen was the most prolific author of his time. He put out over five hundred separate books, few of them short. In medicine alone, he produced over twenty thousand pages of text—and that is just what has survived, only about a third of the total. He wrote not only on medicine but also on botany and philosophy, and was not above penning a play or two when things got slow on the science front.

All of his books, thousands upon thousands of pages, went into the great library at Alexandria. From there, he was discovered by the Church. Overwhelmed by the sheer bulk of his knowledge and impressed by the spiritual foundations of Galen's corporeal philosophy, the Church adopted him fully and completely. He was said to have been divinely inspired and infallible, and it became heresy to go against him. He was translated into Latin and disseminated throughout the Christian world. New approved versions of Galen were produced all the time, and no medieval medical office was complete without the sixteen or so volumes that came to constitute the Galenic canon.

Although by the sixteenth century there was a good deal of evidence around that Galen had made some glaring errors, the Church continued to restrict the sciences of medicine and anatomy to the findings of a man who never saw the inside of a human being.

‡

IT WAS IN 1525 that the sanctity of Galen got its first major jolt. The House of Aldus (then being run by the tightwad Torresani, Erasmus's favorite) published a compilation of Galen's work in the original Greek, drawn, of course, from all those manuscripts that had made their way to Italy from Constantinople. In this translation, there were some noticeable differences from the Church-approved texts. Suddenly there were two Galens, and the fight was on. The differences were largely trivial, often only a matter of semantics, but this was the first time that anyone had debated anything at all about medicine in hundreds of years.

Inevitably, some even began to question Galen altogether. The renegade Swiss physician Theophrastus Phillippus Aureolus Bombastus von Hohenheim, who, in a wise professional move, shortened his name to Paracelsus (although reasons for that particular choice remain obscure), began to spout the laughable notion that disease originates from agents outside the body causing a disruption in body chemistry, and not from an imbalance in the humors. Paracelsus, who gained favor and notoriety in Strasbourg when he cured Johann Froben—yes, that Froben, Erasmus's and Luther's publisher—and lost it soon after when Froben relapsed and died, also said that medicines should not be merely herbal but also include animal and especially mineral substances as well—in fact, anything that worked. (Not all of Paracelsus's views were so enlightened. He also claimed that he could turn rocks into gold and that the stars foretold the optimum time to administer an enema. Also, his own personal hygiene was so lax that when he had a new coat made every month and tried to give the old one away, no one would take it because it smelled so bad.) Labeled as a quack and a charlatan by the established medical community, Paracelsus nonetheless remained adamant about his theory of chemical rather than humoric imbalance. For most of his life, despite the praise of Erasmus, whom he also treated, he was hounded from place to place and died in poverty.

Galen notwithstanding, almost every student of medicine or anatomy in the sixteenth century realized that nothing could move forward without firsthand observation. The spur for this observation turned out to be not so much a thirst for scientific knowledge as a thirst for profit.

By the 1530s, the medical profession had a firmly established hierarchy. At the very top were physicians, whose authority sprung primarily from their ability to read Latin. Much as the Church had used Latin to keep knowledge of the Scriptures from the laity, physicians since Hippocrates had used Latin to keep medical knowledge from anyone but themselves. Being a physician largely meant being a scholar—someone who could read and interpret the old texts—learning from books rather than empirically.

Directly under the physicians came the surgeons, and then the barbers. Surgeons were craftsmen, members of a guild with requirements for entry and set prices for their services. They had some book learning, but not nearly as much as physicians. As the people who were actually treating wounds, setting bones, or cutting people open, they were, by necessity, empiricists, much like the ship captains who preferred heresy to shipwreck.

Barbers were at the bottom of the ladder—they knew no Latin and their skill was minimal. They were, however, cheap. Anyone who couldn't afford a surgeon got a barber. More disquieting for the surgeons, physicians often opted for the less expensive barber when contracting for a dissection. The competition sometimes boiled over. At the University of Paris, "the resentment of the surgeons was expressed in a complaint to the faculty...in which it was asserted that the barbers had independently obtained the body of an executed criminal, and that certain members of the faculty had not only demonstrated its anatomy, but furthermore in French rather than in Latin." "Independently obtained" meant that they stole it.

It was soon clear to the surgeons that the only way they could maintain their competitive edge on the barbers was to make sure that their knowledge of the body was *so* much better that no one who could afford to would ever choose the cheaper alternative. And the only way to ensure better knowledge was to have more dissections.

Although empiricism was pushing hard against tradition at the University of Paris in 1536, the university lagged somewhat behind its Italian counterparts in its use of human dissection as a research and teaching tool. Human dissections, although allowed, were still reasonably rare. Bodies were difficult to come by—only the corpses of executed criminals were permissible. And dissections were expensive. You had to pay the executioner, his assistants, and the boatman who brought the body across the river, then buy breakfast for everyone including the two men who had cut off the cadaver's head and buried it in secrecy so as not to offend the populace. You also had to rent a table and buy vinegar to wash the body. When it was over, there was the mess to clean up and payment to the priest to allow you to bury the bits and pieces of the body that were left, with a little extra for a Mass for the soul of the dead criminal.

Dissections were performed in a corner room of the medical school that could be sealed off from the rest of the building by a heavy wooden door. It was round, about thirty feet across, and rose straight up to a peaked roof about fifty feet high. Students could observe close in from ground level or from a walkway set about fifteen feet up. There was a row of large windows behind the walkway and another row of windows between the walkway and the roof. These windows provided the only ventilation for the entire room, the only way to rid the room of the smell.

The two most distinguished professors of medicine at the university during Servetus's tenure there were Jacobus Sylvius and Jean Guinter of Andernach. Both men were leaders of Parisian academic medicine, particularly of anatomy, but they had very different methods of instruction. Sylvius, by all reports a dour, foul-tempered bigot, was nevertheless by far the more popular teacher. He once had nine hundred copies of a book printed up as required reading for his general studies course; they all sold out in a few days and more had to be printed. It was common practice at the time for the professor to sit in a high chair during dissections and read to the observing students from Galen (in Latin, of course) while a barber or surgeon actually cut up the body. Since the barbers didn't understand Latin, however, they never knew what it was they were supposed to be displaying at any one time. (One student complained that he could have learned more from "a butcher in his stall.")

Unlike his fellow physicians, Sylvius got right in there and cut up the body himself. Because he didn't get too many human bodies, he was more likely to dissect dogs (which were plentiful). He also employed other, somewhat more unorthodox means of acquiring specimens. A writer of the period who audited Sylvius's class wrote:

I recall having heard the eloquent Jacobus Sylvius lecture on Galen's *Use of parts* to a remarkable audience of scholars of all nations...I have seen him bring in his sleeve sometimes a thigh or sometimes the arm of someone hanged, in order to dissect and anatomize it. They stank so strongly and offensively that some of his auditors would readily have thrown up if they had dared; but the cantankerous fellow with his Picard head would have been so violently incensed, threatening not to return for a week, that everyone kept silent.

Sylvius was responsible for identifying valves in the veins as well as a number of other important blood vessels and muscles, but he remained a staunch Galenist. When faced with obvious errors in the Galenic model, he asserted that Galen had been right but that the human body had changed over the years, "and not for the better." The thigh bone had become straighter, for example, because people had come to wear tighter pants. To Sylvius, the only possible improvement in medical science was a better, more literal translation of Galen's original Greek texts.

Guinter de Andernach taught much more in the traditional mode. Although he was a kindly man, friendly to his students, his principal contribution to their education was unintentional. Because he himself did not dissect the corpse, he left more of the work to his student assistant. The student assistant was responsible for preparing the cadaver for dissection, which meant at the very least a space close to the barber during the actual lecture. In some cases, it even meant actually taking charge of the knife. This represented an invaluable opportunity to see what was in the body up close. Dissections were crowded, and those in the back, while removed from the stink, were also removed from the lesson. The student chosen for this honor was always at the very top of the class. He was christened "archdeacon of students" by the others.

Guinter had two such student assistants, one right after the other,

whom he felt compelled to cite for excellence. The first, Andreas Vesalius, he described as "a young man by Hercules, singularly proficient in
anatomy."

✣

IF ANYONE COULD BE SAID to have been bred for greatness in the
field of medicine, it was Vesalius. Family lore had it that his great-great-
grandfather, Peter Witing, was physician to Emperor Frederick III. His
great-grandfather, Johannes de Wesalia, was professor of medicine at
the newly opened University of Louvain as well as city physician of
Brussels and court physician to Charles the Bold. It was Johannes who
was granted the family heraldic symbol. Since these were unfortunately
assigned based on the family name, Vesalius's family wound up with
three weasels. Johannes was also responsible for accumulating the family fortune, which was considerable, and for the purchase of a large estate in Brussels.

Johannes's eldest son, Everard—Vesalius's grandfather—advanced
the family's social position still further. *He* became physician to Emperor Maximilian, his wife, Mary of Burgundy, and their son, Philip the
Fair, later married to Juana the Mad and father to Charles V. Everard,
who died young, probably in his thirties, was actually knighted, which
was rare for a doctor.

In spite of this pedigree, Vesalius almost didn't make it because
Everard never bothered to marry Vesalius's grandmother, and so their
son, Andries Van Wesele, Vesalius's father, was born out of wedlock. Illegitimacy (outside the papacy) was a major handicap in those days,
and Andries's expectations were thus necessarily reduced. He rose only
to the position of apothecary, although he was apothecary to Charles V
and, as such, had to follow the court around from place to place. This
meant that he was rarely home, which wasn't so bad since instead of
living on the beautiful Van Wesele estate, Vesalius and his parents had
been forced to set up housekeeping in the much more déclassé neigh-

borhood of Bovendael. Bovendael, which was basically skid row, was conveniently located near the Montagne de la Potence, which was a wooded area where they tortured and executed criminals. In those days, they couldn't be bothered to cut down the bodies after they'd killed them, so the Van Wesele family always had a clear view from their sitting-room window of decaying, stinking corpses, half-eaten by birds. A more direct source of inspiration for a budding anatomist would be hard to come by.

Vesalius, born in 1514, would probably have ended up an apothecary like his father, but fate took a happy turn. As reward for all those years spent following him around and dispensing potions, Charles removed the stain of illegitimacy from Andries's family by royal edict. The way was now paved for Vesalius to become a great man.

After a brief stint at the University of Louvain in 1533, Vesalius was off to the much more prestigious University of Paris, where his keen enthusiasm for anatomy won him the coveted position of assistant to Guinter. As bodies were scarce, Vesalius, no doubt drawing on childhood experiences, developed his own unique form of studying. At night, he and some friends would sneak down to the charnel house and gather up any loose bones they might find lying around. Then they would blindfold each other and attempt to identify each bone simply by touch. Vesalius was a whiz at this game, although there was additional competition. "I was gravely imperiled by many savage dogs," he reported later.

Vesalius, as a Belgian and a subject of Charles, had to leave Paris in 1536 when the emperor invaded France. He finished off his course of study at the University of Padua, where, upon graduating in record time, he was immediately hired as professor of surgery and anatomy. Wherever he went, he made a practice of learning as much about the human body as possible. He stole bodies, bit by bit, from gallows and stakes by the side of the road, boiled the bones to soften them, and then reassembled the skeletons. He sometimes kept corpses in his apartment for up to three days before holding private anatomies for his

The only accurate portrait of Andreas Vesalius, age twenty-eight, taken from the Fabrica

students—this in an age before refrigeration and air-conditioning. And he never, ever missed the opportunity to perform an anatomy:

> When I returned from my visit to France I was invited by the physician of the Countess of Egmont to attend the autopsy of an eighteen-year-old girl of noble birth who, because of an enduring paleness of complexion and difficulty in breathing— although otherwise of agreeable appearance—was thought by her uncle to have been poisoned. Since the dissection had been undertaken by a thoroughly unskilled barber I could not keep my hand from the work, although except for two crude dissections lasting three days, which I had seen at school in Paris, I had never been present at one. From constriction of the thorax by a corset the girl had been accustomed to wear so that her waist might appear long and willowy, I judged that

the complaint lay in a compression of the torso around the hypochondria and lungs. The attendant women left to shed their corsets as quickly as possible.

And on another occasion:

The handsome mistress of a certain monk of San Antonio here [in Padua] died suddenly as though from strangulation of the uterus or some quickly devastating ailment and was snatched from her tomb by the Paduan students and carried off for public dissection. By their remarkable industry they flayed the whole skin from the cadaver lest it be recognized by the monk who, with the relatives of his mistress, had complained to the municipal judge that the body had been stolen from the tomb.

Vesalius could not help but notice that what he saw in his anatomies often did not correspond with accepted doctrine. In many key areas, Galen had been completely wrong. But it wasn't until 1540, at a public dissection in front of two hundred people in the Church of San Francesco in Italy, that Vesalius finally declared, as his biographer Charles O'Malley wrote, that "if his statement did not agree with Galen's, he would nonetheless demonstrate that he was right and Galen was wrong... It was sufficiently novel and sufficiently irritating to the conservative members of the audience so that they felt called upon to demonstrate their displeasure by marching out of the hall."

Then, in 1543, Vesalius did something that no one had had the nerve or the skill to do before—only twenty-nine years old, he published a book called *De Humani Corporis Fabrica* (*On the Structure of the Human Body*), in which he recorded his observations without regard to Church dogma. It was the very same year that Copernicus published *On the Revolutions of the Celestial Spheres.* The *Fabrica* was printed in folio and is one of the great books of science and perhaps the most important book ever published in the field of medicine. Vesalius described hundreds of parts of the body that had never been described before, including the heart. He charted the course of veins. But more than that, he ceaselessly refuted Galen. The lobed liver was gone, as was the compound lower jaw. The femur was now straight, and bile ducts and the uterus were accurately depicted for the first time.

But however overpowering the scholarship, what made this book so unique were its illustrations. The *Fabrica* ran to 663 pages, of which 277 were woodcuts of muscles, blood vessels, organs, and nerves. These were illustrations of such incredible beauty, accuracy, and detail that although the artist or artists remain anonymous, prevailing thought credits them to the workshop of Titian. The title page illustration, an engraving depicting Vesalius dissecting a cadaver in the midst of a packed and enthralled crowd of students, is one of the most famous in printing history.

(The original woodcuts were carefully preserved and protected, surviving numerous wars, plagues, and panics. They were lost for a time, only to be rediscovered in 1893, hidden in the library at the University of Munich. Then, after four hundred years, these priceless pieces of art were destroyed, along with the one-of-a-kind skeleton of the giant carnivorous dinosaur Spinosaurus, by Allied bombs in World War II.)

The *Fabrica* was an instant sensation. The illustrations in particular were so convincing that Galenic theory crumbled almost from the day it was published. With one exception, Vesalius's description of human anatomy remained the standard for over four centuries. But that exception was enormous. Galen had postulated that blood moved from one side of the heart to the other through pores in the heart wall. In all of his autopsies, Vesalius had failed to observe these pores, yet in this one instance only he did not trust his own eyes. Rather he concluded that the pores in the septum did exist but were simply too small to be seen. So Vesalius missed entirely the heart's role in circulating blood through the body, and therefore also the functions and importance of the circulatory and respiratory systems, and without these there could be no real advancements of medical knowledge.

Title page of the 1543 edition of the Fabrica

The *Fabrica* was the pinnacle of Vesalius's career. The very next year, his father died and left him a sizable inheritance, and he gave up research and academia to accept the more prestigious position of personal physician to Charles V. He got married, built a big house, and re-laxed into his new role. When Charles abdicated in 1556, Vesalius moved to Spain to become court physician to his successor, Philip II.

But Vesalius's devotion to anatomy ultimately had its price. There was a rumor that while in Spain, during the dissection of a young no-bleman, Vesalius touched the heart with his pointer and it suddenly beat. Another rumor claimed that while he was dissecting a young woman who had died of a strangled uterus, she suddenly but briefly sprung back to life, much to the consternation of her relatives. What-ever the reason, in 1564 he felt obliged to resign his office and make amends by undertaking a pilgrimage to Palestine. He made it there, but on the return trip he was shipwrecked on a deserted island. The man who gave the world the human body died miserably and alone, some-where off the coast of Greece. ‡

CHAPTER NINE

THE MAN WHO replaced Andreas Vesalius as Guinter of Andernach's assistant was Michael Servetus. Guinter considered them equals and called Servetus a young man "distinguished by his literary acquirements of every kind, and scarcely second to any in his knowledge of Galenical doctrine." Nowhere was the versatility of Servetus's genius more evident than in his time at the medical school in Paris. Within three years of taking up an entirely new course of study, one with which he had no previous experience and no family background, during a time when he lectured on at least two unrelated subjects, Michael Servetus, by virtue of one great discovery, became one of the foremost anatomists in the world.

Servetus was an unusual student in a number of respects. Actually, he was not officially a student at all—his name appears nowhere in the ledgers. In order to register, an applicant was required to produce a birth certificate, and Michel de Villeneuve would have been unlikely to submit a document that revealed that he was really the arch-heretic Servetus. He probably bluffed his way in with the promise to produce his proofs at a later date and then either continued to finesse the issue or allowed it to be forgotten. This of course meant that when he left the university three years later, he didn't officially have a degree, either.

Yet it is clear that he was there, that he did study medicine and complete the course brilliantly. Graduate students, then as now, were encouraged to teach as a supplement to their income, and Servetus, editor of Ptolemy, began to lecture on geography and astronomy, as well as mathematics. Apparently he was an engaging speaker, because his lecture series became very popular and was well attended by many important people, including an ambitious and talented young priest by the name of Pierre Palmier.

After his first year, Servetus felt himself sufficiently advanced in his studies to compose a pamphlet on digestive aids entitled *The Syrups*. The full title was *A Complete Account of Syrups Carefully Refined According to the Judgment of Galen to which, after a full discourse on concoction has been added the true method of purgation, as well as an exposition on the aphorism: Medicate that which has been concocted.* After the author's name, Michael Villanovanus, was appended modestly, "You who are going to concoct the crude humors and restore health to the human body. Observe the teachings of this book."

Title page of The Syrups

Syruporum vni-
VERSA RATIO, AD GA-
leni cenſuram diligenter
expolita.

Cui, poſt integrã de concoctione diſceptationem,
præſcripta eſt uera purgandi methodus,cum ex-
poſitione aphoriſmi:Concocta medicari.

Michaële Villanouano authore.

Γρὸς τὸμ φιλία τρομ.
Εύροα ποιήσωμ τά τε σώμαϊα,τά τε πεπάνωμ
Ωμὰ χυμῶμ,τάυτης ᵭόγματα ἴᵭι βίβλᵃ.

P A R I S I I S
Ex officina Simonis Colinæi.
I   5   3   7

The Syrups was little more than an extremely accurate translation of Galen. In the Galenic model, food is taken into the stomach, then "concocted," or cooked, to provide energy. Any unused portion then passes into the blood and is circulated by the veins through the body, where the food undergoes a second "concoction" by the body's heat. As the concocted food flows with the blood, each organ or body part assimilates what it needs for nourishment, then passes whatever is left to the next part, and on and on, until every part of the body has had its shot. Anything still unused is then expelled in the traditional manner.

When everything works properly, the result is a balance in the blood of the four humors. Eat a bad lobster, however, and the balance is disrupted. Disrupted balance means incomplete assimilation, and that in turn could lead to putrefaction of the blood. As part of the treatment to restore balance, "syrups," or sweetened herbal or fruit liquids that encouraged heat in the stomach to aid digestion (read: purgative), were employed.

Despite pithy passages on such processes as the generation of pus and bile, Servetus's little tract has no current medical relevance whatever. At the time, however, it was considered a very helpful manual, and it went to six printings, making its author a nice bit of money while adding to his reputation as a medical scholar.

Servetus was now the author of a popular book, an instructor in a popular lecture series, and the archdeacon of students in the medical school. He was more secure than he had ever been before. But as a biographer would later write, he was also saddled with "a genius for indiscretion," a trait that he brought forth with gusto now. He began in his lectures to criticize some of the faculty for lack of talent or sufficient education. Specifically, his complaint was that these professors did not study astronomy, and that no physician's education could be complete without it. In those days, astronomy was a broadly defined discipline that included the effects of weather. It also included astrology, one branch of which was called "judicial astrology" and was, in fact, little more than fortune-telling.

Servetus, as passionate and bull-headed when he was wrong as when he was right, thought it laughable that medical professors were too shortsighted to grasp that the stars affected the timing of cures. As always, he expressed his opinions colorfully and often. He called his professors "the plagues of society," among other things.

The medical faculty, understandably, did not appreciate his remarks, and the dean of the school had Servetus in his office several times, objecting to his language and warning him not to incorporate horoscopes or the influence of the stars into medical treatment. Servetus reacted by preparing a scathing pamphlet in which he attacked the medical faculty even more vociferously. When the faculty learned that Servetus was preparing a written diatribe, they went to the Parlement of Paris and petitioned them to prevent Servetus from publishing his tract. When Servetus learned that the faculty had sued to suppress his pamphlet, he rushed it into print by promising a larger fee to the publisher and then made sure that it was distributed for maximum impact and embarrassment to the professors.

Then it was again the professors' turn. They bypassed the Parlement and went directly to the Inquisition, demanding that Servetus be cited for heresy, not because he was criticizing them, of course, but for practicing judicial astrology. While this degree of heresy was not nearly as heinous as, say, denying the Trinity, who but Michael Servetus could then have walked in under an assumed name, calmly faced a tribunal that would have happily sentenced him to death if they had had any idea who he actually was, and argued persuasively (and successfully) that his accusers didn't know what they were talking about?

After the Inquisition tossed out the case, the faculty went back to the civil authorities and demanded that the pamphlet be suppressed and that Servetus be enjoined from lecturing on proscribed topics. There was a trial and Servetus hired a lawyer to defend him. Perhaps he shouldn't have, for although his counsel argued strenuously that his client was a practitioner of astronomy, not judicial astrology, the Parlement disagreed, ultimately accepting the plaintiff's case almost word for word. Servetus was required to recall all the copies of his pamphlet and told to stop predicting the future. However, to show how unimportant they considered the case, the Parlement dismissed the entire matter with what amounted to a finger-wagging lecture. Servetus was told to be polite to his professors, and his professors were told to treat him with gentleness, as parents treat their children.

Servetus left Paris soon afterward. He had not spent the requisite four years at medical school to get his degree, which could not have been conferred anyway, but he had learned pretty much all he needed to know. In fact, he had learned more. After observing at most two or three anatomies, Servetus had made a stunning intellectual leap. It would be one of science's great deductions, the very thing that Vesalius, a brilliant observer but a far less intuitive thinker, had missed. Servetus's discovery would later be called "a bridge between the medieval world and the modern."

He would not publish it for another fifteen years.

‡

AFTER SERVETUS LEFT PARIS, he returned for a brief time to Lyon before setting up practice as a country doctor in nearby Charlieu in the spring of 1538. Charlieu didn't have too many doctors educated at the University of Paris, so he was accepted almost immediately by the town's leading citizens and his practice thrived. There is even a hint of a romantic connection with a local girl.

But not everybody in town was pleased that the brilliant Dr. Villenueve had decided to settle down there. Professional jealousy was apparently expressed in a much more direct fashion in those days. Servetus was attacked one night on his way to tend a patient, by marauders representing a competing doctor. There was a sword fight in the dark. Servetus succeeded in driving off his attackers, slicing one up in the process. He himself was slightly wounded. As a result of this incident, he was arrested (no doubt at the instigation of the other doctor) but was released two or three days later.

After this experience, he began to look around for a new place to practice. His old student, Pierre Palmier, had recently been appointed archbishop of Vienne. Vienne, on the Rhône about twenty miles south of Lyon, was an important ecclesiastical city. Four previous bishops had been elevated to sainthood, and one had been elected pope. Palmier, who had the heart of an ecclesiastic but the soul of a humanist, was now the leader of the church for the entire province of Dauphiny. When he heard of Servetus's availability, he stepped in and asked him to transfer to Vienne, even offering him apartments at his own château.

(The tradition of referring to the French heir to the throne as "dauphin" originated in Dauphiny. Dauphiny had been a separate principality, but in 1349 Humbert, the sovereign, "having had the misfortune of dropping his only son into the Rhône," entered a monastery and gave his country to the French king, Philippe de Valois, on the condition that the eldest son of the king from then on always be referred to as "dauphin." In addition, royal edicts were not to be in force in Dauphiny unless they were submitted independently, with the king referred to as "Dauphin of Vienne.")

In Vienne, as in Calvin's birthplace of Noyon, social as well as ecclesiastical life revolved around the archbishop. Servetus could count not only on getting a lot of business, but on meeting the very best, most educated, wealthiest people in the province, which included renewing his old acquaintance with Cardinal de Tournon, by then perhaps the most powerful Church official in France. More than that, Vienne was the site of a new branch printing office of the Trechsels' publishing house. If he moved to Vienne, Servetus could continue to edit, which he obviously enjoyed, as well as practice medicine.

He accepted Palmier's invitation and within two years had gained a reputation, through his own hard work and humanitarianism, as one of the leading doctors in the province. Among his patients were not only Palmier but also Guy de Maugiron, lieutenant governor of the province and a commander in the king's council. As had Champier before him, Servetus treated the poor as well as the rich, and when plague struck Lyon in 1542, he ignored the personal risks and dedicated himself to caring for the sick.

✠

MICHAEL SERVETUS SETTLED into the most idyllic period of his life. He was celebrated as a physician and mixed freely with the highest levels of local society. He had money, position, and the leisure to pursue the studies necessary to a rich intellectual life. His reputation as a scholar commended him to other men of letters and ensured that he was in demand as an editor of important works.

His first assignment for the Trechsels in Vienne was a second edition of the *Geography*, which Servetus dedicated to Palmier, who evidently assisted in the work. "For you," he wrote, "are the one among our church dignitaries I have known who, loving letters and favoring learned men, have given particular attention to geographic science. I am also incited to my work by the many favors I have received at your hand." As beautiful as the 1535 edition had been, the 1541 was even better. The paper was of a higher quality, the woodcuts were improved, maps were added, and the commentaries supplemented.

This second edition was as significant for what was omitted as for what was added. Opposite the map of Palestine, for example, where formerly had been inserted the refutation of the milk and honey legend, there was...nothing, no commentary whatever. As for the passage where Servetus had cast doubt on the king's ability to cure scrofula by touch, "I have never seen this" was replaced by "I have heard this is so." But nowhere was the new, kindlier Michael Servetus more in evidence than in the few lines he appended to the address to the reader:

This world and all its kingdoms wouldst thou know,
What mighty rivers to blue oceans flow,
What mountains rise, what cities grace the lands,
Thick-peopled, rich with toil of busy hands,—
—If such lore thou hast a mind to call,
Open this book, and there survey it all.

Then, in 1541, he was asked to edit a one-volume edition of the Pagnini Bible.

✚

THE PAGNINI BIBLE WAS THE work of Santes Pagnino, a Dominican friar born in 1470. Pagnino devoted twenty-five years of his life to the completion of a Latin version of the Bible translated from the original Greek and Hebrew and divided, for the first time, into chapters. It ran to seven volumes and was sponsored by Popes Leo X and Clement VII.

Although Pagnino intended his Bible to be a literal rendering of the original Scriptures, the participation of the Church ensured that any questionable passages would come down on the side of orthodoxy. The Bible was published in Lyon in 1527, and Pagnino spent the last seven years of his life in the city.

When Pagnino died, a local burgher decided to finance a new, one-volume edition of his Bible to commemorate his death. Whoever undertook to edit the project would obviously require a thorough knowledge of Hebrew, and Servetus came up as the most likely candidate.

Up until this point, Servetus had maintained his image as a devout Catholic. He went to Mass like everybody else and counted the archbishop and the cardinal as his friends. He could easily have lived out the rest of his life in comfort and success. There is every indication that he intended to do so ... until he accepted the job as editor of the Pagnini Bible.

The first Servetus edition of the Pagnini Bible was actually rather tame, sticking largely to the traditional interpretation of the Scriptures. However, he could not resist including a preface in which he criticized biblical scholars for not accepting the Scriptures in their literal form but instead insisting on seeking more mystical meanings. He didn't specifically mention the Trinity, of course, so no one made the connection. He went on to say that a study of Hebrew and ancient Jewish culture could clarify many of the inconsistencies that had grown up around orthodox interpretation:

> They who are ignorant of the Hebrew language and history are only too apt to overlook the historical and literal sense of the sacred Scriptures; the consequence of which is that they vainly and foolishly expend themselves in hunting after recondite and mystical meanings in the text where nothing of the kind exists.

No one seemed to take issue with this statement, and soon after, Servetus signed a contract to undertake the much more arduous task of editing a full seven-volume edition. It would take him three years. In this larger edition, he made significant alterations in the translation in order to demonstrate that the Scriptures were not being applied literally by either Rome or the reformers. He attacked the notion that passages in the Old Testament prophesied those in the New. One correction in particular was to cause a stir. In Isaiah 7:14, there is a passage that officially read, "Behold, a virgin shall conceive and bear a son." Servetus corrected the misapplication of the Hebrew and substituted the proper translation, "a young marriageable woman," for "virgin." As a result of the changes, the Villanovanus edition of the Pagnini Bible was put on the restricted list in Louvain and also prohibited by the Inquisition in Spain.

It did not, however, affect Servetus's status in Vienne. He remained publicly admired and respected. But privately, his interest in theology

was rekindled. All the old passions came surging back. Furiously, secretly, he began once again to scribble down his own thoughts on the
nature of Christianity.

‡

IN ADDITION TO WORKING for the Trechsels, Servetus freelanced for
other publishers. One of these, Jean Frellon, for whom Servetus translated Latin grammars into Spanish, was a practicing Catholic who privately leaned toward the reform movement. The two became friends,
and Servetus, once again in the grip of his own theological fury, violated his own rule and discussed religion.

Servetus, with his encyclopedic knowledge of the Scriptures, was
getting the better of Frellon in every argument. Casting around for a
more competent authority to help him pursue the discussion, Frellon
had an idea. He happened to be a good friend of one of the great biblical scholars in Europe, he told Servetus. He was sure that his friend
would find Dr. Villeneuve's ideas interesting, and that the doctor would
find his friend to be the perfect person with whom to discuss these
lofty matters. Frellon even offered to write a letter of introduction.

Servetus agreed. He enclosed a letter of his own with that of
Frellon.

The letters were addressed to the Reformer of Geneva, John
Calvin. ‡

ΛFTER THE AFFAIR of the Placards in 1534, Calvin had fled to Basel. He stayed about a year under the alias Martianus Lucanius (an anagram for Calvinus), and it was here that the *Institutes* was first published by Thomas Platter. The preface was an open letter to Francis, "the Most Christian King of France," and was a defense against the charge then being put forward by the king that the Paris reformers were all extremists.

By early 1536, Francis was again seeking to court the German Protestants as a potential second front against Charles, and had invited Bucer and Melanchthon to Paris, supposedly to help devise a plan of reform for the French Church. Bucer and Melanchthon refused. As it seemed, however, that Francis might be forced to soften his domestic opposition to the Protestants, Calvin decided to lay the groundwork for his return to France. He left Basel for Italy and the court of Renée, the duchess of Ferrara. The duchess was the daughter of Louis XII, and cousin and partisan of Marguerite. Many of the French reformers who had not fled to Basel had found refuge instead with Renée, and Calvin, still hoping for a high position in the reform movement when it moved back to France, knew that her patronage would prove helpful. He secured a job as her private secretary under the pseudonym Charles Despeville and made the acquaintance of other useful people, such as the poet Clément Marot, whose poems he would later borrow, set to music, and publish in a book as psalms appropriate for church choirs.

Unfortunately, the duchess was married to Duke Hercules II, son of Lucrezia Borgia, grandson of Pope Alexander VI, and an orthodox of the old school. Hercules was not pleased with his wife's new court. Calvin saw trouble ahead, and when Francis declared a six-month amnesty in May 1536, he immediately left for Paris. (He showed excellent timing, for soon afterward, when one of Renée's entourage publicly refused to go to Mass, Hercules called in the authorities and had everybody in the house arrested. Renée had to resort to pleading with the pope to save her house guests, while her husband petitioned him to have them all burned. The duchess won that round.)

Francis's amnesty allowed any known dissenter to return to France without fear of prosecution, but anyone who wished to stay in the country beyond the six months had to reaffirm allegiance to Rome. Calvin used this grace period to sell the property in Noyon that he had inherited from his father, gather up his younger brother Antoine, his half-sister Marie, and a few other sympathetic townspeople, and head for Strasbourg.

However, after Charles's invasion of Provence, there was fighting along the route to Strasbourg. Calvin and his band ended up being diverted and spending a night in Geneva instead.

✣

SIXTEENTH-CENTURY GENEVA was a brawling, hard-drinking commercial center, a town of middle-class merchants and tradesmen, prosperous without being wealthy, more Cleveland than cosmopolitan. For more than a hundred years, Geneva had been ruled by a prince-bishop appointed by the duke of Savoy. Savoy, part of the Holy Roman Empire, was located in the Alps, south of the city. The Genevans had long wanted their independence.

In 1526, the Genevan bishop, Pierre de la Baume, corrupt, inept, and inconsistent in policy (there is nothing worse for business than inconsistency in policy), failed to quell an uprising by the local patriotic party, known as the "Eidguenots." The Eidguenots (from which we get the later

"Huguenots"), sensing weakness, approached the neighboring Swiss cantons of Bern and Fribourg and formed a triple alliance aimed at kicking out Pierre, and with him the duke of Savoy. The bishop fled, but the duke sent troops and Pierre was reinstalled in 1533 with the help of Catholic Fribourg, which double-crossed Geneva and remained loyal to Rome.

Pierre hadn't been back in power six months before he was forced to escape again. However, this time when Catholic Savoy, aided by Charles, sent an army, Protestant Bern, aided by Francis, sent an opposing one. By May 1536, it was all over—the Genevans had their city to themselves.

The Genevan clergy, who by and large had supported the bishop, were now held in extreme disfavor by the Eidguenots, who threw their support instead behind Guillaume Farel, an expatriate French preacher and former member of the Cercle de Meaux. Farel had been in the city since 1532. He immediately called for the end of Mass and the destruction of relics and idols. Those Catholic clergymen remaining in town were given the choice of exile or conversion. Most left and Geneva became officially Protestant.

Three months later, Calvin rode into town on his way to Strasbourg, intending to stay only the one night. He stayed, more or less, for the rest of his life.

✝

WHEN FAREL, WHO HAD READ the *Institutes*, was told that its author was in town, he rushed over to meet him. Farel needed help. Although the Genevan citizenry had voted to "live by the Gospel," they were having trouble with the particulars. There was no real discipline within their church, and Farel needed to organize the new theories into a coherent whole. Who better to aid an aging, overburdened preacher than a gifted young man of energy and spirit who had already set the philosophy down on paper so expertly?

But Calvin was not seeking a position in Geneva. He was working on a new, updated *Institutes*. The first edition had almost sold out, and there was even talk of a French version. Calvin needed time to write and study, and he preferred the more sophisticated Strasbourg. He declined the invitation, claiming that he was too shy, his temperament was unsuitable... he just wasn't the right choice.

But Farel hadn't fought the bishop, fought Fribourg, fought the local clergy, and even fought Bern only to be stopped by one man's self-deprecation. He had been spit upon, beaten up, and put in fear of his life, all to get Geneva to this moment. When blandishments failed, Farel used theatrics. He stood up, glared down at Calvin, raised his arm, pointed a finger at him, and brought down God's curse like Zeus on the mountaintop. Years later, Calvin could still recall the incident:

> Wherever else I had gone, I had taken care to conceal that I was the author of [*The Institutes*]; and I had resolved to continue in the same privacy and obscurity, until at length Guillaume Farel detained me at Geneva, not so much by counsel and exhortation, as by a dreadful curse, which I felt to be as if God had from heaven laid his mighty hand upon me to arrest me... Farel, who burned with an extraordinary zeal to advance the gospel, immediately strained every nerve to detain me. And after learning that my heart was set upon devoting myself to private studies, for which I wished to keep myself free from other pursuits, and finding that he gained nothing by entreaties, he proceeded to utter the imprecation that God would curse my retirement and the tranquility of the studies which I sought, if I should withdraw and refuse to help, when the necessity was so urgent. By this imprecation I was so terror-struck, that I gave up the journey I had undertaken.

So John Calvin stayed to preach in Geneva.

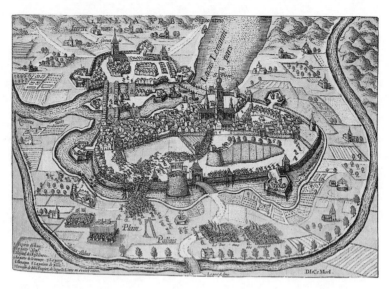

The walled city of Geneva

✝

FAREL MADE CALVIN PASTOR at one of the city churches. In addition
to weekly sermons, he was responsible for all the mundane aspects of
church life—weddings, baptisms, funerals, and the organization of
church functions. But that was not why Farel had asked him to come,
nor why he had stayed. They both had bigger plans, and on January 16,
1537, they brought them forward in a document entitled "Articles concerning the Organization of the Church and of Worship at Geneva."

The Articles provided a blueprint for standardizing church services
and membership throughout the city. Among their proposals was a call
for communion to be celebrated once a month, for psalms to be sung
at services, and for the establishment of a children's choir. But it also
contained some less benign demands. Farel and Calvin required that
the civil authorities give over the right of excommunication completely
to the church. They also called for the appointment of certain qualified
persons to spy on the rest of the community, this to ensure that every-

one was behaving in an upright, austere fashion at all times. Only then could they be eligible for communion and therefore admission to the church. Most controversial of all was the requirement that every living soul in the city of Geneva take a solemn pledge that ran to twenty-one paragraphs, affirming their faith in Calvin's interpretation of the Scriptures as it applied to everything from God and law to prayer, salvation, and behavior. Refusal to take the oath was to be punishable by loss of citizenship and banishment.

The plan was submitted to the civil government, which then consisted of three layers. At the top were four syndics and a city treasurer, elected by the male citizens of Geneva. The syndics also sat on the twenty-five-member *Petit Conseil* (Little Council), which met three times a week to administer the affairs of the city, deal with foreign issues and capital crimes, and handle finances. Then there was the *Deux Cents*, the Council of Two Hundred, which met once a month to discuss legislation and was legally the ultimate authority, but for all intents and purposes was ruled by the Little Council. So it was to the Little Council that Calvin and Farel brought their articles. The council was unwilling to risk disrupting the fragile faith of the newly converted city, so it approved the plan and the Council of Two Hundred followed suit.

But it is one thing to adopt legislation, another to enforce it. There were already any number of laws on the books to which nobody paid the least bit of attention, and many on the Council of Two Hundred expected that Calvin's articles would suffer the same fate. But they had not reckoned with the commitment of their new ministers. For over a year, Calvin and Farel pushed for administration of the pledge. In July 1537, they ordered the police to roust the populace in groups to force the oath on them. Nonetheless, many continued to refuse.

Over the next six months, opposition to Calvin's policies grew. Finally, in January 1538, the Council of Two Hundred decreed that, pledge or no pledge, no one could be excluded from taking communion. Then, in February, when the general election was held, the citizens of Geneva voted in new syndics, and a Little Council vehemently opposed to the ministers.

The situation worsened. Calvin and Farel were harassed. Obscene ditties were sung outside Calvin's house and gunshots fired under his windows. Matters came to a head on Easter Sunday. Calvin and Farel refused to administer communion on the grounds that the congregation was contaminated because not everyone had taken the pledge. There were riots in the streets.

That was enough. Genevans hadn't fought ten years to be rid of Savoy so it could be replaced by this. On April 23, 1538, the Council of Two Hundred gave Calvin and Farel three days to get out of town. Calvin's response to his banishment: "Well and good. If we had served men we would have been ill-requited, but we serve a Good Master who will reward us."

There was public rejoicing in the streets of Geneva as Calvin and Farel rode away.

‡

THEY WENT TO BERN TO report their injuries at the hands of the councils, and from there to Zurich and a general meeting of Swiss reformers. The ministers at Zurich listened to Calvin's version of events and agreed with his interpretations. They instructed Bern to send an embassy to Geneva and use its influence to see if matters couldn't be smoothed over. Bern intervened as requested, but to no avail. Geneva was adamant. No more Calvin. He was turned back before he reached the city's walls.

He and Farel, now unemployed and homeless, went to Basel to stay with friends. Soon after, Farel accepted a position as pastor at Neuchâtel, where he had preached before coming to Geneva, and he urged Calvin to come with him. But Calvin, tired and humiliated, preferred to retreat into his books.

Then Bucer and Capito, still in Strasbourg, urged Calvin to fulfill his original intention of accepting a pastorship in their town. Calvin paid a visit in July, but loath to subject himself to the pressures and conditions that he had so recently experienced in Geneva, he refused Bucer's offer. The older reformer then took a page out of Farel's book. "God will know how to find the rebellious servant, as he found Jonah," he thundered.

September found Calvin in Strasbourg, pastor of a congregation composed primarily of French refugees.

‡

LIFE IN STRASBOURG WAS MUCH more to Calvin's taste. There were none of those ugly scenes and difficulties that had characterized his relations in Geneva. Strasbourg had gone over to the reformers early, in 1524, and already had a solid church organization in place by the time Calvin got there. There was therefore no need to struggle with the government for the enactment of religious rules (although there was no pledge, and the civil authorities retained the right to excommunicate). Nor was Calvin looked to as the sole, or even the primary, reformer— that role was Bucer's. Calvin's parish was small, just a couple hundred displaced countrymen. *Ecclesiola gallicana,* he called it—the little French church. It was small enough that he knew everyone, and he didn't have any trouble with discipline; the congregation didn't seem to mind that he quizzed them on faith before administering communion at Easter, and they wholeheartedly embraced his passion for song at worship. In fact, the little French church became known for its choir.

During this period, Calvin ate little and slept less. His work consumed him; he often wrote late into the night. He was very thin and had stomach problems. By his own admission, he was short tempered. His friends proposed that he marry in order to reduce his irritability— this was a simpler time—and have someone look after his needs and his health. He rejected the first three candidates but settled finally on a widow with two children. This arrangement was apparently successful because he now had time to publish a number of other books on religion, and his reputation grew.

Then, in 1539, came the updated *Institutes*. It began:

The Epistle to the Reader

In the First Edition of this work, having no expectation of the success that God has, in his goodness, been pleased to give it, I had, for the greater part, performed my office perfunctorily, as is usual in trivial undertakings. But when I perceived that almost all the Godly had received it with a favor which I had never dared to wish, far less to hope for, being sincerely conscious that I had received much more than I deserved, I thought I should be very ungrateful if I did not endeavor, at least according to my humble ability, to respond to the great kindness which had been expressed toward me, and which spontaneously urged me to diligence...I may add, that my object in this work was to prepare and train students of theology for the study of the sacred volume, so that they might both have an easy introduction to it, and be able to proceed in it, with unfaltering step, seeing I have endeavored to give such a summary of religion in all its parts...Strasbourg, 1 August 1539.

The new *Institutes* ran to over a thousand pages. The Sorbonne had it burned in the streets of Paris.

It was a hit.

‡

BUT WHILE CALVIN'S STAR was on the rise, Geneva's was starting a long, hard slide.

Soon after the Little Council ousted Calvin and Farel, church discipline disappeared, and Geneva went back to the old ways. There were brawls in the street; drunkenness (and worse) was up and church attendance was down. Nobody paid any attention to the replacement ministers. Politically, there were problems as well. In a dispute with neighboring Bern over the rights to some border land, Geneva sent two syndics as head of a delegation to negotiate a treaty. The syndics were given strict instructions that they ignored, and Bern got everything it wanted. When the syndics returned to Geneva, they found themselves disgraced and had to flee for their lives. The two remaining syndics also got themselves into trouble. One killed a man in a street fight and was executed, the other died falling out of a window while trying to escape the fate of the first. So within two years, the most powerful opposition to Calvin had self-destructed.

All of a sudden, the disgraced, banished reformer, now perhaps the most well-known Protestant authority in Europe, didn't look quite so bad.

Following the events in Geneva carefully, the Church in Rome decided that the city might be ripe to be brought back into the Catholic fold. The pope had the archbishop of Carpentras, Cardinal Jacopo Sadoleto, a learned and important man, well respected by all, write a letter to the city gently pointing out the errors of their previous religious leaders and urging them to reconsider allegiance to the pope. The letter caused an uproar, not because the Genevans were actually considering Sadoleto's offer—they weren't—but because the pope's interest in their city could mean nothing but trouble. Worse, there was no one in that whole town of burghers and merchants with the education and erudition necessary to respond to the archbishop in kind. In its extremity, Geneva turned to the one man it knew could face down the pope. They asked John Calvin to draft their reply.

No matter what Geneva had done to him in the past, Calvin had no intention of sitting by and watching it slip back to Rome for lack of adequate legal representation. He wrote a letter to Sadoleto—a masterful letter, a work that earned him as much praise as did *The Institutes*—turning the archbishop's arguments back on him. "It [was] a week's work," he wrote to Farel.

Calvin's letter was successful. Soon after, Geneva experienced an abrupt change of heart. According to the still-unidentified author of a famous 1724 pamphlet, *An Anonymous History of Michael Servetus, Burnt Alive at Geneva for Heresie*:

> One of the town ministers, that saw in what manner the people were bent for the revocation of CALVIN, gave him notice of their affection . . . : The senate of two hundred being assembled, they all crave CALVIN. The next day a general convocation. They cry in like sort again all; we will have CALVIN, that good and learned man, CHRIST'S minister . . . they saw that the name of CALVIN waxed everyday greater abroad; and that, together with his fame, their infamie was spread, which had so rashly and childishly ejected him.

But Calvin refused to return. He dreaded the place, he wrote to friends. The Genevans promised to conform to his ideas, to "keep Calvin always." They bought him a nice big house on a pleasant street, voted him a hefty executive salary of 500 florins a year, and threw in twelve measures of wheat and two *bossets* (250 gallons) of wine (this last undoubtedly for his guests, since Calvin didn't drink). They offered to move his wife and the two children and all the household goods free of charge.

So, finally, Calvin agreed to come back. But this time, he got a contract. It was a very good contract—he wrote it himself.

It was called the *Ordonnances écclésiastiques (Ecclesiastical Ordinances)* of the Church of Geneva, and it was among the most ambitious, comprehensive, and oppressive sets of laws ever to be enacted voluntarily by any community. It was Calvin's old Articles, now made both broader and more specific, written by a man who understood the law thoroughly and had the upper hand. The *Ordinances* of 1541 and their subsequent companion laws ("Ordinances concerning the polity of the churches under the Seigneury of Geneva that are thought to be useful, submitting everything to the discretion of Messieurs" of 1546 and 1547) were Calvin's prescription for the perfect society. He intended Geneva to act as standard bearer in the quest for the restoration of the godly life on earth.

The *Ordinances* established four orders—pastors, teachers, elders, and deacons—and listed the qualifications and duties of each of these positions. It provided for free mandatory public education and the establishment of a college, for a communal hospital available to all, and for physicians and surgeons for the poor.

Calvin's reforms worked. Murder, mayhem, prostitution, and general lawlessness were so greatly reduced that the city acquired a reputation as a paragon of piety, sobriety, and hard work. Protestants all over Europe viewed Calvin's Geneva as epitomizing the superiority of reform over the corruption of Catholicism. Geneva, rather than Basel, became the destination for wealthy and educated French religious refugees, and the city's population swelled with the minority émigrés.

But order, as it always does, came with a price. The world is wicked, Calvin insisted, and the wicked require discipline. This too was provided for in the *Ordinances*. The most significant element of Calvin's new regime was the enactment of his old plan to establish an official network of spies, a religious secret police. A group of laymen approved by Calvin became responsible for ferreting out the sins of the rest of the community and reporting them to the authorities. On a weekly basis, any whose behavior fell short of the required standard were brought to Calvin's attention. The police operated on commission—a portion of any fines assessed as punishment went to them.

The practical result of all of this godly work was that Geneva, which had previously enjoyed its beer and wine, its prostitutes and its gambling, suddenly found itself the Singapore of the sixteenth century. Nathaniel Weiss, a nineteenth-century French freethinker, described Calvin's Geneva:

> One burgher smiled while attending a baptism: three days' imprisonment. Another, tired out on a hot summer day, went to sleep during the sermon: prison. Some working men ate pastry at breakfast: three days on bread and water. Two burghers played scuttles: prison... A blind fiddler played a dance: expelled from the city. A girl was caught skating, a widow threw herself on the grave of her husband, a burgher offered his neighbor a pinch of snuff during divine service: they were summoned before the Consistory, exhorted and ordered to do penance... A burgher said "Monsieur" Calvin instead of "Maitre" Calvin; a couple of peasants, following their ancient custom, talked about business matters coming out of church: prison, prison, prison... Two boatmen had a brawl, in which no one was hurt: executed. Most savagely of all were punished any offenders whose behavior challenged Calvin's political and spiritual infallibility.

But the severity of the new regime in Geneva was not restricted to matters of law. It applied to matters of conscience as well. Calvin received many letters asking for his advice or help. While he provided spiritual comfort to many of these petitioners, his rigidity and utter conviction of his own godliness could lead to appalling callousness. At one point, a woman of high birth wrote to Calvin seeking asylum on the grounds that her husband, a powerful nobleman who had in the past physically forced her to attend Mass and make vows to the saints, had now threatened to drown her or have her thrown in a secret dungeon for life. If she came to Geneva, she asked, "and her return were demanded by the king [of France] or by her husband, would you [Calvin] give her up, for it is certain that he would not come to look for her, unless it were for the purpose of amusing himself by having her burnt or doing her slowly to death in a permanent dungeon."

Calvin replied that although "when persecution arises it is permissible for a partner to flee after she has fulfilled what is her duty," he was sure that "the noble lady who requests our advice is very far from having reached this point." Calvin added that since "when pressed to defile herself with idolatry she yields and complies . . . she has no excuse for leaving her husband." Only, he concludes, "if, after having put to the proof the things we have said, she finds *her husband is persecuting her to the death*, then she may avail herself of the liberty which our Savior grants to His followers for escaping from the fury of the wolves."

This was the John Calvin with whom Michael Servetus began a correspondence. ‡

PART II

‡

Servetus
and Calvin

CHAPTER ELEVEN

THE LETTERS BETWEEN Michael Servetus and John Calvin
began in 1546 and continued for more than a year. Servetus's
first note was direct and polite. Could Calvin please explain the
relationship of Jesus to God, the nature of regeneration as it
applies to the Kingdom of Heaven, and the role faith plays in such institutions as baptism and the Lord's Supper?

Calvin's response, which he signed under his old alias Despeville,
was cold, condescending, and officious. In it he wrote:

> We believe and confess that Jesus Christ, the man who was
> crucified, was the Son of God, and say that the Wisdom of
> God, born of the Eternal Father before all time, having be-
> come incarnate, was now manifested in the flesh...you own
> him as the Son of God, but do not admit the oneness, save in
> a confused way. We, who say that the Son of God is our
> Brother, as well as the true Immanuel, nevertheless acknowl-
> edge in the One Christ the Majesty of God and the Humility
> of man. But you, confounding these, destroy both.

Calvin's dismissiveness provoked an immediate reply, the tone of
which was now anything but deferential. Instead, Servetus wrote to the
Calvin he knew from the old days in Paris. He lectured, was familiar,
often abusive. He belittled Calvin's knowledge and interpretations of
Scripture, and he backed up every argument with citations.

Calvin, who had people flogged for failing to address him as "Master," and who was used to the most slavish kind of toadying, was furious. He replied to Servetus in kind, then dashed off a letter to Frellon:

> I have been led to write to [Servetus] more sharply than is my wont, being minded to take him down a little in his presumption; and I assure you that there is no lesson he needs so much to learn as humility. This may perhaps come to him through the grace of God, not otherwise, as it seems. But we too ought to lend a helping hand. If he goes on writing to me in the style he has hitherto seen fit to use, however, you will only lose your time in soliciting me farther in his behalf; for I have other business that concerns me more nearly, and I shall make it a matter of conscience to devote myself to it, not doubting that he is a Satan who would divert me from studies more profitable. Let me beg of you therefore to be content with what I have already done, unless you see most pressing occasion for acting differently.
>
> Recommending myself to you and praying God to have you in his keeping, I am your servant and friend—
>
> CHARLES DESPEVILLE
>
> [GENEVA] THIS 13 OF FEBRUARY 1546

Servetus was not deterred. He continued to pester Calvin with letters, passionately urging acceptance of his arguments. He also sent him a copy of his new manuscript. This manuscript was a fuller, sharper, more detailed recounting of the arguments he had first put forth in *De Trinitatis Erroribus*. Calvin replied that he was far too busy to write a book in response but sent Servetus a copy of *The Institutes* and told him that all the answers he was looking for could be found inside.

Servetus, the editor, was not one to let this opportunity pass by. He read Calvin's book very carefully, and then he took it apart, line by line, scribbling comments in the margins, like a professor grading the term paper of a not particularly accomplished student. He sent the now-annotated *Institutes* back to Calvin. He even offered to fulfill a long-postponed commitment and come to Geneva for a face-to-face debate.

When Calvin's *Institutes*, which had won him so much fame and glory, which was second only to the Bible in his opinion, was returned to him with insulting notes plastered all over the margins, he felt much as Francis had felt when he saw the placard on his bedroom door. "There is not a page of this book that is not befouled with vomit," he wrote to a friend.

Jerome Bolsec, who at the time was a prominent citizen of Geneva, and who was later to have problems of his own with the Reformer, wrote:

> Since which time Calvin, greatly incensed, conceived a mortal antipathy to [Servetus], and meditated with himself to have him put to death. This purpose he proclaimed in a letter to Pierre Viret of Lausanne, dated the Ides of February [1546]. Among other things in this letter, he says: "Servetus desires to come hither, on my invitation; but I will not plight my faith to him; for I have determined, did he come, that I would never suffer him to go away alive."

Calvin reiterated this sentiment in a letter to Farel in Neuchâtel:

> Servetus wrote to me lately, and beside his letter sent me a great volume of his ravings, telling me with audacious arrogance that I should there find things stupendous and unheard of until now. He offers to come hither if I approve; but I will not pledge my faith to him; for did he come, if I have any authority here, I should never suffer him to go away alive.

In 1547, according to Bolsec, Calvin wrote one more letter, this one not to a friend but to an enemy, the noted French pursuer of Protestants, Cardinal de Tournon. In his letter, Calvin revealed to the cardinal that the doctor Michel de Villeneuve of Vienne was actually the arch-heretic Michael Servetus.

If Bolsec was correct, Calvin timed his letter to take advantage of some significant changes on the French political landscape. After a long illness, Francis had finally died. His eldest son, Francis, and his youngest, Charles, were already dead. The new king was the middle son, Henri II, a dark, cold man, personality traits likely acquired as a result of having been sent to prison in Spain when he was seven. He was never his father's favorite, and there is some suspicion that his elder brother was poisoned. With the advent of Henri, Tournon fell out of favor and was demoted from advisor at court to archbishop of Lyon. Calvin was sure that Tournon would not pass up the opportunity to regain some favor by mercilessly prosecuting a high-visibility heretic.

But Calvin was evidently unaware that the doctor and the cardinal were friends. Tournon, who thought that Calvin was the most evil man on earth, did nothing. He is reputed to have laughed at the idea of one heretic trying to turn in another.

Servetus continued to write to Calvin, thirty letters in all, some promoting his own views, some criticizing Calvin's. In his eleventh letter, Servetus attacked Calvin's concept of original sin. "All that men do, you say is done in sin," Servetus wrote, "and is mixed with the dregs that stink before God and merit nothing but eternal death. In this, you blaspheme. Stripping us of all possible goodness, you do violence to the teaching of Christ and his apostles, who ascribe to us the power of being perfect: 'Be ye therefore perfect, even as your Father in Heaven is perfect.' (Matthew 5:48)."

The last three letters contained discussions of a subject that would have great significance later—the role of the true Christian in the administration of justice and the maintenance of social order. Servetus agreed that the Christian man had the right, even the duty, to become a magistrate or leader of the people. But, he stressed, this role must be discharged with God's mercy. What hope was there if all a citizen who had transgressed could look forward to was death? Christ bid an adulteress to "Go unto him and sin no more." Banishment and excommunication, both of which were commended in the Scriptures, even for heresy, were preferable to a punishment that made repentance impossible.

It seems that Calvin replied to some of these letters and not to others. But there is no doubt he was seething. Servetus's language did not moderate over time, and he did little to hide the fact that he believed Calvin was perverting the Christian ethic every bit as much as the pope was. In the course of the correspondence, Servetus asked repeatedly for the return of his manuscript, but Calvin refused to send it back. In 1550, he again tried to goad the Catholics in France into taking action. In *De Scandalis,* a monograph denouncing unorthodox scriptural interpretations, Calvin asserted that Villanovanus was in fact Servetus. Either by oversight or contrivance, the authorities in France still did nothing.

☩

SERVETUS WORKED ON HIS MANUSCRIPT in secret for six years; not until 1552 was it finally ready for publication. It ran to almost eight hundred pages and was entitled *Christianismi Restitutio* (*The Restoration of Christianity*). The title was a slap at Calvin's *Christianae Religionis Institutio,* much as *De Trinitatis Erroribus* had been a slap at Saint Augustine. Servetus left no doubt as to the book's purpose. On the title page, he wrote:

The whole apostolic church is summoned to the threshold. Once again there is restored knowledge of God, of the faith of Christ our justification, of the regeneration of baptism, and of participation in the Lord's Supper. With the heavenly kingdom restored to us, the wicked captivity of Babylon has been ended, and the Antichrist with his hosts destroyed.

Title page of Christianismi Restitutio

Underneath, in Hebrew, was written, "And at that time shall Michael stand up. And war broke out in heaven." The Michael to whom he referred was not himself but rather the archangel Michael, with whom Servetus felt at least a strong bond and perhaps even a transmuted identity. Servetus believed that the Apocalypse was at hand, and this was his declaration of war, a call to revolution against the abominations unto God and the tyranny imposed by both the pope and the Reformer.

The task we have set ourselves here is truly sublime; for it is nothing less than to make God known in his substantial manifestation by The Word and his divine communication by the Spirit, both comprised in Christ, through whom alone do we learn how divineness of the Word and the Spirit may be apprehended in Man. Hidden from human sight in former times, God is now both manifested and communicated to the world ... to the end that we may see him face to face as it were in Creation, and feel him intuitively but lucidly declared in ourselves. It is high time that the door leading to knowledge of this kind were opened; for otherwise no one can either know God truly, read the Scriptures aright, or be a Christian.

In the body of the work, all the old themes were there: the injustice of infant baptism, the contortions of the Scriptures, the myth that was the Trinity, but most of all, the assertion that God existed in all people and things. In contrast to his earlier books, his language was sophisticated, and each argument was laid out in scrupulous (and often suffocating) detail. There were discourses and dialogues, the latter featuring Michael and Peter, the same two names he had used in *Two Dialogues on the Trinity*.

The book was to be published anonymously, but the manuscript contained several laughably obvious clues. At one point in the dialogues, Peter says to Michael, "I perceive you are Servetus." Also opting for maximum provocation over discretion, Servetus included, right up front, the text of the thirty letters that he had written to Calvin.

‡

SERVETUS HAD A MANUSCRIPT, now he needed a publisher. The heretical nature of the work was obvious, so the Trechsels were out of the question. Frellon was a possibility, but that would mean compromising a friend if the Inquisition reacted badly, a distinct possibility.

Instead, Servetus sought printers outside of France who might be sympathetic to his views. He sent the manuscript to a friend of his, a publisher named Martin Borrhaus in Basel. Borrhaus wrote back:

> The Grace and Peace of God be with you, dearest Michael! I have received your letter and your book; but I fancy that on reflection you will see why it cannot be published in Basel at the present time. When I have perused it [more carefully] I shall therefore return it to you by the accredited messenger you may send for it. But I beg you not to question my friendly feelings toward you. To what you say besides I shall reply at greater length on another occasion. Farewell! Thy
>
> MARRINUS
>
> BASEL, APRIL 9, 1552

Borrhaus did not express any surprise at the content of the book, so he must have been aware that his friend Michael (either as Villanovanus or Servetus) held these extreme views. It is also unlikely that this was the only person in whom Servetus had confided—there seems to have been a network of like-minded individuals, although it is impossible to say how big or far-flung this network was. But it is clear that for much of his time in Vienne, Servetus had been leading a double life.

Finally, five months later, he found a pair of brothers-in-law, Balthazar Arnoullet and Guillaume Geroult, who had recently established a small printing firm in Lyon with a branch in Vienne. Geroult handled the editorial end, and Arnoullet took care of the business side. During his last sales trip to Geneva, Geroult had run afoul of the Ordinances and been accused of "sexual irregularity." He had been dragged in front of Calvin himself, where he was publicly humiliated, then fined and banished. The temptation to get even by publishing *Christianismi Restitutio* (especially after Servetus agreed to foot the entire cost of printing and pay a bonus on top of it) overwhelmed caution. Geroult outflanked his brother-in-law, a Calvin supporter, by withholding information as to the true nature of the material.

Still, Arnoullet should have suspected something. None of the work was done by the firm's regular employees, nor was it done in their regular print shop. Instead, Geroult set up a secret press in a cabin in the woods and staffed it with pressmen hired specifically for the job. The author edited his own work. As soon as each page was typeset, the manuscript leaf from which it had come was burned. The title page was notable in that neither the author's nor the publisher's name appeared (although, once again unable to resist, Servetus appended the letters "M S V" as a colophon).

Finally, after four months, a thousand octavos (this was a book for the people) were ready for shipment. On January 3, 1553, the first batch of five hundred books, hidden in bales of hay, was dispatched by horse cart to Frankfurt for sale at the upcoming book fair. Another shipment went to a printer in Lyon for safekeeping. A third was sent to a bookseller in Geneva. ‡

ALMOST NOTHING HAPPENED in Geneva that Calvin did not know about. Very soon after its arrival and before it could ever go on sale, he had a copy of *Christianismi Restitutio* in his hands.

By 1553, with the threat of Savoy and the pope's interference only a distant memory, Genevans were once again rankling at the extreme restrictions on their day-to-day lives. Their displeasure was enhanced by the fact that the many French refugees who now chose to resettle in Geneva seemed to be gobbling up all the good jobs.

Calvin's opposition called itself *les enfants de Genève*, children of the republic, and had formed the Patriot Party, which became known as the "Libertines." Among its leaders were veterans, or sons of veterans, of the wars against Savoy, such men as Ami Perrin and Philabert Berthelier. The Libertines' strength was concentrated in the civil government, in the Little Council and the Council of Two Hundred, while Calvin dominated the Consistory, the roster of pastors.

By early 1553, the escalation of hostilities between the two sides had brought them to the brink of outright war. The previous year, Calvin had excommunicated Berthelier, and the Little Council had been moving closer and closer to negating the Ordinances by reinstating him. By the time *Christianismi Restitutio* had settled in Calvin's hands, the situation was tenuous, and there was a possibility that despite his international renown he would once again be kicked out of Geneva.

When he saw the book, he knew that regardless of what happened in the city, he could at least be rid of Servetus and, with some deft maneuvering, might even persuade his enemies to handle the entire messy affair. But he could not be seen as taking a personal hand in the matter. After all, the letters at the beginning of the book were to him, and his involvement could easily be interpreted as a personal vendetta and not a theological dispute. This might provide just the embarrassment that the Libertines were waiting for.

Calvin resolved upon a plan. First he banned the book in Geneva. Then he ripped out the first sixteen pages of his copy and summoned a loyal subordinate, a Genevan merchant named Guillaume de Trie.

A few days later, on February 26, 1553, Trie sent a letter to his cousin, Antoine Arneys, who lived in Lyon. Trie was originally from Lyon himself—in fact, he had been a sheriff there—but had fled four years earlier as part of the French religious migration. Arneys remained staunchly Catholic, but the cousins had kept up a correspondence. Religious differences being what they were, relations between the two had sometimes been strained, each using his letters to undermine the theological position of the other.

The French inquisitors had recently arrested five students from Switzerland on grounds of spreading heresy, and Arneys, in his previous letter, had accused the reformers in Geneva of perpetuating a system that led to chaos and disorder. Trie replied:

> My dear cousin, I express my sincere thanks for your beautiful admonishments which you made trying to brief me on the situation here. I do not doubt that they came from your feelings of deep friendship. I see, however, (thank God) that the vices are corrected better here than by your regulations. We would not suffer that the name of God be blasphemed and that the wrong doctrines and opinions are spread without repression. You tolerate among you a heretic who deserves to be burned wheresoever he may be. When a man says that the Trinity . . . is a Cerebus and an infernal monster, and when he

disgorges all the villainies possible to think of against all that the Scriptures teach us about the eternal generation of the Son of God...I ask in what place and in what esteem would you hold him?...I have to speak frankly...one should not be content simply to put to death such men, but they should be most cruelly burned. Please show me where is the zeal you are so proud of and where is the enforcement of law by your splendid hierarchy you so glorify? The man of whom I speak has been condemned by all the churches you reprove, yet you tolerate him among you to the point that he could print his books full of blasphemies that I need say no more.

Just in case Arneys (or whoever else might subsequently see the letter) was a bit slow at picking up the hint, Trie did say more:

This man is a Portuguese Spaniard, named Michael Servetus by his real name but who is at present using the name of Villeneuve and who practices medicine. He had lived during a certain time in Lyon, and is now at Vienne, where the book about which I talk has been printed in the printing office of a certain Balthazar Arnoullet. And in order that you would not think that I speak without foundation, I am sending you the first leaf [sixteen pages] for your information.

‡

WHEN ARNEYS GOT HIS cousin's letter, he reacted precisely as Calvin had anticipated and forwarded the letter and the sixteen pages to the local authorities. They, in turn, sent the material directly to the President of the Ecclesiastical Court of the Holy Apostolic See, the Inquisitor General of the Faith in the Kingdom of France and Gaul, a ferocious zealot and dogged persecutor of heretics, the Dominican friar Matthieu Ory.

Ory, essentially the head of the national religious police, wasted no time in contacting the vicar of Lyon, Benoit Bautier. Agreeing on the need for speed and stealth but mindful of the chain of command, on March 13 Ory drafted a letter to an aide to Cardinal de Tournon, who, now unwelcome at court, was staying at the Château de Roussillon, just south of Vienne.

I wish to inform you in high secret about certain books that are being printed in Vienne and which contain execrable blasphemies against the divinity of Jesus Christ and the Holy Trinity and whose author and printer are in the region. The reverend Vicar and I have seen the book and we agreed that one of us or we both should go and talk to the Monseigneur . . . The reverend Vicar writes to you about this in such a secret that your left hand should not know what your right hand is doing. We ask you only to ask orally Monseigneur the Cardinal if he knows a certain physician named Villanovanus and a printer Arnoullet, because the matter concerns them both.

Upon reading the letter, Tournon summoned Bautier and the vicar of Vienne and instructed the latter to deliver a written order to Guy de Maugiron, lieutenant governor of Dauphiny. It instructed Maugiron to proceed on the charges "with extreme diligence and . . . under the strictest possible secrecy." Tournon went on to add, "I am sure of the zeal which you have, and that you will not spare even your own son in this matter for the honor of God and his Church."

Maugiron, a friend and patient of Dr. Villeneuve, was in a tricky spot. The doctor had cured his son of a fever, tantamount in those days to saving someone's life. Maugiron was in no position to ignore a direct order from a cardinal, but neither was he prepared to forget who had really spared his son.

Nonetheless, on March 16 the trap appeared set. The local judges convened at Maugiron's house and sent a message to Dr. Villeneuve that they needed to speak to him on a matter of great importance. After two hours, the doctor still had not appeared and the judges began to be concerned, but then Villeneuve arrived, bidding those assembled good day with an air of casual self-confidence. When questioned, he denied that he was Servetus or that he had ever engaged in heretical behavior. Furthermore, as a longtime resident of Vienne, well known by the town's prominent churchmen—including the archbishop and the cardinal—he was at a loss to explain how such scurrilous accusations could possibly have been lodged against him. When the judges informed him that they intended a search of his home, he made no objection whatever.

The search turned up nothing—not a book, a document, or a note. Not a single piece of evidence, including the letters from Calvin, was left to connect Villeneuve to Servetus. There were two copies of a paper on astrology written by Michael Villanovanus, but since they were in the house of Michael Villanovanus, that could hardly be considered incriminating.

The next day, the judges went to the printing house of Arnoullet and Geroult, confronted Geroult (Arnoullet was out of town), and questioned him for hours. Geroult denied any knowledge of any heretical tract. The judges then examined each of the printers and compositors individually, as well as each of their wives and all of the servants in the house. They showed the printers the pages that Arneys had received in the mail. The terrified printers denied ever seeing them before. The characters were not the same as those they used in their typesetting, the paper was different, and they had not produced an octavo in over two years. A check of the Arnoullet catalog confirmed all that they had said. The printers were then warned that if they revealed details of the investigation to anyone, they would stand trial for heresy.

The judges had one last card to play. They waited for Arnoullet to return and then accosted him before he could speak to anyone. The astonished Arnoullet appeared completely baffled by the accusation... as, in fact, he was, since Geroult had told him nothing about the book.

At this point, the judges faced a dilemma. If they dismissed the matter as a case of mistaken identity and then were found to be wrong, they might well have to face the wrath of Ory and the Inquisition themselves. On the other hand, Dr. Villeneuve was a long-standing and respected member of the community, a fact that he himself had taken pains to point out, and an unfounded persecution might have equally unpleasant consequences. The judges decided to throw the matter up the line and referred it to Archbishop Palmier. Palmier refused to accept on the basis of an unsupported accusation that his friend, doctor, collaborator, and former teacher had deceived him. He summoned Ory to Vienne personally. If he was going to go on with this, he told the Inquisitor, he had better be absolutely sure.

Feared and powerful though he was, Matthieu Ory was not about to commit himself to prosecuting such a well-connected citizen without more proof. He returned to Lyon to indulge in a bit of counter-espionage. He called in Arneys and dictated a letter in which Trie was asked to send along a copy of the entire book.

Instead of sending the book, Calvin decided to provide a more definitive form of proof without abandoning what politicians in a later era would call "plausible deniability." The letter that Trie sent on March 26 in reply to Arneys's request was a masterpiece of misdirection.

My dear cousin,

When I wrote the letter that you have communicated to those whom I charged with indifference, I did not suppose the matter would go so far. I simply meant to call your attention to the fine zeal and devotion of those who call themselves the pillars of the Church, although they suffer such disorder in their midst, and persecute so severely the poor Christians who wish to follow God in simplicity [this referring to the five students]. Inasmuch as this glaring instance had been brought to my notice, the occasion and subject seemed to me to warrant mentioning the matter in my letters. But since you have disclosed what I meant for you alone, God grant that this may the better serve to purge Christianity of such filth, such deadly pestilence. If they really wish to do anything, as you say, it does not seem to me that the matter is so very difficult, though I cannot for the moment give you what you want, namely the printed book. But I can give you something better to convict him, namely two dozen manuscript pieces of the man in question, in which his heresies are in part contained. If you show him the printed book, he can deny it, which he cannot do in respect of his handwriting. The case then being proved, the men of whom you speak will have no excuse for further dissimulation or delay.

The manuscript pieces of which Trie wrote were the letters that Servetus had written to Calvin and the scathing marginal comments with which Servetus had notated Calvin's *Institutes* seven years before. Since there could be no doubt as to the source of this material, Calvin had Trie write the following:

All the rest is here right enough, the big book and the other writings of the same author, but I can tell you, I had no little trouble to get from Calvin what I am sending. Not that he does not wish to repress such execrable blasphemies, but he thinks his duty is rather to convince heretics with doctrine of other means, because he does not exercise the sword of justice. But I remonstrated with him and pointed out the embarrassing position in which I should be placed if he did not help me, so that in the end he gave me what you see. For the rest I hope by and by, when the case is further advanced, to get from him a whole ream of paper which the scamp has had printed, but I think that for the present you have enough, so that there is no need for more to seize his person and bring him to trial.

Even after Ory received this reply, the Inquisition still refused to act. There was no real proof, he claimed, that Michel de Villeneuve was Michael Servetus or, even if he was, that it was he who had written *Christianismi Restitutio.*

When Calvin learned of this, he knew that if he was to force Ory's hand, he would have to supply even more compelling evidence, although each time he sent something new, his own participation in the affair became more obvious.

On the last day of March, he had Trie make one last try.

> My dear cousin,
>
> I hope that I shall have satisfied your requests in part at least by sending you the handwriting of the author. In the last letter which you received you will find what he says about his name, which he disguised, for he excuses himself for having assumed the name Villeneuve when he is really Servetus alias Reves, on the ground that he took the name from that of his native town. For the rest I will keep my promise, God willing, that if there is a need I will furnish you with the manuscripts which he has printed, which are in his handwriting like the letters ... As for the printer, I am not sending you the proofs by which we know it is Balthazar Arnoullet and his brother-in-law, Gerard Geroult, but we are well assured nevertheless and he cannot deny it ... When you have finished with the letters, let me have them back.

If this letter had not spurred the inquisitors to action, it is possible that Calvin would have been forced to drop the entire matter. He was running out of options. He certainly was in no position to cross the border himself, travel to Vienne or Lyon, and harass Matthieu Ory until he arrested the heretic.

As it turned out, he didn't have to.

On April 4, Tournon, Ory, Palmier, and other members of the local ecclesiastical hierarchy met at the Château de Roussillon. Ory was finally willing to press the case. There was compelling evidence that Villeneuve was the heretic Servetus, and he and the printer Arnoullet must be arrested without delay. Tournon and Palmier had no choice but to agree.

It fell to Palmier to handle logistics. After dinner, the archbishop and his vicar returned to Vienne. Word was sent to Arnoullet that Palmier wished to see a copy of his newly printed New Testament. When Arnoullet showed up with his book, he was dragged off to prison.

Dr. Villeneuve, however, was not at home. He was, in fact, in the midst of a house call—he had left his home at night to tend to a sick patient. That patient was none other than Guy de Maugiron, the lieutenant governor, the same Maugiron who had warned the doctor three weeks before that his house was going to be searched, thus allowing him to destroy any incriminating papers that may have been lying about. The sheriff was sent to Maugiron's with instructions to tell the doctor that there were many sick and wounded prisoners at the palace and ask if he could possibly come and tend to them? The doctor replied that he would be pleased to offer whatever assistance he could.

When he arrived at the palace, he was arrested.

‡

DESPITE THE SERIOUSNESS of the charges, the terms of imprisonment were not severe. Although the jailer was instructed to watch the prisoner closely, the doctor was given his own suite of rooms, his valet was allowed to continue to attend him, and visitors were permitted.

Early the next day, Palmier informed Tournon of the arrest and asked if Ory wished to come to Vienne for the interrogation. Now that he had official sanction, Ory took off at a gallop and almost wore out his horse, arriving by midmorning. He then set off for the prison with Palmier's vicar and the sheriff. Palmier himself did not attend.

At the interrogation, in response to queries about his background, Villeneuve—he still insisted he was Villeneuve—gave a brief history of his life, which focused almost entirely on the period after he enrolled at the University of Paris. He omitted completely all of his dealings with the Protestants. He identified himself only as the author of works on medicine and geography. He was shown the pages of Calvin's *Institutes* that referred to baptism but was asked only to interpret the passage, not questioned about the marginal notes. He replied in a manner consistent with accepted dogma. When he was then asked about the handwriting of the notes, he said that he wasn't sure since it had happened so long ago, but that the handwriting might be his. Regardless, however, since the *Institutes* was itself heretical, he took the position that all the notes had been proper.

Once again the judges were unsure what to do. They could hardly fail to agree with someone who had been so lacerating to the arch-heretic Calvin, and the explanations of the accused seemed reasonable enough. They adjourned the interrogation until the following day.

The next day, they confronted the prisoner with the letters from Servetus to Calvin. This time, they heard a slightly different story:

> My Lords, I tell you the truth. When these letters were written, at the time I was in Germany about twenty-five years ago, a book was printed in Germany by a certain Spaniard called Servetus. I do not know where from in Spain, nor where he lived in Germany...Having read the book in Germany when I was very young, about fifteen to seventeen, it seemed to me that he spoke as well or better than the others. However, leaving all that behind in Germany, I went to France without taking any books, merely with the intention of studying mathematics and medicine, as I have since done. But having heard that Calvin was a learned man, I wanted to write to him out of curiosity without knowing him otherwise...requesting that correspondence should be confidential...to see whether

he could not convince me or I him... *When he saw that my questions were those of Servetus he replied that I was Servetus. I answered that although I was not, for the purposes of the discussion, I was willing to assume the role of Servetus,* for I did not care what he thought of me, but only that we should discuss our opinions. On those terms we wrote until the correspondence became heated and I dropped it. For the last ten years, there has been nothing between us and I affirm before God and you sirs that I never wished to dogmatize or assert anything contrary to the Church and the Christian religion.

The proceedings were adjourned, but even the accused knew that this tortured explanation would not hold and there was now no longer any question of the ultimate outcome. As soon as he was returned to the prison, Villeneuve sent his valet to a local monastery to collect a debt that was owed him. He also instructed the boy to bring him a gold chain, six gold rings, and other valuables. Minutes after the valet returned with the money, Ory informed the jailer that security was to be tightened and that Dr. Villeneuve was to speak to no one without express permission.

At 4 A.M. the next morning, the jailer was up to take care of his own small vineyard on the grounds when he heard Dr. Villeneuve call to him. When he got to the cell, he found the doctor dressed in his fur-trimmed, floor-length bathrobe and black velvet nightcap. Villeneuve asked for the key to the gardens so that he might take a walk (a euphemism for going to the bathroom). Although ordinary prisoners were chained in their cells, it was permissible for one of high position to walk about, so the jailer gave him the key, then left to go back to his vines and allow the doctor some privacy.

The garden was on the third floor, but it contained a terrace that looked out over the courtyard of the palace. Between the terrace and the courtyard was the roof of a shed. Michel de Villeneuve went to the very end of the terrace and took off his bathrobe and nightcap. Underneath he was fully dressed. Leaving the robe and cap under a tree, he noise-lessly leapt from the terrace onto the roof, and from there down to the courtyard. Michel de Villeneuve, physician and longtime resident and respected citizen of Vienne, once more became the heretic Michael Servetus and, slipping out the Rhône gate, disappeared into the night.

‡

IT WAS AFTER 6 A.M. when the jailer's wife got up and made the rounds of the cells. She noticed immediately that Dr. Villeneuve was missing. She ran and got her husband, and together they searched the garden and the grounds. When it became clear that the prisoner had escaped, the jailer's wife, fearing repercussions, put on quite a show. She screamed, she beat her breast, she beat her children, she beat the servants and all the prisoners then at hand. She tore her hair. Finally, she clambered up onto the neighbor's roof and wailed.

The judges, informed that their prisoner had fled, ordered that the palace gates be closed and all the nearby houses searched. The search turned up nothing. Although everyone in the surrounding areas was questioned, only a peasant woman had seen the fugitive, dashing through the woods just outside the city. The judges then immediately seized all of the prisoner's papers and effects, and claimed all the money that he had in the bank.

The sheriff was put in charge of the investigation, although he eventually fell under some suspicion as well. It seems Dr. Villeneuve had cured his daughter of a dangerous illness.

‡

AT THE BEGINNING OF MAY, Ory got a tip, possibly through the old Calvin-Trie-Arneys pipeline, that Arnoullet had two printing presses in the countryside that he had said nothing about.

When Ory and the police arrived at the cabin in the woods, they found three printers at work. They confronted them with the pages of *Christianismi Restitutio.* The printers got down on their knees and admitted printing the book although they claimed to be ignorant of its contents. The author had corrected the proofs himself, they said, and in any event, none of them spoke or read Latin. After they had heard of the arrest, they told the sheriff, they realized what the book really was but were afraid to speak for fear of being burned. The printers added that ten days after the printing had been completed, on January 13, five bales of books had been sent to a typecaster in Lyon named Pierre Merrin at the request of the author.

Arnoullet, who had been released, was once again thrown into prison, but Geroult had already fled. The next day, the inquisitor questioned Merrin at his shop. Merrin readily admitted that he had received the five bales with the label: "From Michel de Villeneuve, Docteur en Médecin, to Pierre Merrin, caster of type, near the Church of Our Lady of Comfort." The same day, Merrin said, a Vienne churchman named Jacques Charmier had arrived and said that Dr. Villeneuve had asked that the bales be stored until called for, and that they contained blank paper. No one had contacted him since.

The inquisitor took the bales back to Vienne and confronted Charmier, who insisted that he never had any idea of their true contents. Nonetheless, he was sentenced to three years in prison, as was Merrin. The printers were not excused for their ignorance of Latin and were given prison terms as well.

On June 17 the civil tribunal declared the fugitive Servetus guilty of scandalous heresy, sedition, rebellion, and evasion of prison. He was sentenced in absentia to pay one thousand livres to the king, have all his property and possessions confiscated, then, if he was caught, to be burned at a slow fire until his body was reduced to ashes. In the absence of the actual prisoner, the sentence was to be executed in effigy.

The next day, the sentence was carried out. Servetus's picture was hung for a moment to "dull its sensibilities," and then burned along with all the books by Michael Servetus that the Inquisition could get its hands on, which included the five bales that contained half of the copies of *Christianismi Restitutio*.

As for Arnoullet, he remained in prison for four months. On July 14 he wrote to his agent asking him to go to Frankfurt and destroy every remaining copy of *Christianismi Restitutio*, so that not a single page could be found.

Calvin, as he expected, was later accused of complicity in the arrest of Michael Servetus. He replied, "They say I did nothing else than throw Servetus to the professed enemies of Christ as to ravening beasts, that I was responsible for his arrest at Vienne in the province of Lyon. But how should I come to such familiarity with the satellites of the pope? To be on such good terms?" ‡

CHAPTER   THIRTEEN

DESPITE BEING PERHAPS the most wanted man in France, Michael Servetus once again succeeded in vanishing without a trace. He had a large circle of friends and admirers in Vienne, some of whom certainly helped him, but no one was ever accused. Servetus later said that after he left the city he went south, but no evidence of his actual whereabouts has been found. In a time of no fingerprints, no mug shots, no Identi-Kits, no police artists, and only the most limited communications between civil authorities in different sections of a country, it was almost impossible to track a fugitive unless he behaved ostentatiously, told people who he was, or was spotted by someone who knew him personally. Once he had cleared the area around Lyon, Servetus, traveling with a good deal of gold, could have gone almost anywhere. If he had traveled south toward the Mediterranean, even his dark skin would not have stood out.

The choice of a final destination, someplace where Servetus could be confident that his past would not catch up to him, was more problematic. He had mentioned earlier in his life that he considered the New World a place where intellectual and religious freedom might be pursued. But even in Europe, there were a number of locations where his ideas had gained sufficient popularity to ensure his safety. One of the most prominent of these, ironically, was Naples, in Catholic Italy, where Servetus had learned that a large community of Spaniards was set to embrace him. Instead of traveling down the Rhône, however, and taking a ship from Marseilles or traveling through Savoy and then down along the coast of Italy, Servetus chose a route that has puzzled scholars for centuries.

In order to begin his trip south to Naples, Servetus went north, to John Calvin's Geneva.

✝

CALVIN'S POSITION HAD worsened considerably over the course of the year. In March the Libertines had succeeded in gaining complete control of the Little Council, and the syndics asked the Consistory for a list of all persons who had been excommunicated and the reasons for each ban. The list contained, as everyone knew, the names of a goodly number of leading Libertines, including Berthelier. The ministers said they would rather resign. The issue remained unresolved, but the Council began to nettle Calvin in any way it could—overturning his rulings, ignoring his dictates, even coughing during his sermons. On July 24 a beaten Calvin asked to be allowed to resign. The Council refused. The last thing they wanted was Calvin traveling about the country denouncing the godless Genevans and drumming up support for himself, a tactic he had used to good effect in the past. A toothless Calvin in Geneva was far preferable.

Calvin, stuck where he was, hunkered down. He refused to reinstate Berthelier even after the Council let it be known that it intended to vote to restore him. This, as both parties knew, could well be the final blow, the one that broke the power of theocracy in the city. And there seemed to be no way out. Only an immense turn of fortune, some might say a miracle, could save Calvin now.

Then, on Saturday, August 12, Michael Servetus came to town.

✝

HE ARRIVED ON FOOT and took a room at the Inn of the Rose. He claimed later that he had only intended to stay for one day and had asked the host and hostess at the inn to help him rent a boat to take him up Lake Geneva to Lausanne, where he might link up with the Zurich road, from whence he would then head south to Italy.

But the next day was the Sabbath, when there would be no boats. Nor could Servetus simply remain at the inn. Church attendance was mandatory. Failure to attend would be conspicuous and might easily result in arrest. Yet of all the churches in Geneva, Servetus seems to have chosen the Madeleine, the very one where Calvin himself was preaching. According to the city records, he was recognized "by certain brothers" and arrested.

Calvin had his miracle. Personified in this one fugitive was the very reason that Geneva had invited him to return in the first place—unmitigated sin.

And what were the Libertines to do? Although one of its leaders, Ami Perrin, was a friend of Geroult—Geroult had even dedicated a book to him—the Libertines as a political group had no love of Servetus. If they supported Calvin, however, they were admitting that their enemy was needed to defend the city from heresy. If they sided with the heretic or even asked for leniency on his behalf, they would fall prey to that age-old epithet, "soft on crime." The situation was far from hopeless, however. Calvin was not known for subtlety. It was always possible that now, with control of the city hanging in the balance, he might be baited into overplaying his hand and the Servetus case might turn out to be enough of a fiasco to ruin him.

It was to be the ruin of the Libertines instead.

Calvin did not for a second back away. Servetus was immediately thrown into a lice-infested cell with the windows shuttered closed. Within hours, all Geneva knew of the arrest. "It seemed good to make him a prisoner," the city records read, "that he might no longer infect the world with his heresies and blasphemies, seeing that he was known to be incorrigible and hopeless." No one bothered to mention that making him a prisoner was itself a violation of law, since Servetus had committed no crime in the city.

According to the Codex Justinian, the legal code under which Geneva operated at the time, in cases such as this, the accuser must be imprisoned along with the accused until he could produce evidence to support his charges. If no evidence was forthcoming, under the *lex talionis* (the law of retaliation), the accuser would then suffer the punishment set aside for the crime. In this case, of course, the punishment was death.

Although Calvin wanted public recognition for leading the moral crusade against Servetus, he had no intention of taking himself out of circulation by going to jail. Instead, he had his cook, Nicolas de la Fontaine, act as accuser in his place. (Calvin's supporters later insisted that Fontaine was a secretary, but Fontaine had been a cook before he fled France. In any event, Calvin referred to him as *Nicolaus meus*—"my man Nicolas.")

Also according to the law, a formal charge had to be presented within twenty-four hours of arrest or the accused would be set free. The very next morning, Servetus was brought before the *lieutenant-criminel*, Pierre Tissot, for arraignment. Fontaine formally declared himself Servetus's accuser and presented a list of thirty-eight charges. He said that he had brought the charges because he felt he must defend Calvin and the church at Geneva. A few days later Calvin would admit that he had drawn up all thirty-eight specifications himself.

In order to meet the deadline, Calvin had been forced to work through the night, and, as a result, the charges were hastily written and very general. They ranged from publishing heretical literature to the accused's blasphemous beliefs to his lack of respect for church doctrine. Perhaps the most questionable charge was that which accused Servetus of violating the law by escaping from the Catholic Inquisition in Vienne. Most of the French population of Geneva had committed this same crime. Then there was count thirty-seven, one on which a good deal of time was spent. It read, "Likewise, that in the person of Mr. Calvin, minister of the word of God in this church of Geneva, he had defamed in a printed book, the doctrine that is preached, uttering all the injurious and blasphemous words that can be invented." In other words, he had insulted Calvin.

If there was ever a man temperamentally unsuited to navigate treacherous political waters, it was Servetus. Still, here he was on comfortable ground. He answered the theological arguments one by one, in each case bringing his vast biblical knowledge to the fore. No one in the room was any match for him. He insisted that the Trinity had been invented at Nicaea and that it was extrabiblical, and he defied his accusers to produce a single passage in the Scriptures to refute his position. This challenge he was to maintain against all comers for the remainder of the trial.

As to the charge that he had escaped from Vienne, Servetus freely admitted that he had done so but was careful to point out that he had been a prisoner only because he had been denounced to the authorities there by Calvin and Trie, and that the Catholics would have burned him at the stake if he stayed. When he got to count thirty-seven, that he had been abusive to Calvin, Servetus countered that it was Calvin who had been abusive to him, referring to him as "a dog" and "a beast" and worse, and he had merely "responded in a like manner."

After the interrogation, Fontaine presented copies of the 1535 Ptolemy, the Pagnini Bible, and both a printed and manuscript copy of *Christianismi Restitutio* to the court. The manuscript copy was the one that Servetus had sent to Calvin for comment seven years earlier. The printed copy had sixteen handwritten pages replacing those that had been sent to Lyon by Trie. The sixteen pages were in the handwriting of one of Calvin's servants. The secretary had used the manuscript copy as his source.

At the end of the day, Tissot agreed that there were sufficient grounds to proceed further.

The next morning, Servetus was brought before the Little Council, now empanelled as a criminal tribunal. He was again asked to respond to the charges one by one, which he did, this time being even more forceful about Calvin's betrayal of him to the Catholics and the abuse that he had endured at the Reformer's hand. Fontaine moved that the prisoner be tried for heresy, since his responses to the charges had been only "frivolous songs." After Fontaine's one night in jail, he also asked to be released from custody. The court agreed on both counts. The trial was ordered to commence the next day, and Fontaine would go free on bail. That bail was immediately posted in the form of Calvin's brother, Antoine, who served as Fontaine's guarantor. Now officially a defendant, Servetus was remanded to his cell and relieved of his possessions, which included ninety-seven pieces of gold, a gold chain, gold coins, a diamond, a ruby, and some other jewels.

On the third day, the next phase of the proceedings began, a kind of extended pretrial hearing. If Fontaine could make a strong enough case to the Council, he would be released entirely with his bail vacated, and the public prosecutor would take over the case. Two new players were present in court. One was an attorney, Germain Colladon, there to speak for Fontaine. Pious and austere, Colladon was another French expatriate and one of Calvin's closest associates in Geneva. He was sufficiently intimate with the Reformer to later write of Calvin's home life and his day-to-day routine. The other newcomer was a member of the Council, none other than the excommunicate leader of the Libertines, Philibert Berthelier.

Colladon had come prepared to confront the accused with the precise theological arguments of which Fontaine was incapable. Instead, he and Berthelier immediately went at each other. The subject was Calvin; it was as if the defendant wasn't even there. There is no record of their exchange, but the arguments became so heated that court was adjourned early.

The first two and a half days of the trial had not gone well for Calvin. Fontaine had been no match for Servetus's scholarship, and Colladon was not sufficiently feared to control the courtroom. Servetus was showing no contrition and had demonstrated that he was quite capable of using the trial as a forum to air his views. Worst of all, his very lack of political skills seemed to be working in his favor. There were indications that some members of the court were beginning to look favorably on this solitary Spaniard who was so obviously pious and passionate in his beliefs.

So on the afternoon of August 16, John Calvin personally presented himself before the Council and demanded to be heard.

He came in, this mere twig of a man, thin, bent over, almost cadaverous, with the long Frankish nose, the wisp of a beard, and the smoldering stare that itself was enough to break most men. He walked slowly to a place at the front of the room, trailed by his ministers.

Calvin faced Berthelier and the others and told them that Servetus had more than demonstrated the repugnance of his opinions and there was no doubt whatever that these opinions had already infected many and would continue to do so if left unchecked. He demanded an immediate guilty verdict from the Council. In that moment, wrote Robert Willis in *Servetus and Calvin*, "the issue, though continuing to be debated on the ground of speculative theology, was ... transferred to the domain of politics, on which there was only one practical issue involved, as to who or which party that divided the state of Geneva should have the upper hand."

Berthelier and the others on the Council refused Calvin's demand. The trial would continue.

The next morning, Calvin was seated at the prosecutor's bench next to Colladon, with a number of other ministers close at hand. Once again, Colladon began the questioning of the prisoner, trying to shake the foundations of his arguments. Once again, Servetus was more than equal to any line of questioning. The frustration at the prosecutors' bench was apparent.

Calvin stood up.

There would be no surrogates now. It was to be Calvin and Servetus. After almost twenty years, they would finally have their debate. If the stakes had been high for Calvin on that day in Paris in 1534, they were all that much higher for Servetus now.

The exchanges were sharp, fast, and erudite. There was perhaps no other person in Europe who could have matched up to either of them. The subjects of these exchanges were often so esoteric than no one in the courtroom save the participants could follow them. One of these, recorded by Calvin, turned on the differences between Divine substance and the substance of living beings and other material things.

> *Servetus*: All things, all creatures are portions of the substance of God.
>
> *Calvin (annoyed, he claimed, by so palpable an absurdity)*: What, poor man, if one stamped his foot on this floor and said he trod on God, would you not be horrified in having subjected the majesty of God to such unworthy usage?
>
> *Servetus*: I have not a doubt but that this bench, this table, and all you can point to around us is the substance of God.
>
> *Calvin*: Then must also not the Devil be substantially of God's substance?
>
> *Servetus (smiling impudently, according to Calvin)*: Do you doubt it? For my part, I hold it as a general proposition that all things whatsoever are part and parcel of God, and that nature at large is His substantial manifestation.

Calvin let it drop there. As they both knew, he himself had often claimed that God was present everywhere, and Luther had said, "God is present in all created things, and so in the smallest leaflet and tiniest poppy seed."

At every turn, Calvin attacked and Servetus countered. As to the charge that in the *Geography* he had slandered Moses with his remarks about the Holy Land, Servetus noted that he had not written the passage and besides, it was difficult to slander Moses with observations about contemporary Palestine. Servetus also held fast to his critique of the Trinity. Prior to the Council of Nicaea, he maintained, no doctor of the Church had used the word *Trinity*: "if the Fathers did acknowledge a distinction in the Divine Essence, it was not *real* but *formal* ... the *per-*

sons were nothing more in truth than *dispensations* or modes, not distinct entities or *persons* in the accepted meaning of that word."

Other than the Trinity, the most contentious point on which Servetus was accused was his denunciation of infant baptism. This debate cut deeper than theological esoterica or even a question of man's relationship with God. By denying that children under twenty were capable of mortal sins, Servetus not only recognized that childish indiscretion was not the equal of adult criminality, but he left room for both improvement by man and forgiveness by God. To Calvin, on the other hand, God's law was God's law, and no one was immune. Exempting those under twenty would only encourage them to commit adultery, theft, and murder. "[Servetus] is worthy that the little chickens, all sweet and innocent as he makes them, should dig out his eyes a hundred thousand times," he wrote. No, children who committed indiscretions must be damned right along with their elders.

As his final piece of evidence, Calvin produced the copy of the *Institutes* that he had sent to Servetus, minus the samples he had sent to France. He showed the Council the scabrous notations in the margins. "There is not a page of this book that is not befouled with vomit," he repeated.

The Council ruled that the trial should proceed to the next phase.

‡

CLAUDE RIGOT, ATTORNEY GENERAL for the city of Geneva and titularly a Libertine, took over the prosecution. In order to allow Rigot time to prepare, a four-day adjournment was ordered. Calvin used this time well. He denounced Servetus from the pulpit and lobbied furiously among members of the Council who either supported him or were not firmly allied with his opponents. With the protection of God's word once more the cause, the old fire-breathing Calvin was back.

He used the full range of his magnificent intellect to argue against the heretic. It mattered little that the issues seemed purely speculative, involving matters that the members of the Council did not pretend to understand, he said. Servetus was the enemy of religion itself and thus threatened the very cornerstone of civilized society. The Catholics at Vienne had already tried and convicted him—should the Council of Geneva show itself less zealous than the papists of France in protecting the name of God and their own true faith? Simply put, by holding to opinions that ran counter to those generally accepted by Christians everywhere, Servetus was proclaiming his own heresy.

When Calvin heard that after all of this, members of the Council were still wavering, he made it known that he was contacting reformers in other cantons to enlist their support. If Servetus went unpunished, Geneva would stand alone in its godlessness.

Servetus was no longer denying authorship of his works, only that they were heretical or that they had caused any harm among the faithful. When questioned about *Christianismi Restitutio*, he admitted that copies of the book had been shipped to Frankfurt. Calvin, while continuing to insist that Servetus had slandered him, wrote the following in a letter to the reform ministers:

> I doubt not that you have heard of Servetus, the Spaniard, who more than twenty years ago infected Germany with a villainous book, full of sacrilegious error of every kind. The scoundrel having fled from Germany and lain concealed in France under a false name, has lately concocted a second book out of the contents of the first, but replete with new figments which he has had printed in Vienne, not far from Lyons. Of this book we learn that many copies have been sent to Frankfurt. It were long did I enumerate the many Errors, the prodigious blasphemies against God, that are scattered over its pages. Imagine to yourselves a rhapsody made up of the impious ravings of every age; for there is no kind of impiety that this wild beast from hell has not appropriated. You will assuredly find in every page matters that will horrify you. The

author is now in prison here at the instance of our magistracy, and I hope he will soon be condemned and punished. But you are to aid us against the further spread of this pestiferous poison. The [bearer of this] will tell you where the books are bestowed and their number; and the bookseller to whom they are consigned will, I believe, make no objections to their being given to the flames. Did he throw any obstacle in the way of this, however, I venture to think you are so well disposed, that you will take steps to have the world purged of such noxious corruption.

When the trial reconvened on August 21, Rigot was still not ready, so Fontaine and Colladon sat at the prosecutor's bench. A motion by members of the Council to abandon further prosecution of Servetus was defeated. Colladon questioned Servetus on the printing of *Christianismi Restitutio*, trying to find out if Arnoullet was as ignorant of the contents as he claimed. During the session, Calvin suddenly burst into the room. He took his place at the bench, placing a stack of biblical texts in front of him. He pointed to the sources that he claimed demonstrated that the word "Trinity" had been used before Nicaea and assailed Servetus for corrupting the meaning of the essence of God. The two argued through most of the session, once more to a stalemate. During the afternoon, Calvin abruptly left, leaving the books for Servetus to see for himself.

Just before the day's adjournment, Servetus asked for writing materials in order to prepare a rebuttal. The Council allowed him a pen and a single sheet of paper.

The Council also decided to contact the other cantons on its own to ask informally for opinions, and even, astoundingly, to contact the Catholic authorities at Vienne. The first of these moves was welcomed by the defendant. Two years earlier, in a similar case, Jerome Bolsec, whom Calvin wanted to execute for questioning predestination, had been spared after reformers in other cities proclaimed the sentence too harsh. Bolsec, however, was a far less formidable intellectual force and, further, had agreed to keep his mouth shut afterward and discontinue any public pronouncements about Calvinist doctrine.

When Servetus returned to court on August 23, Rigot took over. Fontaine, Colladon, and Calvin were gone. Servetus submitted his single sheet of paper to the Council. Rather than take notes on the arguments, he had used the paper to draft a motion. "Michael Servetus," he wrote, "humbly showeth that the prosecution of a man for the doctrine of the Scripture, or for any question arising from it, is a new invention, unknown to the apostles and their disciples and to the ancient church. As it appears, first from the Acts of the Apostles, chap. xvii and xix, where such accusers are cast off, and referred to the churches when there is no crime in the case, and 'tis only a matter relating to religion." He then cited the case of Arius himself, who had merely been banished by Constantine after the First Council of Nicaea.

This was two arguments in one. In addition to the historic precedent that banishment was the appropriate punishment for Scriptural deviation, Servetus was also pointing out that since he had committed no crime in Geneva, the law clearly stated that he could not be prosecuted in the city, only thrown out.

Lastly, he wrote, "In conclusion, my Lords, insomuch as I am a stranger, ignorant of the customs of this country, not knowing either how to speak or comport myself in the circumstances under which I am placed, I humbly beseech you to assign me an Advocate to speak for me in my defense. Doing thus, you will assuredly do well, and our Lord will prosper your Republic."

The folly of the Libertine strategy was now apparent. Banishing Servetus would accomplish nothing other than leaving a known heretic on the loose in Switzerland under the Libertine aegis. Granting him an advocate was even worse. Under Genevan law, had Rigot granted Servetus the right to an attorney, he could no longer seek the death penalty, leaving banishment as the only option.

Instead, Rigot claimed that Servetus's argument against the death penalty was a confession of guilt, that he would not argue against the application of such a penalty unless he knew he deserved it. As for a lawyer, Servetus was known to be a liar and a seducer, and people such as that did not deserve attorneys, who would merely aid them in lying and seducing more effectively.

Rigot then presented a revised list of thirty charges. These were not theological at all—Rigot was no theologian—but aimed at proving that as a disreputable character, Servetus was a menace to society. Had Servetus not communicated with Jews? Was he not a Jew himself? Had he not read the Koran and become friendly with infidel Turks? While in Basel, had he not caused public disruption? Had he not also been discommodious with Bucer and Oecolampadius? Had he not come to Geneva solely to disseminate his blasphemous ideas? Had he not lived a besotted and dissolute life? Had he not fled the lawful authorities of France? While in France, had he not attended Mass as a loyal Catholic? Had he not lived a life of sexual profligacy while avoiding the holy institution of marriage?

This approach was ham-fisted and not a little silly, and Servetus had little difficulty with either the prosecutor or his questions. He easily demonstrated that he had lived a moral and pious life, and that his only encounters with the authorities had been on speculative grounds. To the last charge, Servetus revealed that he had been operated on for a rupture at age five and been impotent ever since, an assertion that may or may not have been true.

On August 28, Rigot abandoned his thirty charges and substituted a new list of thirty-seven. These charges were similar to the original thirty-eight, except that they were much more finely drawn and demanded a high degree of theological knowledge. They were made to appear as if Rigot had drawn them up himself—Calvin was referred to only in the third person—but as Willis noted:

> The articles now brought forward by Rigot and the questions
> founded on them are in the handwriting of the amanuensis

usually employed by Calvin to make copies of his letters and papers; and beyond question were all dictated by Calvin himself. He perceived he could trust Rigot no further without risk of failure, and so resumed the position he had taken with Trie, his servant Fontaine, and even in person.

Rigot was on unfamiliar ground and Servetus once again fended off the attack, but captivity was beginning to have its effect. He had now been shut up for over two weeks in a cell usually reserved for murderers and common thieves. There was no ventilation, no sanitary facilities, and little light. It was infested with vermin and lice. He had not been allowed a change of clothing, and the food was inadequate and vile. On orders of the prosecutor, he was held in seclusion, not allowed to see anyone save the jailer on days when court was not in session.

Also, either by coincidence or design, the pace of the trial had slowed markedly. There was another adjournment until August 31. Then the courier from Vienne arrived, accompanied by the jailer and a captain. The jailer had come specifically to ask that Servetus absolve him of any complicity in the April escape. Servetus readily did so. The attitude of his friends had changed. The courier presented a letter from Maugiron, the man whose family Servetus had tended in sickness, who said that he "rejoiced to know that Villeneuve is now in the hands of Messieurs de Genève, and I thank God for the assurance I feel that you will take better care of him than did the Ministers of Justice at Vienne, and award him such punishment as will leave him no opportunity for dogmatizing, or writing and publishing heretical doctrines in time to come." The letter also said that Henri II had awarded Servetus's property, valued at over four thousand crowns, to Maugiron's son, the baron de Igé.

The captain told the court that Vienne could assure Geneva that if the prisoner were returned, he would be punished there, and no further proceedings in the latter city were necessary. When asked if he wished to return, Servetus fell on the floor in tears and begged that he might be judged in Geneva.

✝

THAT WAS IT FOR RIGOT. At the next session of the court, the attorney general was replaced by Calvin himself. But there was to be no face-to-face confrontation. Servetus was given paper and the list of charges and was then returned to his cell to prepare written responses in Latin. Latin was chosen because the Council had now decided to officially include the opinions of other reformers in their decision. The responses were to be sent to Bern, Basel, Zurich, and Schaffhausen. If Servetus knew of the Bolsec case, and he well might have, this latest development would have rekindled his hopes.

If so, then Servetus, like the Libertines, underestimated Calvin's resolve. Calvin remembered the Bolsec case too. Although he said publicly that he welcomed the action, privately Calvin was anything but pleased, and he counterattacked. In a letter to Henri Bullinger in Zurich, he wrote that he resented the Council questioning his theological authority. "Our magistrates," he added, "cause you this trouble against our will. They have reached such a point of madness that they question everything we say. So if I assert that it is light at noon they begin to have their doubts about it." He also wrote private letters to the reformers in each of the other cities, stressing the enormity of Servetus's heresy and how vital it was that nothing interfere with swift and certain punishment. If Servetus escaped with his life, who knew where he would next choose to spread his filth?

On September 3, Servetus submitted his responses to the Council. His ability to write with clarity and logic and cite Scriptural support for his arguments was, under the circumstances, astonishing. To Calvin's assertion that his view of man becoming deified on earth degraded God, Servetus responded that Calvin's doctrine of predestination, "by making a slave of our will, turns us into logs and stones." But regardless of scholarship, it was mutual vitriol that most marked these exchanges. Calvin said that Servetus was "a dog wiping his snout," and Servetus likened Calvin to Simon Magus, a first-century magician known as the father of heresy. When Calvin submitted a twenty-three-page rebuttal to Servetus the following day, Servetus returned the pages with comments like "imposter," "hypocrite," and "miserable wretch" scribbled in the margins. To Calvin's assertion that Tertullian, a second-century Carthaginian biblical theorist whose works obviously predated Nicaea, recognized a real distinction in the persons of the Trinity, Servetus wrote, "You lie. Nothing of the sort was ever heard of in Tertullian, but only a disposition."

Servetus's stunted public relations instincts were not improving with incarceration. He seemed unaware that this sort of language, instigated by Calvin or not, would work against him with the other reformers. Calvin, on the other hand, had learned from experience how to play to his audience. He had his ministers submit a memorandum to the Council. "Servetus thinks the judges will not know how eloquent he is and what an unabashed reviler unless at the outset he calls Calvin a homicide and afterward vomits many insults upon him."

But there had been a more ominous development for Servetus, one of which he was completely unaware. On Saturday, September 2, with its singularly bad sense of timing, the Council had finally decided to rescind Calvin's excommunication of Berthelier. Six weeks earlier, they might well have made it stick. Now, however, a rejuvenated Calvin appeared before the Council and told them that he would die a hundred times before he allowed Christ to be subjected to such abuse. The Council ignored him.

The next day, the tension in the congregation was palpable as everyone crowded in, waiting to see what would happen in the head-to-head duel when Berthelier appeared for communion. This was religion as theater. Calvin, who could plainly see a number of prominent Libertines in the audience and assumed Berthelier was there too, stood at the pulpit and exclaimed, "If anyone comes to this table who has been excluded by the Consistory, I will do my duty with my life." He then went to the communion table to await the confrontation. No one moved. The crowd looked about, but still Berthelier did not make his presence known. Finally it became clear why. Berthelier had stayed home.

With that moment of surrender, Servetus was doomed. He was not going to be the vehicle by which the Libertines embarrassed Calvin—he had become an embarrassment himself. Now on the run, the last thing the Libertines wanted was to be branded as supporters of heresy. Except for one or two diehards like Ami Perrin, the Libertines wanted nothing more of Servetus than to be rid of him. The only chance to avoid complete disaster was to show that they could be every bit as pious and ruthless about defending the name of God as was Calvin.

There was another halt in the public sessions. Servetus was now shut up in his cell, incommunicado, twenty-four hours a day. When the proceedings seemed to drag to a halt entirely, he began to grow desperate.

Still unaware of the change in the political landscape, on September 15 he addressed another petition to the Council:

> I humbly beg that you cut short these long delays and deliver me from prosecution. You see that Calvin is at the end of his rope, not knowing what to say and for his pleasure wishes to make me rot here in prison. The lice eat me alive. My clothes are torn and I have nothing for a change, neither jacket nor shirt, but a bad one...It is a great shame, the more so that I have been caged here for five weeks and [Calvin] has not urged against me a single passage [from the Scriptures].
>
> My Lords, I have also asked you to give me an advocate as you did to my opponent, who was not in the same straits as I. You permitted it to him, but not to me and you have liberated him from prison. I petition you that my case be referred to the Council of Two Hundred with my requests, and if I may

appeal there I do so ready to assume all the cost, loss and interest of the law of an eye for an eye, both against the first accuser and against Calvin, who has taken up the case himself.
Done in your prisons of Geneva. September 15, 1553.

MICHAEL SERVETUS IN HIS OWN CAUSE

In reply to the petition, the Council, demonstrating their piety and
ruthlessness in defending the name of God, made only the empty gesture of allowing Servetus, whose money had been confiscated, a change
of clothes at his own expense.

Servetus, still unaware that nothing he said or did would matter
any longer, continued to send notes to the Council. On September 22,
he challenged Calvin directly:

Messieurs, there are four great and infallible reasons why
Calvin should be condemned:

1. This first is that a matter of doctrine should not be
   subject to criminal prosecution as I can amply show
   from the ancient doctors of the Church.
2. The second is that he is a false accuser.
3. The third is that by his frivolous and calumnious reasons he opposes the truth of Jesus Christ.
4. The fourth is that in large measure he follows the doctrine of Simon Magus. Therefore as a sorcerer he
   should not only be condemned but exterminated and
   driven from the city and his goods should be adjudged
   to me in recompense of mine.

To this, Servetus included a list of six questions that the Council
should ask Calvin, all detailing his role in betraying him to the Inquisition in Vienne and his use of Trie as his agent.

When this petition was ignored without a reply, Servetus seemed finally to grasp that friends, justice, and hope had abandoned him. On October 10, this last, sad request came from the prisoner:

> Honored sirs, It is now three weeks that I have sought an audience and have been unable to secure one. I beg you for the love of Jesus Christ not to refuse me what you would not refuse a Turk who sought justice at your hands. I have some important and necessary matters to communicate to you.
>
> As for what you commanded that something be done to keep me clean, nothing has been done and I am in a worse state than before. The cold distresses me because of my colic and rupture, causing other complaints that I should be ashamed to describe. It is great cruelty that I have not permission to speak if only to remedy my necessities. For the love of God, honored sirs, give your order whether for pity or duty. Done in your prisons of Geneva, October 10, 1553.
>
> MICHAEL SERVETUS

By October 23, after a month's delay, replies from the other cities were in hand and translated from Latin into French. All the ministers agreed. Michael Servetus was spouting heresy of the vilest sort and must not be allowed to continue. Although just how he should be suppressed was unspecified and no one directly recommended execution, there was also no one saying that an excessively harsh sentence should be avoided. Calvin, "that most sincere servant of God," was praised highly by each of the four.

Servetus was put under a special guard—two new warders to watch him twenty-four hours a day. If anything happened to the prisoner, these guards would pay with their lives.

On October 26, the Little Council met. Perrin, the last of the Lib-

Magnifiques seigneurs

Il y a bien troys semmaines. que Je desire et demande auoyr audiance, et nay Jamays peus lauoyr. Je vous supplie pour lamour de Iesu Christ, ne me refuser ce que vous ne refuseries a vn turc. en vous demandant iustice. Jay a vous dire choses dimportance, et bien necessaires.

Quant a ce que m'aues commande, quon me fit quelque chose pour me tenir net rien a rien este faict, et suys plus pietre que Jamais. Et dauantaige le froyt me tormente grandamant a cause de ma colique et rompure, la quelle mengendre daultres pauretes que ay honte vous escrire. cest grand cruaulte, que Je naye conget de parler seulement pour remedier a mes necessites. pour lamour de dieu messeigneurs donez y ordre. ou pour pitie, ou pour le deuoyr. Faict en vous prisons de Geneue le dexieme doctobre 1553.

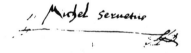

Michel Servetus

A nineteenth-century facsimile of Servetus's last letter from prison. The original is in the Geneva archives.

ertines willing to speak out, moved that the trial be transferred to the
Council of Two Hundred. When this was voted down, Servetus was
condemned without dissent: "We condemn you, Michael Servetus, to
be bound and taken to Champel and there attached to a stake and
burned with your book to ashes." Calvin wrote, "We tried to change the
mode of his death, but in vain."

According to Calvin, Servetus received the news of his sentence
with disbelief and frantic self-pity, moaning and crying out "Misericor-
dia!" [Mercy!] He then begged for an audience with the Reformer,
which Calvin granted.

During this meeting, Calvin held out the possibility that if Servetus
were to publicly renounce his views, he might die more quickly and
mercifully. Servetus was himself worried that in a moment of extreme
pain, he would recant and lose his soul. He begged Calvin to be allowed
to die by the sword. Calvin refused.

> When [Servetus] was asked what he had to say to me he
> replied that he desired to beg my pardon. Then I protested
> simply, and it is the truth, that I had never entertained any
> personal rancor against him. I reminded him gently how I
> had risked my life more than sixteen years ago to gain him
> for our Savior. If he would return to reason I would faithfully
> do my best to reconcile him to all good servants of God...I
> told him that I would pass over everything which concerned
> me personally. He should rather ask the pardon of God
> whom he has so basely blasphemed in his attempt to efface
> the three persons in the one essence...But when I saw that
> all this did no good I...withdrew from the heretic who was
> self-condemned.

The Council wasted no time. The next day, October 27, 1553,
Michael Servetus was led to the stake. Even now, his enemies would
not leave him alone. Every step of the way, Farel walked next to him,

whispering in his ear, urging him to confess his errors and be spared the flames. Servetus prayed silently in reply.

Finally, they arrived at the hill at Champel, with its stake and pile of green wood. Servetus was seated; an iron chain was wrapped around his body and a thick rope wound several times around his neck. The crown of straw and leaves and sulphur was placed on his head, and his book was lashed to his arm.

The fire was lit. Servetus shrieked. At the end of the half hour that it took him to die, he was heard to moan, "Oh Jesus, Son of the Eternal God, have pity on me!"

He had remained true to his beliefs. Otherwise, he would have said, "Oh Jesus, Eternal Son of God."

Every important political, religious, and military figure in Geneva had walked in the procession, then stood for thirty minutes and watched the horror of Michael Servetus's death. All except one.

John Calvin stayed home.

‡

THROUGHOUT BOTH TRIALS and all the minute examinations of *Christianismi Restitutio,* one passage on page 171 in Book V was overlooked. There was no reason that anyone in Vienne or Geneva should have noticed it, since its theological significance was minimal.

Almost as a throwaway, when discussing the nature of the divine spirit, Servetus had drawn on some observations he had made while a medical student in Paris.

> The substantial generation of the vital spirit is composed of a very subtle blood nourished by inspired air ... It is generated in the lungs from a mixture of inspired air with elaborated, subtle blood which the right ventricle of the heart communicates with the left. *However, this communication is not made through the middle wall of the heart as is commonly believed, but*

by a very ingenious arrangement, the subtle blood is urged forward by a long course through the lungs; it is elaborated by the lungs, becomes reddish yellow and is poured from the pulmonary artery into the pulmonary vein. Then in the pulmonary vein it is mixed with inspired air and through expiration it is cleansed of its sooty vapors. Thus finally the whole mixture, suitably prepared for the production of the vital spirit, is drawn onward from the left ventricle of the heart by diastole.

This was a description of pulmonary circulation, perhaps the single most important statement about the workings of the human body in fifteen hundred years. No one had ever described the true function of the heart before. It was the great intuitive leap that Vesalius had failed to make.

The pages from Christianismi Restitutio *where pulmonary circulation is first described*

Between pages 169 and 173 of *Christianismi Restitutio*, Servetus told of how he had unraveled this mystery by deducing that the pulmonary artery "was not made of such sort and such size, nor does it emit so great a force of pure blood from the heart itself into the lungs merely for their nourishment." He recognized that blood changes color in the lungs due to the absorption of something in the air. "Not merely air," he wrote, "but air mixed with blood is sent from the lungs to the heart through the pulmonary vein; therefore the mixture occurs in the lungs."

Servetus theorized that once blood mixes with air, it "is then transfused from the left ventricle of the heart into the arteries of the whole body." This is greater circulation, a process not even guessed at in the sixteenth century. He went farther still and anticipated the discovery of capillaries, which would not be confirmed until the development of the microscope almost two centuries later. The blood in the brain was "elaborated and completed in the very slender vessels or hair-like (*capilaribus*) arteries...These vessels in a very remarkable way are woven together very finely and even if they are called arteries are nevertheless the termination of arteries...It is a new kind of vessel."

If these paragraphs had gotten out into the world, they would have changed the face of science, and Michael Servetus would have been hailed as one of the great medical minds in history. When William Harvey finally received credit for this same breakthrough some seventy-five years later, it launched the modern age of medicine and vaulted Harvey into the ranks of the immortals of science.

‡

AFTER THE EXECUTION, Calvin instructed the printer Robert Estienne to hunt down any remaining copies of *Christianismi Restitutio* and see that they were burned. It was Calvin's intention to eradicate Servetus's ideas along with the man.

He almost succeeded. ‡

THE EXECUTION OF Michael Servetus, while rescuing Calvin from his immediate political difficulties, created an unexpected challenge to his moral authority. The reaction to the barbarity of the execution was far more intense and widespread than he had anticipated. Servetus might have been a Quixotic figure with views repugnant to many, but his extraordinary bravery and refusal to recant even at the moment of greatest agony spurred a wave of admiration among theologians across Europe. Although the sentence (if not the method) had been approved by other churches in Switzerland, Calvin now found himself fending off charges of excess and intolerance. He had not been prepared for the large number of highly placed, respected intellectuals, both in and out of the Church, who did not believe that even a heretic should be executed merely for the expression of conscience, particularly in such a horrific manner.

An official in neighboring Bern wrote a letter to Calvin denouncing him for his approval of the sentence of burning, and a pastor in his old home town of Noyon sent him a scathing note observing that what he had done was worse than anything done by the Inquisition in either Spain or France. Genevans, too frightened to speak out publicly, employed the old familiar tactic of composing little uncomplimentary couplets that were sung *sotto voce* at night in alleys.

It was in Basel where criticism was harshest. Basel still held great sway as the soul of enlightened humanism, and disapproval there could not be ignored. Bullinger, Calvin's most fervent supporter, entreated him to respond. He must seize the initiative and publish a defense of his actions. He must denounce Servetus so aggressively and pervasively that no one could possibly question the propriety of his behavior. "See to it, dear Calvin, that you give a good account of Servetus and his end, so that all may have the beast in horror," he wrote, to which Calvin replied, "If I have but a little leisure I shall show what a monster he was."

So, early in 1554, Calvin published a short tract entitled *Defense of the True Faith of the Sacred Trinity Against the Hideous Errors of Michael Servetus, Spaniard.* It was a ferocious diatribe in which Servetus was portrayed not as a theological dissenter but as an enemy to all religion and a threat to civilization itself. "Knowing the poison to be deadly in its kind," wrote Calvin, "and having regard to the amount of stupidity and confusion which God, to avenge Himself, inflicts on all who despise his doctrine, I have felt myself compelled as it were to take up the pen, and in exposing the errors of the man to furnish grounds for better conclusions. When Servetus and his like, indeed, presume to meddle with the mysteries of religion, it is as if swine came thrusting their snouts into a treasury of sacred things." Calvin bragged about causing Servetus's arrest, initiating the prosecution, and drawing up the charges that he had first passed off on Fontaine.

The pamphlet was published in both Latin and French and seemed at first to have little tangible impact. Calvin's supporters praised his candor and vigilance, while his detractors called the *Defense* self-serving and hypocritical. Indirectly, however, it turned out to be of great benefit to Calvin. Emboldened by the hope that the outside world had at last turned against their enemy, the Libertines under Perrin made one last pathetic attempt to obliterate the French influence and secure Geneva for the Genevans. One night, a bunch of them got drunk and decided to set fire to a house rumored to harbor armed Frenchmen. When they got there, an alert syndic appeared, carrying his baton of office. Perrin made as if to snatch the baton away—signifying that he, and not the syndic, represented the law—but in a move that epitomized the

Libertines' political fumbling, paused in mid-grab. With that hesitation, Geneva lost what little remained of its opposition party. When a second syndic showed up, the patriots lost their nerve entirely and fled into the night to permanent exile in Bern.

After the affair of the baton, there was no more unrest in Geneva, and Calvin consolidated his control of the city. He ordered the entire Council of Two Hundred to stand up, raise their right hands, and swear allegiance to the Reformation. The Little Council was subjected to a Cultural Revolution–like program of regularly scheduled meetings for "mutual correction," during which they were required to point out one another's sins and faults (a directive that the councilors followed enthusiastically, although not necessarily in the spirit of brotherly solicitude that Calvin claimed to have intended). Immediately before elections, Calvin focused his sermons on the personal qualities that he felt were necessary to hold public office, leaving no doubt as to his own choices for syndic. His authority was so complete that when Geneva got its first dentist, the man was not allowed to practice until he had first worked on Calvin.

Discipline was even more rigorously enforced than before. The merest breath of discontent meant a whipping, a tongue pierced with hot iron, or banishment. Mental illness was no excuse—an obviously deranged woman who thought Calvin was her husband was kicked out of town. Calvin took an especially dim view of adultery, a transgression with which he had some personal acquaintance, since apparently two of the loosest women in Geneva were his brother Antoine's wife (who was caught in the act with Calvin's hunchbacked servant) and his own stepdaughter, Judith. Judith tended to flaunt her sexuality, and after one of her more public affairs, "for days [Calvin] was too ashamed even to leave his house."

Calvin's personal problems, however, had no effect on his growing reputation. Religious refugees continued to pour into the city. These newcomers were more than willing to put up with the rigors of the regime, since many of them were coming from places from which they had just barely escaped with their lives. The political energy of the Reformation became more and more concentrated within Calvin's realm.

But Calvin had never intended that his vision be restricted to one city or even one country. When Geneva was secure, he turned his attention to the battle for the soul (and souls) of Europe.

Now a veteran of twenty years of struggle, Calvin once more took up the weapons that had forged Protestant success—books, reading, and education. The public elementary school system in Geneva became acknowledged as the best in Europe. He founded the University of Geneva to nurture a new generation of reform scholars; he trained missionaries and then sent them out to spread the word, not just in Europe, but everywhere in the known world. The Calvinist scholar John T. McNeill wrote, "It was not only the future of Geneva but that of other regions as well that was affected by the rise of the Geneva schools. The men who were to lead the advance of the Reform church in many lands were trained in Geneva classrooms, preached Geneva doctrines, and sang the Psalms to Geneva tunes."

Calvin did not simply rely on missionaries to spread the word. Copies of the *Institutes* flooded the Protestant centers of England, the Netherlands, and Germany and made their way surreptitiously into every Catholic country in Europe. Calvin's great insight was his awareness that the best way to mold the minds of the common people was to have them do the very thing that the Catholic Church had forbidden for centuries. Thus he encouraged the translation of the Bible into vernacular languages and its distribution to merchants, artisans, and farmers. In 1560, printers in Geneva published a Bible in English and shipped it off to Elizabethan England, where it became hugely successful and led directly to the King James version in the following century.

By the time John Calvin died of tuberculosis in 1564, he had become an industry unto himself, exporting revolution. His aim was nothing less than the annihilation of Catholicism. And he might well have succeeded except for one remarkable man who single-handedly shouldered the Catholic colossus and turned it from the brink of extinction, perhaps the most influential figure in Church history after Christ himself.

✝

IÑIGO DE OÑEZ Y LOYOLA was Calvin's mirror image. Physically, they were both small, thin, frail, short-tempered, and constantly beset by illness. Spiritually, both were intense, committed, indomitable, and utterly convinced of their godliness.

Loyola was born in northern Spain, Basque country, in 1491, the youngest of thirteen children. He had studied for the priesthood as an adolescent, but before he was ordained, he was recruited as a page to Juan Velásquez de Cuellar, treasurer to Ferdinand and Isabella for the kingdom of Castile. It didn't take long for him to abandon spiritual pursuits for the much more glamorous life of a courtier. By his own admission, he became obsessed with extravagant dress, drinking, gambling, and whoring about, all to the greatest extremes possible.

Although barely five feet tall, Loyola loved swordplay and was a fierce and fearless fighter. When Velásquez died in 1517, Loyola joined the army. In 1521, during Francis's invasion to reclaim Navarre, the French besieged the fort at Pamplona. The commander wanted to surrender, but Loyola, a junior officer, urged him to fight on and then heroically led the resistance. On May 20 he was hit in the legs by a cannon ball. His left calf was torn open and his right shin broken. After Loyola's fall, the garrison surrendered.

Loyola had been so brave that he was treated with great solicitude by the French. Instead of sending him to prison, they set his leg, and French soldiers carried him home on a litter. The leg had been set incorrectly, however, and had to be rebroken and reset, all without benefit of anesthesia. This second setting was not much better than the first. A knob of bone protruded at the top of his shin. With that deformity, it would have been impossible to fit into the high, tight calf boots

that were all the fashion at court, so Loyola had the offending knob sawed off, also without anesthesia. Then, in an attempt to match the now-foreshortened right leg to the normal left, he demanded that the leg be stretched out by weights. The pain of all this was excruciating and went on for week after interminable week. (It didn't even work— he was left with a limp for the rest of his life.)

Eventually, Loyola developed a fever, and the doctors told him that he was going to die. Then, on June 29, the eve of the feasts of Saints Peter and Paul, the fever broke, and from there he slowly regained his strength. But he still faced months of recuperation, confined to his bed.

Excruciating pain was replaced by mind-crushing boredom. In order to help pass the time, Loyola requested some of the swashbuck-ling romance novels that he favored, but they didn't have any, so instead he was given a book on the life of Christ and one on the saints. With no other choice, he spent his days devouring each and, when he was done, began to consider what it might take to become a saint himself. He could fast longer than this one, become more pious than that one, endure more than a third.

He convalesced until March 1522, lying in bed and planning. After his body had healed, he left the castle, placed his sword and dagger on the altar of a Benedictine shrine, gave all his clothes and worldly possessions to the poor, and, dressed in sandals and sackcloth, carrying only a staff, began a pilgrimage to Jerusalem. On the way, Loyola stopped at a town called Manresa but having no money was forced to put up in a cave outside the city.

He lived in the cave for ten months, determined to purge himself of sins of the flesh. He fasted so severely that his digestive system became permanently damaged. He prayed, scourged himself (self-flagellation with a whip or branches), and undertook other extreme forms of penance. When he emerged, austere and ascetic, his focus was on Christ alone. With the endurance and will forged from two years of almost unendurable hardship, he set out to remake the Catholic Church.

It took over fifteen years. Loyola (who abandoned Iñigo for the Latinized Ignatius) was beaten, thrown in jail, kicked out of two universities, expelled from Jerusalem, and brought in front of the Inquisition but eventually found himself at the head of a small group of believers at the University of Paris. He was there at exactly the same time as Servetus and Calvin, but they ran in far different circles. Loyola's group took vows of chastity and poverty and adopted the Ignatian practices of begging, fasting, and going barefoot. In 1539, he had a vision in which God said to him, *"Ego vobis Romae propitius ero"* ("I will be favorable to you in Rome"), and he set off to see the pope.

‡

IN ROME, THE HEDONISTIC appeal of the Renaissance papacy was fading. The sacking of Rome and the spread of Protestantism were seen as God's condemnation of the degeneracy of the Church. It had finally become clear that despite its numerical superiority and material advantages, and regardless of Protestant squabbling, if Rome did not find a way to match Calvin's commitment, brilliance, and intensity, it might well lose Europe.

When Pope Clement VII died in 1534, there were rumblings that the next pope should move aggressively to clean up the mess. Instead, in a more or less rigged election, the cardinals elevated the sixty-six-year-old Alessandro Farnese, who had just missed being pope twice before.

The genial and easygoing Farnese, who became Pope Paul III, had been educated at the court of Lorenzo the Magnificent and enjoyed art, culture, and food. In his first official act, he confounded both his supporters and detractors by appointing a six-cardinal commission to study the state of the Church and recommend reforms. Each of the six was known for scholarship, piety, and disgust with the old order.

The commission worked for three years. In their report, they recommended such obvious changes as abolishing the sale of benefices and indulgences, renewing the commitment to chastity, particularly by bishops and cardinals (and, by implication, popes), and curbing the rampant nepotism in Rome.

Paul welcomed these recommendations, apparently with total sincerity. He did not, however, seem to understand that they applied to him as well. At the same time as he was preaching austerity and a renewal of faith, he was giving parties, lavishing money on the arts, and undertaking grand (and expensive) new projects. He plotted, seized territory, and installed relatives in positions of power.

Loyola succeeded in obtaining an audience with Paul, who found the vision of a new order of paramilitary zealots who swore total allegiance and obedience to him alone irresistible. Loyola, an indefatigable attacker, stressed the need for the Church to aggressively recruit converts and just as aggressively woo the faithful. Paul, who had his own ideas, had the perfect job for his new recruits, dubbed the Society of Jesus.

For some time, the idea of a general council to reconcile with the Protestants had been making the rounds. This kind of sweeping diplomacy appealed to Paul, but the prospect of a peaceful Germany and an unoccupied Charles once again facing Rome had caused him to rethink the idea. Instead, he had proposed a council of internal reform. He issued invitations in 1536 to all significant parties, both within the Church and without, including every Catholic monarch in Europe.

It had taken nine years, but in December 1545 the nineteenth ecumenical council, the Council of Trent, was convened. As his personal representatives, the seventy-eight-year-old pontiff sent two young members of Loyola's group. Although Loyola himself did not attend, the influence of the Jesuits (a nickname originally bestowed by Calvin, who did not mean it as a compliment) became overwhelming. They were tougher, more focused, more dedicated, and more pious than anyone else there, and as a result, for the first time there was a genuine movement toward reform within the Church.

Loyola now had his opportunity and he was not a man to let it pass by. By the time of his death in 1556, the Society of Jesus had taken control of over one hundred universities throughout Europe, and would come to dominate Catholic education (including the English College at Rome). Within fifty years, Loyola's order would have missions as far away as India, China, Japan, Africa, and the New World. The confessor to the king of France would be a Jesuit.

With it all, perhaps Loyola's greatest achievement was in changing the Church's attitude toward reading. Almost since the religion had been founded, Church leaders had tried to restrict common people's access to books. Literacy was discouraged, and censorship was employed regularly to keep those who could read from actually doing it. The Bible was forbidden, of course, as was anything that the Church deemed heretical—the works of Servetus being prominently featured in this category. Censorship had been mostly random, however. A book or author forbidden in one province might be allowed in another. In 1559, under the new pope Paul IV, who as Cardinal Caraffa had been a member of the council of six that had recommended Church reforms, and then of another council of six that reinstated the Inquisition, the first official papal list of forbidden books was published.

It was called the *Index Librorum et Auctorum*. It forbade the reading of forty-eight editions of the Bible deemed heretical, including all those in vernacular languages, as well as anything at all printed by sixty-one different publishers. No book printed in the previous forty years that lacked an author's name, the name of the printer, or place or date of publication could be read by a Catholic. From that date forward, any book lacking official ecclesiastical approval was forbidden.

In the wake of Paul's order, thousands of books were burned—ten thousand in Venice in a single day. Still, the list was so restrictive, and the penalties for transgression so extreme, that within months even conservative members of the Curia lobbied for change. After Paul died, the Council of Trent redrafted the *Index* to make it more specific, and in 1571 a special congregation was formed to maintain the list and make periodic revisions to keep it up to date.

Loyola went at the problem from an entirely different direction. Censorship had not worked, and with more and more books available to more and more people, it was not likely to work in the future. So if you can't prevent someone from doing something that displeases you, try to ensure that they do it under conditions that are to your liking. Like Calvin, he *wanted* the faithful to read, the more the better. The trick was persuading them to read what the church deemed desirable and avoid that which it didn't.

To accomplish this, Loyola, for once, chose the carrot instead of the stick. He demanded that the leaders of the order write and be published. Not just write, but write in a clear and accessible way. The use of vernacular languages should be encouraged, not banned, since that was the way to get the most material into the hearts and minds of the most Catholics in the shortest period of time.

The Jesuits took up the call. Books poured out of universities and monasteries. The emphasis on printing spread. Peter Canisius, one of the Society's key early leaders and the man often credited with having saved Catholicism in Germany, urged the order to create a college of authors. He lobbied for the appointment of cardinals and bishops who could write for the masses to defend the faith against Protestants. He entreated the pope to grant yearly subsidies to the Catholic printers of Germany, and to permit German scholars to edit Roman manuscripts. He oversaw the translation of foreign writings into German. He persuaded the city council of Catholic Fribourg to establish its own press, and he secured special privileges for printers who would print literature favorable to the order.

It all worked. Largely because of Loyola and his followers, the Counter-Reformation, as it came to be called, halted the spread of reform and saved Catholicism.

In addition to spurring internal reform, the Council of Trent destroyed the last hope for compromise with the Protestants. Tolerance was surrender. Gone were the lightning strikes and finger-in-the-dike diplomacy that had characterized the first half of the century. Protestants and Catholics—Calvinists and Jesuits—dug ecclesiastic trenches, two great armies prepared to pound it out. And they did, in one of the bloodiest and most barbaric centuries in human history.

To know the history of Europe over the next hundred years is to marvel that the human race survived. It is impossible to cite every instance of savagery, cruelty, and degradation undertaken in the name of God, but certain events stand out to give an overall sense of the insanity. One occured in France, where, in spirit, Calvin and Loyola came up against each other in battle for the first time.

‡

IN 1559 HENRY II DIED, and the crown of France fell to his eldest son, Francis II, just fifteen years old. Francis relied heavily on the judgment of his chief minister, Charles de Guise. The Guise family were rich, powerful, and disciples of the new, militant Jesuit Catholicism.

But Calvin had made a point of concentrating on his homeland as well. By 1559, the Calvinists—or Huguenots as they were called, after the Eidguenots, the Genevan patriots who had led the revolt against Savoy—had made significant inroads, particularly in the south, Marguerite's old territory. The Huguenots were led by the Bourbon family, headed by Jeanne d'Albret, queen of Navarre, Marguerite's daughter, and every bit as militant as Charles de Guise. She gathered a large army around her under the command of General Condé and Admiral Coligny.

Then, in 1560, at the age of sixteen, Francis died and was succeeded by his ten-year-old brother, Charles IX. Because he was underage, the queen mother, Catherine de' Medici, a direct descendent of Lorenzo the Magnificent and Pope Leo X, was appointed regent.

Catherine, a Renaissance Catholic, feared the Jesuit Guises and used the only force at hand—the Protestant Bourbons—to try to keep them under control and herself in power. In the short term, the result was a tentative, unexpected, legislated religious tolerance. But tolerance cannot be imposed by fiat, and the resultant jockeying for political power eventually erupted into three separate wars of religion between 1562 and 1570. Desperate for peace, Catherine finally sought to cement a treaty by marrying off her beautiful Catholic daughter Marguerite to Jeanne d'Albret's very Huguenot son, Henry, king of Navarre.

In August 1572, five thousand Protestants traveled to Paris at the express invitation of the royal family to attend a wedding that was to heal the wounds and make France one. The city was so crowded that revelers were forced to sleep in the streets.

The Guise family, in the spirit of Loyola, turned apparent defeat into opportunity. They convinced Catherine that the Huguenots were planning to murder her and take over France. The new allies first bungled an assassination attempt on Coligny, the most influential Huguenot at court and a father figure to Charles, now twenty-two, then went to work on the weak-minded king. Catherine cornered her son and hammered at him until late into the night. Charles finally broke down and shrieked, "Kill them! Kill them all!"

The Guises were happy to comply. They had the gates to the city locked to prevent escape and, at 3 A.M. on August 24, Saint Bartholomew's Day, turned the Catholic soldiers loose on Paris.

The result was a frenzy of slaughter rarely seen even in the most ferocious battles of war. Of the five thousand Protestants who had come to Paris, perhaps fewer than ten percent escaped alive. They were killed with swords, clubs, and knives; thrown from windows or drowned in the Seine. Bodies were hacked at and dumped in the streets. The killing soon went beyond religion as Parisians used the massacre as an excuse to get rid of anyone against whom they held a grudge. Husbands murdered unfaithful wives; landlords rid themselves of unwanted tenants; businessmen killed rivals. The dead choked the streets, and drainage channels ran red with blood.

The killing went on for three days as thousands of bloated cadavers, rotting in the summer heat, filled Paris. Insects and crows descended to share the feast. In some parts of the city, it was impossible to get from one place to another without navigating over and around stinking corpses. The king himself had to wade through the dead to get to the Louvre.

The massacres spread across France. When it was all done, as many as thirty thousand Protestants had been slaughtered.

Catholics across Europe rejoiced. Pope Gregory XIII and his cardinals attended a solemn Mass of thanksgiving for "this signal of favor shown to Christian people," and ordered a special medal struck to commemorate the occasion.

Henry of Navarre only survived because of Marguerite's protection. He got out of Paris, not to return until decades later at the head of a great army. Even then, he was forced to convert to Catholicism in order to be crowned Henry IV, king of France. "Paris is worth a Mass," he is reported to have said, shrugging, as he became the first in a line that would endure for almost two centuries, until another conflagration in 1789.

While the Saint Bartholomew's Day Massacre was a spasmodic, in-

ternecine bloodletting, what happened in the Netherlands was calculated slaughter imposed from without. In 1555, Charles V had handed
rule of the Netherlands (which included Belgium) to his son Philip,
king of Spain. What the new king inherited was a nation grown wealthy
on commerce and shipping, a people with a refined taste for art and
fashion, leisure and letters, and most importantly, a remarkably tolerant attitude toward religion. Philip, as ferociously Catholic as his father,
was determined to stamp out heresy, and so he brought the Inquisition
to the Netherlands.

In 1567, Fernando Alvarez de Toledo, duke of Alva, descended on
Brussels with an army of ten thousand Spanish career soldiers. Garbed
in black, the tall, dark, and spare Alva saw himself as the wrath of God,
the Avenging Angel of Death. He set up the Inquisition as the "Council of Troubles"—Netherlanders called it the Council of Blood. He established a network of spies and informers. Suspected heretics were
rousted from their beds in the dead of night and arrested. Trials were
only for show—heretics were executed en masse. Ports were closed to
prevent emigration. Anyone caught helping a Protestant to escape was
also indicted as a Protestant and executed. Alva himself invited two of
the leading opposition leaders to a lavish dinner at the palace, let them
eat, and then had them arrested, jailed, and killed.

William of Orange, the leader of the opposition and a Catholic, declared himself a Calvinist to try and enlist foreign support. He raised
army after army and attacked but was unable to dislodge the Spanish.
To discourage continued opposition, Alva had entire towns exterminated. In Gelderland, five hundred men were tied back to back and
thrown into the river to drown. Haarlem, a Calvinist center, was systematically starved. The city held out for seven months, its citizens
reduced to eating rats and leather, before finally surrendering. Thousands of emaciated soldiers and townspeople were slaughtered when
they at last opened the gates.

It was death, terror, and more death. When Alva left the Netherlands in 1573, he boasted that he had executed eighteen thousand

heretics. The devastated Netherlands would not recover until Spain's attention turned to the ultimate in religious butchery, the Thirty Years' War.

In the Thirty Years' War every hatred, ambition, and fear that had been unleashed by the spread of knowledge erupted in an orgy of sustained horror. Although central Europe, mostly Germany, was the battleground, there was not a country in Europe that did not contribute combatants and victims. From 1618 to 1648, Catholic fought Calvinist, Calvinist fought Lutheran, Hapsburg fought Bourbon, nationalist fought imperialist. The wreckage was unthinkable. Cities were revisited again and again by a succession of marauding armies that killed, burned, raped, stole every bit of food in sight, then ruined the fields so that nothing further could be grown. In the Netherlands they had eaten rats and leather to survive; in Germany they ate each other. No statistic is more chilling than this: there were 21 million people living in Germany in 1618, at the start of the war; by 1648, the war's end, only 13 million were left. The plague was not so efficient.

✝

SOMEHOW, IN THE MIDST of the devastation, civilization managed to inch forward. Sometimes it leapt. In 1628, the court physician to King Charles I of England published a seventy-two-page, flimsily bound book entitled *Exercitatio Anatomica de Motu Cordis et Sanguinis in Animalibus* (*On the Motion of the Heart and Blood in Animals*). The text, like the title, was in Latin.

The king's doctor had come up with the ideas in the book thirteen years before but was wary of putting them down on paper. Although no one in England was being burned at the stake anymore, the subject matter promised to be more than a little controversial, and prison or even execution was not out of the question. So, erring on the side of prudence, the author first published his tract not in England but in

Frankfurt. To further hedge his bets, he included a dedication to Charles that was even more fawning than usual:

> Most Illustrious Prince!
> The heart of animals is the foundation of their life, the sovereign of everything within them...from which all power proceeds. The King, in like manner, is the foundation of his kingdom, the sun of the world around him, the heart of the republic, the fountain whence all power, all grace doth flow...
> Accept therefore, with your wonted clemency, I most humbly beseech you, illustrious Prince, this, my new Treatise on the Heart; you, who are yourself the new light of this age, and indeed its very heart.

The dedication was signed, "Your Majesty's most devoted servant, William Harvey."

William Harvey was the last person one would think of as timid. As a student at Oxford, he went armed to class and pulled his dagger at the slightest provocation. He was known as much for brawling as for studying, and his views of women were not, even by the standards of the day, enlightened. "We Europeans know not how to order and govern our Women," he observed. "The Turks, [who favored veils and harems] are the only people who use them wisely." In his sixties he accompanied the king to Edgehill for the battle against Oliver Cromwell and the Roundheads, and had to be dragged away by friends in order to avoid being killed.

But between the whoring and the brawling, William Harvey managed to marry the daughter of the personal physician to Elizabeth I, become a favorite at court, get the best seats at the Globe Theatre, study for five years in Padua under one of the great anatomists of his day, and, in his seventy-two pages, become the first man to fully describe the circulation of blood through the body.

Harvey was that rare combination of dogged experimenter and intuitive theorist, perhaps the most fully formed anatomist since Galen. He brought together a number of pieces of disparate and conflicting information, added some observations of his own, and reconciled the contradictions in a cogent, unifying theory.

Harvey began with the fifteen-hundred-year-old assumption that blood was concocted in the liver and consumed by organs and other parts of the body. Using only simple arithmetic, Harvey concluded that this could not possibly be true. If each contraction of the heart forced one half-ounce of blood along on its journey, in only one half-hour the heart would pump about five hundred ounces, more blood than the entire body contained. Did other anatomists really believe that merely by digesting food, the body could replenish its entire blood supply forty-eight times every day? It was far more likely that the blood supply was constant and that blood was returned to the heart after passing through the body.

This assumption was buttressed by another bit of observation, this one by Fabricius of Aquapendente, Harvey's old professor at Padua. In 1574, four years before Harvey was born, Fabricius had observed during dissections that human arm and leg veins seemed to have tiny one-way valves that arteries lacked. Fabricius, a Galenist, assumed that these valves were "to ensure a really fair distribution of the blood," although why they were found only in veins remained a mystery.

To Harvey, however, this discovery solved a mystery rather than creating one. If, as he hypothesized, blood was constantly circulating through the body, moving out from the heart through the arteries and back to the heart through the veins, then one-way valves were meant to keep blood from backing up and impeding the flow.

Harvey went on to refute the theory that the heart did its work when it expanded, the "bigger is better" notion of muscle function. Rather, he said, it was the contraction that was the key. He described pulmonary circulation, the circularity and balance of the system, and gave the details of his experiments, proving that the system could operate in no other way.

There was one last piece of the puzzle, and here Harvey could not rely on observation or past discoveries. If blood circulated as he suspected, how did it get from the arteries to the veins? In *Christianismi Restitutio*, Servetus had hypothesized the existence of tiny blood vessels, but Servetus had been dead for seventy-five years and his work forgotten. Others who later theorized about pulmonary circulation, such as Realdo Colombo (whose work in the 1560s was cited by Harvey), were either unaware of or unwilling to credit Servetus as a source.

As it turned out, Harvey used exactly the same hypothesis as had Servetus. Although he admitted he could neither prove nor demonstrate the existence of these tiny blood vessels, the rest of the theory was so perfect that he was sure they must exist.

Despite his fears, Harvey's work was celebrated almost immediately in England. In the rest of Europe, particularly among medical faculties, the last Galenic strongholds, there was a good deal of initial skepticism. But Harvey's theories were so elegant, so clear, and so obviously correct, that by the time of his death in 1657, William Harvey was almost universally recognized as the man who brought the study of the human body into the modern age.

With *Christianismi Restitutio* destroyed, Calvin and Loyola dominating the religious landscape, and Harvey acknowledged as the man who had discovered circulation, it seemed certain that Michael Servetus would fade into an all but forgotten footnote. ‡

✝

PART III

The Trail

IN 1665, THE year before the Great Fire, London was a city of coffeehouses and taverns, joints of mutton, pickled oysters, morning drafts of ale, lutes, cards, and ninepins. The years of dour, puritanical Cromwell were over, and on the throne sat the rakish Restoration king, Charles II, whose manners and loose morals fueled the boisterous comedies of the period. "Be silent, good people; I am the *Protestant* whore," the actress Nell Gwyn hollered out the window of her coach at the jeering crowd that had mistaken her for the king's French mistress.

The period was almost unique in history for its combination of sexual and intellectual fervor. In 1661 Isaac Newton had begun studying mathematics and astronomy at Trinity College, Cambridge. In 1662 the king had chartered the Royal Society with ninety-eight "fellows," including Robert Boyle, the father of modern chemistry; Robert Hooke, the great natural scientist, who first coined the word *cell* after looking under a microscope at a slice of cork; and the poet, essayist, and playwright John Dryden. John Milton was writing *Paradise Lost*, and John Locke would write about the rights of man. In the coffeehouses (tea wouldn't take over as the national drink for another century) and taverns, Samuel Pepys met his friends to tell stories, swap verses, gossip about parliamentary ins and outs, and keep a diary that would immortalize it all.

In 1665 London teemed with refugees. Some were Protestants who had fled the Continent; some were Royalists whose estates had been looted and decimated by Cromwell's men and for whom the Restoration provided only hollow triumph; some were Catholics, attracted by Charles's own flirtation with Rome. Expatriates were everywhere, trying to rebuild shattered lives or recoup some small portion of shattered fortunes. They capitalized on the freewheeling commerce both over and under the table while waiting until it was safe to go home. Everything was bought and sold, including remnants of the great estates—furniture, art, jewelry, silver... and books. Books by the thousands. In 1665 it was in London, more than any other city in the world, that the book trade boomed.

Most of these books were themselves refugees, thrown adrift in one of two great conflicts. In England itself, after the Civil War between the Royalists and the Puritans in the 1640s, Cromwell's Parliament had levied heavy fines on Royalist supporters. Some of these were paid by the sale of luxury items, in which libraries often figured prominently. The bulk of the supply, however, came from the Continent. Many of the great libraries of Germany, the Low Countries, and Eastern Europe had been dismantled and shipped in crates to London in hopes that they would be protected against onrushing Catholic armies. During the Thirty Years' War especially, England, largely immune from the horror, had become a place of refuge for both aristocrats on the run and their possessions.

Inevitably, many of the books had been "lost" in transit, only to resurface in shops and stalls that ranged from the snobby and elite to the openly disreputable. At the very top were booksellers lucky enough to own a shop in Westminster Hall. Westminster booksellers catered to the rich and famous. Samuel Pepys's bookseller, Mrs. Michell, took messages for him; she and her husband dined with him on occasion. There were also many respectable booksellers in Saint Paul's Churchyard and at the Temple Gate.

In less savory sections of London, less prestigious (not to mention less honest) bookmen claimed their share of the booming market. They were none too thorough when it came to examining the provenance of any particular volume. Book scouts combed the countryside, pilfering any book that might not already be for sale or that carried too high a price tag. Booksellers often employed agents to cross the Channel and coax a rare book out of a gentleman's library in Bohemia, Germany, Switzerland, or the Netherlands, and into circulation in the London market. Stock came and went so quickly that many booksellers, interested only in quick profit, had no idea of the quality, rarity, or real value of what they were selling.

So it was that in 1665, when a recently arrived Hungarian count named Daniel Márkos Szent-Iványi went browsing at a London bookseller's, he came across a volume of astonishing rarity that the bookseller was offering at an extremely reasonable price.

Count Szent-Iványi was an accomplished humanist scholar from a distinguished family and had been a noted theologian in Hungary before his flight. The Szent-Iványis remain prominent in their nation's affairs today—one of the count's descendents, István Szent-Iványi, served as chairman of the foreign affairs committee of the nation's parliament.

The book Count Daniel Szent-Iványi discovered was an octavo, over a century old, lacking the author's name or a printer's mark. To the bookseller, it had obviously been indistinguishable from the thousands of other ordinary old books that were lying around London.

But Count Szent-Iványi recognized the book immediately. It was *Christianismi Restitutio.*

How the book came to be in London, or even to survive at all, no one knows. Perhaps Servetus had retained a few copies, as authors often do, and sent them off to friends. Perhaps he had given one to the publisher Marrinus from Basel, to whom he had first shown the manuscript and who had called him "dearest Michael," or to John Frellon, who had initiated the correspondence between Servetus and Calvin; or perhaps not quite *all* of the shipment to Frankfurt had been destroyed as Calvin intended. Whatever had happened originally, for over a century someone or some group had protected the book as one would protect an escaped political prisoner. They had kept it hidden, in good condition, away from flood, fire, war, pestilence, and the hands of the Catholics and the Calvinists, until the fortunes of war or theft had brought it to that bookstall in London.

Count Szent-Iványi recognized the book because in his faith *Christianismi Restitutio* was considered a great and important work and Michael Servetus the spiritual center. That faith, Unitarianism, would, in the coming centuries, help inspire some of the greatest minds in history, among them John Locke, Isaac Newton, Ralph Waldo Emerson, and Thomas Jefferson. And one of the people responsible for the establishment of that faith—although nothing could have been farther from his intention—was John Calvin.

‡

IN THE EARLY 1550S, there was a small colony of Italians living in Geneva who had fled their native country to avoid religious persecution. Although they were less tractable than Calvin would have preferred, there were a number of eminent scholars in the group, so, provided that they stuck to the rules, he let them stay and even use one of the town churches. Happy to have a place of refuge, the Italians avoided politics and kept pretty much to themselves.

Then came the Servetus trial. The colony's leaders, like everyone else in the city, followed the proceedings closely. Several of them found themselves swayed by the passion and scholarship of Servetus's arguments. They were encouraged in these views by Matteo Gribaldo, a visiting scholar. Appalled by the trial and the sentence of burning, Gribaldo, a lawyer and judge, spoke out against it and even demanded an audience with Calvin to stop the execution. Calvin refused and used his influence to persuade Gribaldo to leave the city.

A year later Gribaldo was back. He began once more to speak at the little Italian church, now promoting Servetus's antitrinitarianism. Calvin, informed by his network of elders that Gribaldo was gaining more than a few converts, decided to act. He invited Gribaldo to a meeting, ostensibly to congratulate him on being called to chair the law school at a neighboring Swiss university. When Gribaldo got there, Calvin, in the presence of several of his church officials, refused to shake his hand, a way of announcing his suspicions about Gribaldo's piety. Gribaldo saw the danger and quickly left the meeting, and soon after left Geneva for good. Calvin got the word out, however, and Gribaldo was hounded from place to place until he finally died of plague in 1564.

But Gribaldo had been too persuasive to simply fade away. The Italian colony became a group of dissenters waiting for a leader. They got one two years later when the distinguished physician Giorgio Biandrata joined the colony.

Biandrata, born four years after Servetus in 1515, was a Catholic aristocrat who had studied medicine in Pavia. He specialized in "women's diseases" and had published a number of medical books. In the early 1540s, Bona Sforza, an Italian married to Sigismund I, king of Poland, had chosen Biandrata to be her personal physician.

Poland, at the height of its power and as large as France, had been one of the places where Reform had caught on quickly, and Sigismund, a devout Catholic, had been unable to stem the tide. The Catholic clergy in Poland were particularly corrupt, and many young nobles embraced the teachings of Luther and then Calvin, as a means of both purifying the religion and amassing political power and wealth through the seizure of the vast estates owned by the Church.

Queen Bona, who had been only twenty-five when she had married the fifty-two-year-old Sigismund I in 1518, added intellectual ferment to the mix by enticing many accomplished scholars and artists to Poland. Her court became a center for humanist discussion and the exchange of new ideas. As a result, her confessor, while nominally a Franciscan friar, soon became a secret dissident leader, spreading Calvinist literature throughout the country. It was here that Biandrata, her doctor, first became acquainted with the new reformist ideas.

As Sigismund grew older, Bona, every bit as clever as the king and even more ambitious, began to assert herself in affairs of state. When Sigismund arranged the marriage of their son, Crown Prince Sigismund Augustus, to the Hapsburg archduchess Elizabeth, the sixteen-year-old daughter of Charles V's brother, Ferdinand, king of Austria, Bona demonstrated that she had taken more from her ancestry than artistic sensibility.

She doted on Sigismund Augustus, who had developed some odd behavior. Restricted to little girls as playmates by his mother during his childhood, he had developed a penchant for dressing in women's clothing. (He also required the little girls to dress as boys.) "It was a mistake of nature," Bona said once, "to let my daughter [Princess] Isabella come into the world as a girl, and Sigismund Augustus as a boy."

The thought of Sigismund Augustus cohabitating with Elizabeth turned out to be too much for Queen Bona to bear. She did not allow the young couple to sleep or dine with each other. Finally, Bona sent Sigismund Augustus out of the country and denied Elizabeth a separate kitchen. The young princess died from a mysterious illness soon afterward. "Elizabeth surely was not deceased of a common, natural death," a Hapsburg diplomat observed in his memoirs.

After Sigismund I died in 1548, Sigismund Augustus, now King Sigismund II, seemed finally to be taken with a woman on his own. Again against his mother's will, he married Barbara Radziwill, a great beauty from a powerful Lithuanian family. "Now we shall have to beware at mealtimes," he wrote presciently to his new brother-in-law Nicholas, the Black Prince. The newlyweds were not wary enough; Barbara, too, died mysteriously a year later.

Despite the cross-dressing, poisonings, and unnaturally close mother–son relationship, however, Sigismund II turned out to be a remarkably effective king. He expanded the country's borders still farther, to include Lithuania and parts of Prussia and the Muscovy duchies and skillfully manipulated the nobility into agreeing to checks against their power.

Although deeply religious himself and a Catholic like his father,

Sigismund II nonetheless allowed Lutherans and Calvinists to live and pray unmolested, noting that he "wished to be king of both sheep and goats." Even Jews were allowed to live and worship openly in Poland. Most significantly, he made no move against those who had, as a matter of conscience, adopted religious practices that called into question the tenets of both Catholicism and Protestantism.

✣

BIANDRATA SPENT THREE YEARS at Sigismund II's court, becoming more and more committed to the wisdom of religious tolerance. When he finally returned home to Italy in 1551, he began to preach his new convictions. But Italy wasn't Poland, and after five years of increasing pressure and threat, Biandrata moved on to Geneva.

The little Italian church was still questioning the doctrine of the Trinity, and Biandrata was soon questioning it as well. His intelligence and reputation and the force of his personality propelled him to the leadership of the congregation. The teachings of Servetus were central to its philosophy, and Biandrata adopted them fully.

Word of these developments got to Calvin, who was furious. His nemesis had acquired a surrogate. To break Biandrata's power, he imposed a new oath. The entire congregation was required to swear fealty to the Trinity in writing, on pain of banishment. Biandrata refused at first, but under pressure from his own followers, who did not want to lose him, pretended to give in. After signing the oath, he continued his efforts to convert Genevans to antitrinitarianism. Calvin was preparing for his arrest when a sympathizer warned Biandrata of the danger, and he was forced to flee.

He returned to Poland, where he was sure he would be welcome. Antitrinitarianism was sweeping the country. In 1556, a Polish minister calling himself Gonesius, who had discovered the works of Servetus in Switzerland, had publicly denied the Trinity at a religious conference and succeeded in converting Jan Kiszka, the second-largest landowner in all of Poland. Kiszka owned four hundred villages and seventy cities. He appointed Gonesius to be the minister of his local church, set up a printing press to promulgate the new views, and converted all of the churches within his vast territory, some twenty in all.

There were a number of different forms of antitrinitarianism being practiced across Eastern Europe. The differences were marginal, often dealing with literal versus figurative interpretations of a key passage or passages in the scriptures, or whether to accept the sacraments as more than symbolism. Although these differences resulted in a number of distinctly different sects—Socinians, Gonesians, and Racovians, among others—they would all eventually evolve into Unitarians.

When Biandrata arrived, he began to expound on Servetus's views and found that many Catholics as well as reformers were not only in sympathy with his doubts about the Trinity and infant baptism, but were attracted by the prospect of a return to a simpler Christianity based solely on the Scriptures. "Young nobles and ministers attending the universities of Germany, Switzerland, or Italy learned the teachings of Servetus and brought them home for discussion," noted the great Unitarian scholar Earl Morse Wilbur.

Gonesius had established a Unitarian school at Pinczow, about fifty miles north of Crakow, and Biandrata's knowledge of the Scriptures, his experience abroad, and his familiarity with Servetus's beliefs quickly recommended him to the minister. Biandrata, as he had in Geneva, became a leader of the new movement. Soon, two other Genevans from the little Italian colony arrived, having been driven out by Calvin in much the same manner as Biandrata. They added their voices to his.

Calvin, in failing health, wrote letters to everyone of importance he knew in Poland warning them of the danger, urging them to use their influence against Biandrata, but no one in authority took action. Quite the contrary. When Biandrata went from Pinczow to Lithuania, then part of Poland, to spread the new word, he found favor with the late Barbara Radziwill's powerful brother, the Black Prince. Suddenly, the entire reformed church of Poland seemed poised to adopt Servetus's views.

Then, in 1563, Queen Bona's grandson, the sickly young king of Transylvania, fell ill, and she asked Biandrata to attend him. He agreed to become the official court physician and spent the better part of the next twenty-five years there. That period would mark the high point for religious liberalism in Europe, but it would be a disaster for Biandrata.

‡

MOUNTAINOUS AND REMOTE, Transylvania (the name means "beyond the forest") was sparsely populated by wildly diverse ethnic groups—Hungarians, Szekelys, Saxons, Wallachians, Moldavians, Greeks, Turks, Magyars, and Slovaks. The Szekelys could trace their lineage to Attila's Huns. While rampaging through Europe in the fifth century, the marauders apparently enjoyed the view from the hills, and many settled there.

Transylvania was feudal and agrarian. The aristocracy, a handful of families, owned most of the land and all of the peasantry. Transylvanians, by necessity, were a hardy people. Goatherding, practiced by many, was a particularly challenging way to make a living. Solitary goatherds roamed the mountains all winter with a charge of sixty or seventy of their master's goats. They survived on cornmeal left along their route in hollow trees or caves. Nothing communicates the flavor of the country better than this eyewitness account of the life of a goatherd:

> He does not close his eyes all night and building several small fires around the herd to keep away the slavering wild animals, watches them until the morning. Should it start snowing again at night, the shepherd [goatherd] immediately rousts the herd from its rest and keeps them moving back and forth . . . Finally,

after six months of misery, hard even to imagine for a person used to social intercourse, with a face blackened by storms and freezing cold, but with a sound, healthy stomach and in good strength he descends with his herd to the village.

If he lived, that is.

Once a major Roman trade route to the east, Transylvania had emerged as a country of great strategic importance. Bordered by mountains on two sides, it was all that stood between the Hapsburgs and the extraordinary Ottoman leader Suleiman the Great.

Suleiman, also known as "the Conqueror," one of those direct descendants of Osman, had assumed the throne in 1520. At that time the Ottoman Empire was at its zenith, extending from Belgrade to Smyrna, from Sarajevo to the Crimea. As a military leader, Suleiman was brilliant, ruthless, and unstoppable. Each summer, seemingly for sport, he set off westward with his army to invade his European neighbors. He attacked, conquered, exacted a hefty monetary tribute, and then went back home to celebrate the inevitable great victory. This went on year after year, season after season.

Suleiman inevitably went through Transylvania, where he warmed up his troops with a little rape and pillaging. By 1526, the Transylvanians, in an attempt to break the pattern, crowned their former defense minister, John Zapolya, king, authorizing him to pay whatever it took to appease Suleiman. Suleiman seemed amenable, but Ferdinand of Austria, who needed Transylvania as a buffer zone for his own kingdom, had himself crowned king of Transylvania instead. Zapolya (tribute in hand) appealed to Suleiman, and the Hapsburgs soon found themselves out of Transylvania. Thereafter King John I ruled the country, always careful to pay up on time.

Impressed by Zapolya's outflanking of the Hapsburgs, Bona married off her daughter Isabella to him in 1539. No sooner had Isabella borne her husband a son, John Sigismund, in 1540, than Zapolya died. Suleiman, passing through again the following year to accept his yearly payoff, bestowed upon the infant John Sigismund the title King John II of Transylvania. Then, for that year's main event, he moved on and threw Ferdinand's troops out of Budapest, taking over most of Hungary for himself.

✜

KING JOHN II GREW UP to be a highly intelligent young man who spoke eight languages and read and studied humanist works. He was always frail and sickly yet forced himself to ride, hunt, and engage in all the rigorous pursuits that were expected of a monarch. One thing he did not do was get married—the king preferred to spend his nights in the royal bedchamber with his councilor and "friend," Gáspár Békés, an army officer.

When Biandrata arrived, he found the twenty-three-year-old king very weak. John eventually recovered and during his long weeks of recuperation adopted Biandrata as something of a father figure. They talked long and often, the discussions inevitably turning to religion.

By the time he had recovered completely, John II had converted, becoming history's first and only Unitarian king. Unlike almost every other religious group that got its start as a reaction to intolerance, the Unitarians under King John did not themselves become intolerant. Instead, in 1568, the king issued the Act of Religious Tolerance and Freedom of Conscience, which, in the light of what was going on everywhere else in the world (and has in large part gone on since), was astonishing for its perspicacity, intelligence, and sophistication:

> In every place the preachers shall preach and explain the Gospel each according to his understanding of it, and if the congregation like it, well, if not, no one shall compel them for their souls would not be satisfied, but they shall be permitted to keep a preacher whose teaching they approve. Therefore none of the superintendents or others shall abuse the preach-

ers, no one shall be reviled for his religion by anyone, according to the previous statutes, and it is not permitted that anyone should threaten anyone else by imprisonment or by removal from his post for his teaching, for faith is the gift of God, this comes from hearing, which hearing is by the word of God.

With the king's blessing, Biandrata attempted to acknowledge the movement's debt to Servetus by republishing *Christianismi Restitutio* under the title *De Regno Christi primus; De Regno Antichristi Regno secondus.* Biandrata must have at some point seen the original but then worked from notes, as the text was a close approximation but not an exact replication of the original.

For three years, Transylvanians of all religions lived in peace and harmony. The tiny nation was a showplace of tolerance. Then, on January 15, 1571, King John II was critically injured when his carriage overturned on a hunting trip. Two months later he was dead.

John, who had of course died without leaving an heir, named Gáspár Békés as his successor, a choice that would have been widely popular except for an accident of timing. Békés had the misfortune of being out of the country on a diplomatic mission when the king died. Even worse, that mission happened to be to Ferdinand's court. Suleiman, suspecting skullduggery, withdrew his support from Békés and gave it instead to a moderate Catholic, István Báthori.

Suleiman's disapproval doomed Békés, and Báthori was elected. When Békés returned and stirred up a rebellion, his troops were routed and he was forced into exile.

Báthori, who was not especially devout and claimed to favor a continuation of the policies of his predecessor, seemed an enlightened choice. Biandrata approved. He even used his considerable clout to have Báthori also elected king of Poland after Sigismund II died (also without issue) in 1575. On ascending the Polish throne, Báthori willingly submitted to an oath allowing members of all religions to worship in peace.

But, in fact, the Unitarian Camelot was finished. The new king soon decreed that Unitarians would be allowed to practice their faith, but only on the condition that they did not further extend their questioning of traditional dogma. This proved to be a more incendiary condition than first assumed. So tenuous had the Unitarian position become that when Francis David, a prominent Unitarian, asserted that the Lord's Supper was merely symbolic, Biandrata had him arrested before the king could act to suppress the movement entirely. When David was brought to trial, Biandrata himself served as prosecutor. David died in jail shortly thereafter, and Biandrata became an object of loathing within the movement he had done so much to create.

It didn't help Biandrata's reputation that his appeasement strategy failed totally. In 1579, Báthori, in an effort to encourage Catholicism within his borders, asked the Jesuits to send missionaries to work among the peasantry. The Jesuits came but mostly went to work on Báthori. The oath of toleration that he had taken at his coronation was void, they insisted. Not only was a king not bound by promises given to heretics, he was under holy obligation to break them. They finally convinced Báthori of God's will, and Unitarians lost whatever fragile legal standing they had retained.

Jesuits and Calvinists didn't agree on many things, but one thing they did agree on was that liberal Christianity was anathema. Heresy aside, a movement that placed moral responsibility with the individual was an overwhelming threat to centralized power. Thus, even in those areas where control was contested, Unitarians were persecuted.

As for Biandrata, he died, unmourned, in 1588.

‡

WHEN COUNT DANIEL Márkos Szent-Iványi recognized the copy of *Christianismi Restitutio* in a London bookshop almost one hundred years later, the Unitarians' position was, if anything, more precarious than before. In fact, it was that very precariousness that had forced Count Szent-Iványi to be in London in the first place.

In 1638, the Unitarian university at Racow, Poland, a place of learning of sufficient reputation that parents of Catholics and Protestants across Europe sent their sons there for a quality education, had been closed. Then, in 1660, Unitarianism in Poland was officially suppressed. Unitarians were forced to flee to Protestant strongholds throughout Europe, including the Netherlands, Germany, and especially England. That diaspora, more than any other single event, is responsible for the strong and vibrant Unitarian presence in present-day Western Europe and the United States.

In Transylvania, pressure on dissenters steadily increased. Leaders of the Unitarian movement were often imprisoned or executed, and the property of adherents seized. Congregations held on, often by force of belief alone.

When Count Szent-Iványi returned home to Transylvania several years later, he took his copy of *Christianismi Restitutio* with him. It was irrelevant to him that he now possessed the only known copy of an important historic work, something he could have sold to a collector for a hefty sum. Instead, he donated the book to his church, the Unitarian congregation at Cluj, Transylvania's capital. The minister, thrilled to receive so rare a gift, took it and put it away so that it would remain safe. Of course, neither man recognized the importance of, or even especially noted, the critical passage on blood circulation.

Servetus and his discovery were once again lost to the world. ‡

TWO DECADES LATER, in 1689, the Catholic king of England, James II, was deposed, more or less bloodlessly, by the Protestant nobility in what has come to be known as the Glorious Revolution. They replaced James with Holland's William of Orange, who was married to James's Protestant daughter Mary. Parliament then set about enacting a series of laws to curb the monarchy's power and prevent a return to Catholicism.

The great religious question settled, scientific discovery became the major force in English intellectual life. Newton had published the first edition of *Principia Mathematica* three years earlier, Robert Boyle had conducted sophisticated experiments in chemistry, and his assistant, Robert Hooke, had proposed a wave theory of light. Suddenly there was talk of gravity, light spectra, calculus, and the microscope. The staggering pace of these new developments was disorienting for many in the academic community. A backlash set in among a group of traditionalists, who were quickly dubbed "The Ancients" by wits of the day, while those who aggressively championed the new theories—many of them members of the Royal Society—were called "The Moderns."

This conflict came to a head with the publication by Sir William Temple of an essay entitled "Upon the Ancient and Modern Learning." Sir William was a gentleman of considerable stature in seventeenth-century England. He had enjoyed a long diplomatic career, mostly in Belgium and the Netherlands, which culminated in his appointment as ambassador to The Hague. He had become acquainted with William of

Orange while the future king of England was still a boy, and had even taken a hand in arranging his marriage to Mary. Although technically in retirement during King William's reign, he remained an advisor, and several times the king traveled to one of Sir William's various country houses to consult with him.

Sir William, in addition to his estates, maintained a chic town house in London, and an art collection that included masterpieces by Van Dyck, Titian, and Holbein. This combination of money, power, and influence had caused Sir William to develop a rather high opinion of himself and his abilities, which worked to the detriment of self-discipline. He had a habit, for example, of bragging of his sexual prowess, regardless of the audience—in his youth it "had nearly killed him," he often observed. On his death, he left instructions that his heart be cut out and buried in a silver box in one of his gardens, and the rest of him interred at Westminster Abbey.

In 1690, Sir William decided to throw his considerable reputation into the Ancient–Modern debate, and it did not daunt him in the least that he had no scientific training or knowledge with which to support his arguments. He was already a familiar figure in literary circles, having published a number of popular memoirs about his experiences in the Netherlands, so producing a scholarly essay tracking the course of knowledge from the Greeks up until the present day seemed a nice way to keep himself in the public eye. He weighed in with full force on the side of the Ancients.

Sir William began with the unequivocal assertion that books had little impact either in perpetuating or advancing human knowledge. After all, he noted, ancient societies like that in Mexico did not have books, and they did just fine. He went on to chart all of the various branches of learning—philosophy, grammar, rhetoric, poetry, astronomy, physic (medicine), music, architecture, and mathematics—and found that in each case the Greeks were clearly superior in both style and content.

More than this, Sir William brought into serious question the significance of the Moderns' discoveries and even their authenticity:

> There is nothing new in Astronomy, to vie with the ancients, unless it be the Copernican system; nor in Physic, unless Harvey's circulation of the blood. But whether either of these be modern discoveries, or derived from the old fountains, is disputed ... if they are true, yet these two great discoveries have made no change in the conclusions of Astronomy, nor in the practice of Physic, and so have been of little use to the world, though perhaps of much honour to the authors.

Indeed, according to Sir William, the Moderns' insistence on thinking for themselves was positively harmful. "Besides who can tell, whether learning may not even weaken invention, in a man that has great advantages from nature and birth; whether the weight and number of so many other men's thoughts and notions may not suppress his own ... as heaping on wood, or too many sticks, or too close together, suppresses, and sometimes extinguishes, a little spark that would otherwise have grown up to a noble flame."

Those in the academic world allied on the side of the Ancients were thrilled that so eminent an authority as Sir William Temple should take up their cause. They even reissued the works of those early philosophers about whom Sir William had been especially enthusiastic, among them the epistles of a sixth-century B.C. Sicilian monarch named Phalaris, whom Sir William had praised for his "spirit, wit, and genius," to say nothing of his benevolence.

Unfortunately for Sir William, scholars had proved sometime earlier that the letters about which he had been so effusive were fakes. More than that, Phalaris was actually a ruthless tyrant who had his enemies roasted alive inside a huge bronze bull. When he was finally overthrown by Telemachus, the bronze bull was then used to cook Phalaris. The

Moderns seized on the Phalaris blunder with glee, then brought forth a twenty-eight-year-old English country clergyman named William Wotton to take on Sir William.

Wotton, at the time chaplain to the earl of Nottingham, had been a child prodigy, described in a letter to Pepys as "one of the miracles of this age for his early and vast comprehension." Unlike Sir William, Wotton was a thorough scholar and meticulous researcher.

In 1694, Wotton, choosing his title as a direct parody of Sir William's, published *Reflections upon Ancient and Modern Learning*. He examined the same branches of learning, delineating the same inventions or discoveries, eviscerating Sir William's arguments line by line.

Reflections upon Ancient and Modern Learning catapulted Wotton into the frontlines of the battle, and the counterattacks were quick in coming. Sir William wrote a second essay in reply, and angry epithets by the supporters of each flew back and forth in print. Sir William's most powerful ally was his former secretary, none other than Jonathan Swift. Swift, who should have known better, hurled himself into the breach, immortalizing the sniping in an essay entitled *The Battle of the Books*. It began:

The

BOOKSELLER

To The

READER

The following Discourse ... seems to have been written ... when the famous dispute was on foot about Ancient and Modern learning. The controversy took its rise from an essay of Sir William Temple's upon that subject, which was answered by W. Wotton, B.D. . . . In this dispute, the town highly resented to see a person of Sir William Temple's character and methods roughly used by the reverend gentlemen aforesaid, and without any manner of provocation. At length, there appearing no end of the quarrel, our author tells us, that the Books in Saint James's Library, looking upon themselves as parties principally concerned, took up the controversy and came to a decisive battle.

The books then slip from the shelves, don armor, take up lances and swords, and ride horses about the library in combat. In the ensuing fight, the Ancients give the Moderns a proper thrashing.

The Battle of the Books, although hilarious and written with Swift's trademark acid quill, did not advance his standing among his peers. "Wit," Samuel Johnson observed of the essay, "can stand its ground against truth only a little while."

‡

LOST AMIDST ALL THE FUROR was a short paragraph in Wotton's book. In Chapter 18, "Of the Circulation of the Blood," he wrote:

> The first that I could ever find who had a distinct *Idea* of this Matter was *Michael Servetus*, a *Spanish* physician, who was burnt for *Arianism* at *Geneva* near 140 years ago. Well had it been for the *Church of Christ* if he had wholly confined himself to his own Profession!... in a Book of his, entitled *Christianismi Restitutio*, printed in the year MDLIII, he clearly asserts that the Blood passes through Lungs, from the Left to the Right Ventricle of the Heart; and not through the *Partition* which divides the two Ventricles, as was at the Time commonly believed. How he introduces it, or in which of the Six Discourses in which *Servetus* divides his book, it is to be found, I know not, having never seen the Book myself. Mr. *Charles Bernard*, a very learned and eminent Chirurgeon [sur-

geon] of *London*, who did me the Favour to communicate this Passage to me, which was transcribed out of Servetus, could inform me not further, only that he had it from a learned Friend of his, who had himself copied it from *Servetus*.

This was the first time that Servetus's great discovery had been mentioned in print. Although it evoked a certain curiosity, the passage was more or less ignored. There were not too many in England, Ancient or Modern, willing to withdraw even partial credit for the discovery of pulmonary circulation from Harvey and grant it to a Spanish heretic. What's more, Wotton, by his own admission not having seen the actual book, had made mistakes. There were seven discourses, not six, and Servetus had (correctly) written that blood traveled from the right ventricle to the left, not the other way around as Wotton quoted.

But Wotton persisted. He went back to Dr. Bernard to locate the actual copy of the book. Bernard, perhaps the most prominent surgeon in England, who had once had the sheriff of London removed from his post for failing to deliver cadavers of criminals for dissection purposes, directed Wotton to the source of the quote.

Three years later, Wotton produced a second edition of *Reflections upon Ancient and Modern Learning*, in which he updated the Servetus section and noted that he had now seen a transcription of *Christianismi Restitutio* in the library of the bishop of Norwich. The bishop had told Wotton that his transcription had been made from an original. The original had come from the personal library of a German noble, Landgrave (provincial governor) Karl von Hessen-Kassel.

‡

HESSE, IN WESTERN GERMANY, just north of Mainz, had been a Protestant stronghold almost from the time of Luther, but no one knew

Ancient and Modern Learning.

Modern Diſcoveries ; and therefore it is not ſo much as pretended that he knew this Recurrent Motion of the Blood. Which alſo further ſhews, that if *Hippocrates* did know it, he explained himſelf ſo obſcurely, that *Galen* could not underſtand him ; who, in all probability, underſtood *Hippocrates*'s Text as well as any of his Commentators, who have written ſince the *Greek* Tongue, and much more, ſince the *Ionic* Dialect has ceaſed to be a living Language.

Since the Ancients have no Right to ſo noble a Diſcovery, it may be worth while to enquire, to whom of the Moderns the Glory of it is due ; for this is alſo exceedingly conteſted. The firſt Step that was made towards it, was, the finding that the whole Maſs of the Blood paſſes thorough the Lungs, by the Pulmonary Artery and Vein.

The firſt that I could ever find, who had a diſtinct *Idea* of this Matter, was *Michael Servetus*, a *Spaniſh* Phyſician, who was burnt for *Arianiſm*, at *Geneva*, near CXL Years ago. Well had it been for the *Church of Chriſt*, if he had wholly confined himſelf to his own Profeſſion ! His Sagacity in this Particular, before ſo much in the dark, gives us great Reaſon to believe, that the World might then have had juſt Cauſe to

Q. 3   have

230   *Reflections upon*

(*c*) *Vitalis* have bleſſed his Memory. In a Book (*c*) of *Spiritus in ſiniſtro cordis ventriculis ſuam Originem habet, juvantibus maximè pulmonibus ad ipſius generationem. Eſt ſpiritus tenuis, calore vi elaboratus, flavo colore, igneâ potentiâ, ut ſit quaſi ex puriore ſanguine lucidus vapor: generatur ex facta in pulmone mixtione* his, entituled, *Chriſtianiſmi Reſtitutio*, printed in the Year MDLIII. (*d*) he clearly aſſerts, that the Blood paſſes thorough the Lungs, from the Left to the Right Ventricle of the Heart ; and not thorough the *Partition* which divides the two Ventricles, as was at That Time commonly believed. How he introduces it, or in which of the Six Diſcourſes, into which *Servetus* divides his Book, it is to be found, I know not, having never ſeen the Book my ſelf. Mr. *Charles Bernard*, a very learned and eminent Chirurgeon of *London*, who did me the Favour to communicate this Paſſage to me, (ſet down at length in the Margin) which was tranſcribed out of *Servetus*, could inform me no further, only that he had it from a learned Friend of his, who had himſelf copied it from *Servetus*.

inſpirati aëris cum elaborato ſubtili ſanguine, quem dexter ventriculus ſiniſtro communicat. Fit autem communicatio hæc non per parietem cordis medium ut vulgo creditur, ſed magno artificio à dextro cordis ventriculo, longo per pulmones ductu, agitatur ſanguis ſubtilis ; à pulmonibus præparatur ; flavus ejicitur, & à venâ arterioſâ in arteriam venoſam transfunditur ; deinde in ipſâ arteriâ venosâ inſpirato aëri miſcetur & expiratione ſ fuligine repurgatur ; atque ita tandem à ſiniſtro cordis ventriculo totum, mixtum per diaſtolen attrahitur, apta ſupellex ut fiat ſpiritus vitalis. Servet. Chriſtian. Reſtit.

(*d*) Vid. *Sandii Bibliothecam Anti-Trinitariorum*, p. 13.

Realdus Columbus, of *Cremona,* was the next that ſaid any thing of it, in his *Anatomy,* printed at *Venice,* MDLIX. in *Folio ;* and

The passage in the second edition of Reflections upon Ancient and Modern Learning *where William Wotten reveals Servetus's role in discovering pulmonary circulation*

how this copy of *Christianismi Restitutio* came to be in the landgrave's library, including, apparently, the landgrave himself. Nor was this the same copy that Szent-Iványi had purchased in London. That copy had been clean and unmarked. A number of pages in the copy on the landgrave's shelves were damaged, browned in the center as if by scorching, and in one or two cases, burned through. What was most significant about this copy, however, was that at the end, on the three blank pages after the colophon, were handwritten notes. On the first of those three pages, the person who had written those notes had signed his name.

It was Germain Colladon. This was the very copy that Colladon had used at the trial. The notes were references to the text that Colladon, Calvin's friend and surrogate prosecutor of Michael Servetus, had used to organize his prosecution.

It was not unusual for works used as evidence in heresy trials to be stored as evidence, even after the sentence on the accused had been

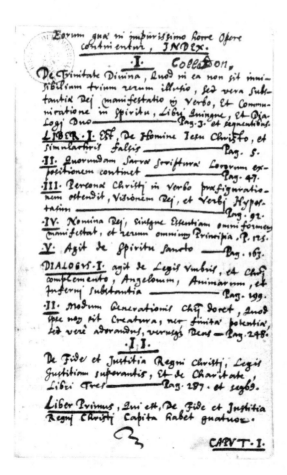

Germain Colladon's notes at the back of Christianismi Restitutio

carried out, so Colladon's retention of the book might not have violated Calvin's direct order to have all copies destroyed.

Sometimes, however, the evidence *was* destroyed with the heretic, and the scorching on the pages led to speculation that perhaps the Colladon copy was the very one chained to Servetus at his execution, and that someone had snatched it out of the flames. The idea that someone had reached into a burning pile of twigs and leaves at a public execution to grab away a forbidden book before it could be consumed and then successfully made his escape through a phalanx of soldiers seemed more than a little improbable. Moreover, the scorching appeared on very few of the almost eight hundred pages, and then only in the center of the page, never on the edges, as would have been the case if the book had actually been placed on or near the flames. A much more likely explanation is that someone, possibly Colladon himself, fell asleep while examining the book, and candle wax inadvertently dripped on an open page. Later theories asserted that the stains had been caused by water, not fire. While there is evidence that the book was exposed to moisture—in the second half there had been a discernible crinkling of the pages—the damage to the browned pages seems certainly to have been caused by heat.

Colladon's copy, then, had either been sold with his effects upon his death or stolen, the perpetrator likely someone of the prosecutor's acquaintance who had access to his private papers. Whether acquired legally or illegally, for motives ideological or mercenary, the book had eventually made its way through the serpentine alleys of the European book trade to end up, as had many priceless volumes, as an anonymous occupant in the library of a nobleman who knew nothing of either the book's significance or its value. Clearly, however, someone with access to the library had known of both and had made copies of the text without bothering to mention it to the landgrave. One of these copies had ended up in the library of the bishop of Norwich.

Then, in 1706, a friend of Hessen-Kassel noticed the book while browsing through his library. Unlike the landgrave, this man was well aware of the death of Servetus and recognized immediately that he had stumbled upon something of great rarity and value. The friend was the great German philosopher and mathematician Gottfried Wilhelm Leibniz.

‡

LEIBNIZ, BY NOW SIXTY, was one of history's few true universal geniuses. By the time he was twelve, he had taught himself Latin and Greek so that he could read the books in his father's library. As an adult, he began the development of symbolic logic and, working independently of Newton, invented calculus. In physics, Leibniz anticipated Einstein by rejecting Newtonian absolutes and arguing that space, time, and motion are relative. He propounded a theory of substance based on a construct called "monads," which he claimed exerted force on one another. He invented a calculating machine capable of performing all four arithmetic operations. He studied Roman law and natural law and applied each to the modern day. He studied Chinese thought and interpreted it for the European mind. In metaphysics, he proposed the "law of optimism," in which he claimed that man lived in the "best of all possible worlds" (a claim Voltaire would later lampoon in *Candide*). As a corollary, he strongly disagreed with Locke's notion that the mind is tabula rasa at birth, to be developed only as experience plays on the senses.

After studying law in Leipzig for five years, he was refused admission to the university's doctoral program in 1666 because he was only twenty. Instead, Leibniz transferred to the University of Altdorf, which immediately awarded him a doctorate in jurisprudence. Although he was shy, bookish, and a pure academic, Leibniz declined a professorship, choosing instead to seek a wealthy patron and work as an independent scholar. He was engaged by the elector of Mainz to propose legal reform, but in 1672 the elector sent him as emissary to Paris to talk Louis XIV out of attacking Germany. Leibniz proposed to Louis that it would be much more profitable to mount a campaign against rich and heretical Egypt instead, and then to build a canal through the isthmus of Suez as a means of transporting riches back to France. (Louis didn't take the advice about Egypt, although Napoleon subsequently did. Napoleon would have built the canal as well if his engineers hadn't miscalculated and told him that a sea-level waterway was impossible.)

Leibniz remained in Paris until 1676, studying philosophy and mathematics. From there he returned to Germany, going to work as librarian, judge, and minister in Hanover for the Brunswicks—the family that would soon spawn kings George I, II, and III of England. While in their employ, Leibniz traveled often. He was by that time sufficiently well known that Peter the Great summoned him to Russia to recommend educational reforms. When he traveled to Italy, Leibniz, although

Gottfried Wilhelm Leibniz

a Lutheran, was offered the custodianship of the Vatican library if he converted to Catholicism (even just for show), but he refused.

Leibniz was a favorite of royalty for his entire adult life. He was particularly popular with young princesses and queens eager to partake of the new intellectual freedom that accompanied the stirrings of enlightenment. Queen Sophie Charlotte of Prussia, only thirty-seven on her deathbed in 1705, said, "I go now to satisfy my curiosity about the basic causes of things which Leibniz has never been able to teach me, about space and the infinite; about being and nothingness; and for the King my husband, I prepare the drama of a funeral, which will give him a new opportunity to demonstrate his magnificence."

In addition to everything else, Leibniz was a passionate and accomplished theological scholar, who believed that free will was central to morality and that man chose goodness or evil. While he never renounced his allegiance to Luther, he rejected parochialism and sought to apply general Christian values across society. He worked actively toward total reconciliation of Catholics and Protestants.

When he read through the copy of *Christianismi Restitutio* in the landgrave's library, he came to understand that it was Servetus, not Harvey, who had discovered pulmonary circulation. He mentioned his discovery in several letters, one of them to an English bishop, but could not pursue the matter. At the time, he was occupied defending himself against charges by the Royal Society in London that he had plagiarized Newton in his writings about calculus (he had not—his version, if anything, was superior). But he made sure to tell his host that the only known copy of an extremely important book sat on his shelves. The Colladon copy of *Christianismi Restitutio* would be anonymous no longer.

Four years after Leibniz died in 1716, leaving behind perhaps the widest range of intellectual achievements since Aristotle, a French duke, François-Eugène de Savoie-Carignan, came to visit Hessen-Kassel. The duke of Savoy was himself a book collector of some note and interested in the works of Servetus. He owned one of the few remaining copies of *De Trinitatis Erroribus* but had never seen the now-famed last copy of *Christianismi Restitutio.* The landgrave ushered his guest into the library to see one of the rarest books in the world, a volume that the great Leibniz himself had pointed out.

It was gone.

Hessen-Kassel looked further; he ordered his servants to do a volume-by-volume search; he interrogated everyone who had access to the library. It was no use—the Colladon copy of *Christianismi Restitutio* had disappeared. ‡

CHAPTER SEVENTEEN

THREE YEARS LATER a Dutchman named Gysbert Dummer traveled to London. He carried with him a thick sheaf of papers about which he spoke to only a trusted few. Dummer had crossed the Channel specifically to engage English printers to typeset this manuscript. He chose England because, at that moment, a combination of forces made it the ideal venue.

In 1695, Parliament had ended state censorship by voting down the renewal of the Licensing Act, which required all printed materials to be approved and then registered by the Stationers' Company, a quasi-government monopoly. In doing so, Parliament also eliminated the taxes on printing and the tariffs on foreign books. Suddenly, books were a lot cheaper, and the audience for the printed word not only became larger but now also included many for whom books had previously been an unaffordable luxury. For conservatives, who had gone along with the measure only grudgingly, this widening of availability could not have come at a worse time.

By the end of the seventeenth century, the advancement of science had become such an accepted force that it was impossible to prevent the wholesale application of reason to human affairs, especially religion. Reason meant choice, and choice meant the rejection of the absolutes on which Catholicism and even most of the reformed sects, particularly Calvinism, were based. It was inevitable that the movement that began with Newtonian logic and the grinding of lenses should eventually put God Himself under a microscope.

As in Servetus's time two centuries before, intellectuals and non-conformists questioning the very cornerstones of established Christianity could disseminate their books and pamphlets to a new and hungry audience. Although two years later a frightened Parliament tried to take back much of the newly gained freedom of the press with the Blasphemy Laws, which threatened anyone who denied the Trinity or the divine authority of the Scriptures in print with three years' imprisonment, the demand for open debate had become so great that the authorities found themselves unable to control the spread of even the most extreme religious literature.

Atheism in particular had grown so prevalent that Richard Bentley, master of Trinity College, Cambridge, and a Newton disciple, felt the need to confirm the reality of God in the prestigious Boyle Lectures (named for Robert Boyle who had funded the series in his will). He merely succeeded in increasing skepticism. "No one," observed a wit at the time, "doubted the existence of God until the Boyle lecturers undertook to prove it."

Two similar dissenting sects were particularly prolific in print. The first, called the deists, had adopted the most purely rational form of religion. Deists believed only in the existence of a divine force. They often reduced God—whom they referred to as the "Supreme Being"—to more of a moral concept than a physical reality, and sometimes used the concepts of God and Nature interchangeably. Less extreme, but still way outside the boundaries of accepted religious doctrine, were the Unitarians, whose faith had spread from the first tenuous beginnings in Transylvania and Poland to Holland, England, and America. Unitarians, with their denial of the Trinity and their faith in a strict adherence to the Scriptures, were a tiny but highly select minority among the dissenters. "It is now certain that Milton was substantially a Unitarian, and that Locke and Newton were at heart no less so," wrote J. M. Robertson in his panoramic study, *A History of Freethought: Ancient and Modern to the Period of the French Revolution.*

Dummer, a Unitarian from Holland, had come to England because his manuscript was too controversial and dangerous to be published almost anywhere else. It was a transcription, made from an original, of *Christianismi Restitutio*.

Dummer hired a local printer named Samuel Palmer, who completed the first five sheets before switching to another printer, Isaac Dalton, with Peter Parris, a Frenchman, in charge of the actual composition. These two had completed proofs up to page 260 when a lexicographer, Samuel Patrick, was engaged to do the correcting.

This was a mistake. Patrick, who had been unfamiliar with the book when he was hired, realized in the course of his work just what it was that he was correcting. He immediately informed Dr. Edmund Gibson, the bishop of London, that heresy was being promulgated in his city. Dr. Gibson, one of a number of conservative clergyman who had managed both to preach and prosper—he died leaving a fortune acquired while in the service of God—immediately sought and received an injunction under the Blasphemy Laws from the Censor of the Press. He then ordered the page proofs seized and publicly burned. On May 27, 1723, Dummer opened his door and found himself face to face with the police. The proof sets that were in his home were confiscated and subsequently burned, and Dummer himself was fined. He was lucky to escape prison.

But the Dummer episode didn't end the new interest in Servetus. The following year, a small book appeared at several London bookstalls. It was entitled *An Impartial History of Michael Servetus, Burnt Alive at Geneva for Heresie*. It bore only the legend "LONDON: Printed for Aaron Ward, at the *King's-Arms* in *Little Britain*. 1724." It was 216 pages long and contained both passages from Servetus's writings and a detailed account of the trial, including a verbatim rendering of both Calvin's charges and Servetus's replies. Sources were shown in the original Latin, Greek, and French, and then translated into English.

The writing was clear and accessible, but as to its impartiality, there might have been some question. In discussing Calvin, the anonymous author observed, "Calvin caused the Papacy of *Rome* to be banished out of *Geneva*, yet he established a papacy of his own; that as there was a

Title page of
An Impartial History

pope at *Rome,* so he was no other than a pope at *Geneva,* not only by establishing an infallibility in the very constitution of the church, but by his maintaining and carrying on of that constitution, together with his own authority, by persecution and blood."

By focusing on the political aspects of Servetus's trial, *An Impartial History* skirted the Blasphemy Laws and as such could be officially frowned on but not suppressed. Copies made the rounds, particularly among England's religious liberals. The author (whose identity has never been firmly established) cited Wotton as the first to note Servetus's discovery of pulmonary circulation. He further noted that he, the author, had "owned a copy of the manuscript for some years."

From the bishop of Norwich to Gysbert Dummer to the author of *An Impartial History*, transcriptions of *Christianismi Restitutio* seemed to be popping up everywhere. But where was the book?

It was about to resurface in the hands of Dr. Richard Mead.

‡

RICHARD MEAD WAS the most prominent British physician of his day. He treated kings, queens, scientists, and poets. He was by Newton's bedside during his final illness and prescribed ass's milk for Alexander Pope. He was the recipient of the "gold headed cane," symbolic of the best of British medicine, passed down from one reigning physician to another. His portrait now hangs in the National Portrait Gallery.

He was born in 1673, the eleventh of thirteen children; his father had been expelled from the Church of England for nonconformity but was wealthy enough to provide private tutors for his brood. Richard attended the best universities, gaining a medical degree in Padua, which still had one of the finest medical schools in Europe, in 1695. He established his practice the next year in the house in which he had been born.

Mead first attained public acclaim at age thirty for a treatise on the ever-popular subject of poison, although Mead's work focused largely on snake venom. The following year, he asserted in a paper that a common, pesky disease known as "itch" was caused by mites, counter to the widely held belief that it was a "constitutional disorder." Such was his reputation after this treatise that a scant two years later, he was scratched into the Royal Society.

He moved to London and quickly established himself as a society doctor. Mead was already making in excess of five thousand pounds a year, a huge sum, when, in 1719, there was an outbreak of plague in Marseilles. Londoners fell into a panic that the disease would strike them as well. At the request of the secretary of state, Mead prepared a pamphlet entitled "A short Discourse concerning Pestilential Contagion and the Methods to be used to Prevent it." It was a clear, concise explanation of the role of basic sanitation in isolating disease and preventing its spread. The pamphlet went through seven editions and calmed public fear. The following year, he demonstrated the value of inoculation as a preventative measure against plague and established himself as the premier medical authority in Britain.

In 1720, he bought a huge house on Great Ormond Street that had enough space to allow him to indulge in another passion for which he had gained notoriety. Richard Mead owned the largest and most comprehensive personal library in England. His collection contained more than ten thousand volumes. Unlike other great bibliophiles, however, most of whom were nobility, Mead opened his house and library to the public, allowing access to anyone who wished to stroll through and look at his books.

Sometime in the late 1720s, that library came to include the Colladon copy of *Christianismi Restitutio.*

The rule of "finders keepers" seems to have been in force. Mead, who was intimate with almost every major book collector in Europe, was doubtless aware that the Colladon copy of *Christianismi Restitutio* had formerly been a star attraction in the library of Karl von Hessen-Kassel. He was also aware that the book had not departed by legitimate purchase. Theft and dubious transference were apparently so common to the trade in rare books that they seem to have been an accepted means of acquisition. In any event, the landgrave's heirs (if they knew) did not protest.

By 1733, Mead's library also contained a copy of the aborted Dummer reprint. Apparently, the police had not been as zealous as Bishop Gibson might have liked. Mead even hired a scribe to copy the unprinted pages to complete his copy in manuscript. This led to speculation that it had been Mead himself who had backed the project, but that he had been too powerful a figure for Bishop Gibson to accuse personally. That assumption lasted for two centuries until a bibliophile named Leonard Leopold Mackall spent two years poring through reams of original documents and concluded that Mead had, in fact, purchased both the original and the reprint some years after Bishop Gibson's order.

Collectors are a fickle breed, however. In the end, Mead, who also collected artifacts, traded his copy of *Christianismi Restitutio* to his friend and fellow collector, a Parisian named Claude Gros de Boze, in exchange for some rare medals. The details of this transaction are unavailable, so there is no way to know if Mead got a good deal. The only thing that is clear is that Richard Mead, the most prominent physician in England, was willing to trade away what was believed to be a one-of-a-kind item of enormous scientific significance for a handful of coins. (He traded away his copy of the reprint as well.)

De Boze kept both copies until he died. He had the original rebound and the page ends gilded, and wrote in large letters on the endpaper opposite the title page that the book had been acquired by de Boze from Richard Mead. His library was purchased by another French bibliophile who subsequently sold the Colladon copy of *Christianismi Restitutio* to yet another collector, Louis-Jean Gaignat, for 1,200 livres sometime in the 1750s. This price reflected *Christianismi Restitutio*'s scarcity and its worth as an oddity in a rich man's library, but it was still an obscure title by a minor figure in history.

Then, in the late 1750s, Servetus became a favorite subject of François-Marie Arouet, who in his teens had adopted the pen name of Voltaire.

‡

VOLTAIRE WAS A TITANIC figure, not only the most influential voice of the eighteenth century but a man who became the conscience of Europe and forced the entire Christian world to examine the foundations of its faith. He regularly spouted heresies that could have had him burned a hundred times over yet enjoyed such respect from kings, queens, nobles, philosophers, and even his enemies, that in time he became invulnerable.

He was born in Paris in 1694, but after two stints in the Bastille in his twenties for lampooning aristocrats, he lived most of the rest of his life in or just outside Geneva. Over the course of his eighty-four years, in addition to thousands and thousands of letters, he composed enough poems, stories, histories, plays, and essays to fill seventy large volumes. In many ways, Voltaire represented the very pinnacle of the printing revolution that had begun three centuries before. One man, through his writing, changed the way the world thought and brought Western civilization to a period called Enlightenment. It was as if Erasmus had been multiplied a thousandfold. There is not remotely a parallel for him in contemporary society.

He was nonetheless a man of contradictions. He was an atheist who often invoked the authority of God. He tirelessly championed tolerance but was a virulent anti-Catholic and anti-Semite and believed that the Reformation had descended into persecution and corruption. He was known for clear thinking but refused to accept any validity whatever in differing points of view. He wrote with enormous wit and had the ability to highlight foibles of human nature with hilarious results, yet he himself became more and more cynical with the passage of time.

But most of all, Voltaire was a man of obsessions, and most of his obsessions centered around what were to him the interlocking concepts of injustice and religion. In the course of his life he threw himself into several celebrated cases of religious persecution, the most famous of which was the Calas affair.

In 1761, in Toulouse (which had not become one whit more tolerant since Servetus's time), a sixty-four-year-old linen dealer named Jean Calas was one of the few Huguenots who had neither fled the city's repression nor been forced to undergo compulsory conversion to

Catholicism. Calas had two daughters and four sons, the oldest of whom, Marc Antoine, had just finished law school. When Marc Antoine found out that only Catholics could be hired to practice in the city, he tried to pass himself off as one but was found out. Depressed that his years of study would be wasted unless he converted, he became a gambler and a drunk. Eventually, he tied a rope to a bar that he had braced between two doorposts and hanged himself.

Despite overwhelming evidence that the death was a suicide (including testimony by Jeanne Vignière, the Calas's Catholic governess), the court in Toulouse held that the elder Calas had murdered his son to prevent him from converting. Calas, who staunchly denied the charge, was tortured in an attempt to get him to admit his guilt. First his arms and legs were stretched until they were pulled from their sockets. An hour later, thirty pints of water were poured down his throat until his body swelled to twice its normal size. Two hours after that, he was tied to a cross in the public square in front of the cathedral, where each of his limbs was broken twice with an iron bar. Through it all Calas swore he was innocent. Finally, he was strangled, and his corpse tied to a stake and burned.

All the family's possessions were confiscated by the town, and Calas's two daughters were forced into a convent. Donat Calas, the youngest son, fled to Geneva and obtained an audience with Voltaire. Voltaire checked Donat's story out and, deciding it was true, committed himself to clearing Calas's name.

Voltaire wrote letters and pamphlets. He badgered his admirers at the French court, who included the king's mistress. He appealed to the senior Catholic officials in France, engaged prominent lawyers, and persuaded others to take up the case pro bono. He took Donat Calas into his home, brought another Calas son to Geneva, and set Madame Calas up in Paris, so that the case would never be far from the consciousness of the authorities. To defray expenses, he began a defense fund among whose contributors were Catherine the Great of Russia; Caroline of

Brandenburg-Ansbach, wife of George II of England; and Augustus III, king of Poland.

It took three years, but finally the magistrates of Toulouse gave in. They cleared Calas's name, fired the judge who had convicted him, released his daughters from the nunnery, and granted the Calas family thirty thousand livres in compensation.

Voltaire said that he never smiled during the entire three years. When the news of the verdict arrived, he wept.

Even before the Calas affair was concluded, Voltaire took up a similar case, again from near the enlightened Toulouse, of a Protestant named Pierre Sirven who had also been falsely accused of murdering his child to prevent her from converting. With Calas as a grim example, Sirven had fled to Geneva, but all his property had been seized. That case took nine years, but Voltaire was once more successful.

Because of his ferocity, the names of Calas and Sirven became famous throughout Europe. In fact, anyone whose cause was taken up by Voltaire soon became known across the continent.

⸭

IN 1749, VOLTAIRE BEGAN work on a project that would occupy him, on and off, for the next twenty years. It was nothing less than an attempt to redefine history. Rather than merely provide a chronicle of events from a Eurocentric point of view, Voltaire traced the route of mankind from barbarism to civilization, overlaying events with philosophy. He devoured traditional histories, making notes, rejecting standard treatments, and creating new ones of his own.

The work had many incarnations and many titles, but Voltaire finally settled on *Essai sur les moeurs et l'esprit des nations depuis Charlemagne jusqu'à nos jours* (*Essay on the Morals and Spirit of Nations from Charlemagne to Our Day*). The final product was a huge and compendious work, acknowledged for its breadth and astounding scholarship, the first attempt to give Oriental and Islamic civilizations their proper credit in the development of European civilization. It was also a ferocious attack on the Christian churches, asserting, among other things, that the persecution of Christians at the hands of the Romans paled when compared to the persecution by Christians of anyone who thought differently than they did. Prominent among the archvillains in *Essai sur les moeurs* was John Calvin.

Voltaire detested Calvin, perhaps more than he detested any other man in history. To him, Calvin personified all that was evil, corrupt, bullying, brutal, and narrow-minded about those who clawed their way to power in the name of God.

Voltaire devoted an entire chapter to Servetus and referred to him often in his correspondence and other writings. He called Servetus a "very learned doctor" and even credited him with the discovery of circulation of the blood. He described Servetus's imprisonment and showed how Calvin had circumvented Genevan law by putting Fontaine up to go to jail in his stead. The burning was described in grisly detail. "I see from my windows," he wrote in a letter in 1759 from his estate in Ferney, high on a hillside above Lake Geneva, "the city where Jean Chauvin, the Picard called Calvin, reigned, and the place where he had Servetus burned for the good of his soul." Servetus, Voltaire concluded in *Essai sur les moeurs*, had simply been murdered by John Calvin, "an assassination committed in ceremony."

In the two hundred years that had passed since Servetus had been led to the stake, there had not been anyone, not even the leaders of the Unitarian movement, who had written so forcefully of his fate. In his passion, Voltaire was motivated not by a love of Servetus—to whom he referred as "mad" and "a fool"—but only by his abhorrence of Calvin. Still, for the first time since his death, the injustice that had befallen Michael Servetus became familiar to the readers of Europe.

‡

BOOK COLLECTING IN THE eighteenth century was not all that different from book collecting now—celebrity sells. As a result of the writings of Voltaire, when the contents of Louis-Jean Gaignat's library were sold at auction after his death in 1769, the Colladon copy of *Christianismi Restitutio* went for 3,810 livres, more than three times what he had paid for it. The buyer was the most famous book collector in France, Louis César de la Baume Le Blanc, Duc de Lavallière.

A hundred years before, no Lavallière would have been able to afford a library, much less a copy of *Christianismi Restitutio*. The Lavallières had been a family of minor provincial nobles, barely passing for aristocracy, when the family fortunes had suddenly been given a big boost.

The Lavallière who had done the boosting was the duke's great-aunt Louise. Louise had been a painfully shy girl of sixteen given to unrealistic romantic daydreams when, by a series of fortunate accidents, she was accepted as a maid of honor to Henriette, sister to England's Restoration king Charles II and wife of Philippe, younger brother of Louis XIV of France. A maid of honor's duties included attending her aristocratic mistress at parties, driving with her in the park, and accompanying her on her various sojourns to the magnificent country chalets and palaces that were the playgrounds of the French court.

It happened that Louis XIV, in his early twenties at the time and married to the devout but not terribly attractive Maria Theresa of Spain, was much enamored of his brother Philippe's vivacious young wife. He and Henriette were often seen chasing each other through the fields by day and taking long intimate walks together at night. Earnest, singularly atrocious love poems were composed by the king for Henriette's appreciation.

Not unreasonably, these innocent pleasures had sparked the malicious rumor that the king was playing around with his brother's wife. Henriette and Louis put their heads together and decided that the king should feign interest in other women to defray suspicion. Henriette then suggested one of her own maids of honor, that mousy little blonde schoolgirl Louise, as a possible candidate for this position. This ruse worked, although not as Henriette had intended. In no time at all, it was Louise who was running through the fields (albeit more slowly, since she had a limp) and taking the long intimate walks with the king.

Louise's tenure as official royal mistress did not last all that long—it was over by the time she was twenty-three. Then, ever conscious of appearances, Louis had Louise live in the same house with the married woman who replaced her in his affections so that no one would suspect he'd changed allegiances. Still, thanks to this diffident schoolgirl from a nondescript family, the fortunes of the Lavallières were assured.

Stung by whisperings about the lowly status of his mistress, Louis legitimized the two children Louise bore him who survived, then heaped riches on her and her family. In 1667, the French Parlement was put on notice of the king's intentions with a letter patent that declared Louise the Duchesse de Vaujours, with the ability to hand down the title and all the wealth that went along with it—which included Vau-

Louise de Lavallière

jours and the barony of Saint-Christophe—"two holdings equally considerable by their revenues"—to her children and her children's children. Louis's generosity did not stop there. Even Louise's brother Jean-François, an anonymous cadet in a minor regiment, was suddenly elevated to command a new company, the Light Horse of the Dauphin, and spent a lot of time with the king.

None of this mattered to Louise, however. She loved Louis and, broken at the thought of losing him, abandoned all those new worldly goods and gave herself over to God, entering the severe, cloistered world of a Carmelite nun, where she would spend the last thirty years of her life, inspiring a long romantic novel by Alexandre Dumas. Neither of Louise's children provided an heir to the new duchy, so the estates passed to Jean-François, who, unlike his sister, enjoyed every minute of his exalted new position. He in turn passed those riches on to his son Charles-François, who then provided *his* son, Louis-César, with the means and the position to create one of the most magnificent private libraries the world has ever known.

✝

LOUIS CÉSAR DE LA BAUME LE BLANC was born Duc de Vaujours on October 9, 1708, while his great-aunt Louise, ill and tired, was approaching the end of her life. He became the Duc de Lavallière, peer of France, at age thirty-one, when Charles-François died.

The new duke quickly became a favorite of the new king, Louis XV, his uncle once removed. He was named captain of the hunt in 1745 and grand falconer of France three years later, both coveted positions in the reign of as obsessive a sportsman as Louis. He was allowed to ask many favors of the king for his friends and neighbors, thereby ensuring that he became a beloved and respected man. Largesse aside, Lavallière seems to have been genuinely popular. He was erudite, thoughtful, and charming. Madame Pompadour, the king's mistress (a position of enormous influence, the duke was well aware), named

Lavallière director of her personal theater at Versailles. All of these honors and all this popularity served to increase his wealth, and by the time he was forty, the duke had more than doubled the family's already hefty fortunes, thus allowing him even greater resources to indulge in his passion for rare books.

The Duc de Lavallière was that most fortunate of collectors, a man with an obsession to own every famous book he could get his hands on and the money to afford to go out and do it. He was a child of the Enlightenment and, naturally, an admirer and correspondent of Voltaire. His tastes ran to science, history, and theology, and away from the more traditional fields of poetry and art.

He began buying rare books in 1738, and by the time he died in 1780 at age seventy-two, Lavallière had amassed a library of more than

Duc de Lavallière

LOUIS CESAR DE LA BAUME-LE-BLANC,
DUC DE LA VALLIERE ;
Né le 9 Octobre 1708. Mort le 16 Novembre 1780.

one hundred thousand books. The collection was divided into the main categories of "Theology," "Jurisprudence," "Science and Arts," "Belles Lettres," and "History." Each main category had numerous subcategories. Under science, for example, there were headings for physics, botany, optics, medicine, anatomy, surgery, chemistry, alchemy, astronomy, and metallurgy, and a section on natural history that was said to be "twice as extensive as that owned by the King." Among the authors represented in medicine, for example, were Galen, Vesalius, Avicenna, Hippocrates, Paracelsus, and even Symphorien Champier.

In theology, the first and most prominent section, there were dozens and dozens of Bibles—Bibles in Latin, Bibles in Greek, Bibles in Hebrew, Bibles in French, Bibles in German, Bibles in other assorted languages, and, for the well-versed, polyglot Bibles. At least fifteen of these were incunabula (literally "cradle" or "birthplace," here meaning books printed before 1501), including a Vulgate Bible by Fust and Schoeffer from 1462. There was also a 1522 first edition of Cardinal Ximenes's Complutensian Polyglot Bible. In addition, the duke owned Psalters, liturgies, books of hours, and the work of virtually every prominent Christian scholar in history. Lavallière was extremely interested in heterodoxy and acquired any number of volumes that had been considered heretical when they were first published. Among the many books in his library by religious dissenters, mystics, and other heretics were a number by Michael Servetus.

The Duc de Lavallière was one of the most prominent Servetus collectors in the world. He owned two editions of the Pagnini Bible edited by Michel de Villeneuve; a copy of *The Syrups*; first editions of *De Trinitatis Erroribus* and *Dialogorum de Trinitate*; both the 1535 and the 1541 editions of the *Geography*; the 1546 manuscript copy of *Christianismi Restitutio*, the one in which Servetus had first mentioned pulmonary circulation (and had mentioned the possibility of emigrating to the Americas); Mead's copy of the Dummer reprint; and, of course, the "*example unique*" Colladon copy of *Christianismi Restitutio*.

Upon his death, Lavallière left the entire library to his only child, a daughter, the Duchesse de Châtillon. The duchess was neither the collector nor the intellectual that her father had been, and she decided to put the library up for auction. It took three years of cataloging and preparation by the most prestigious bookseller in France, the firm of Guillaume de Bure & Son, before the library was ready to be sold. Most of the actual work was done by the late duke's chief librarian, l'Abbé Rive, and his young Belgian assistant, Joseph Van Praet.

Although the auction was to include just slightly more than half of the library's contents, about fifty-six thousand books, it would be the most celebrated sale of rare books in the eighteenth century, and Bure & Son produced a catalog worthy of the occasion. It was printed in two parts with three volumes each, almost one thousand pages, all six books bound in fine hand-tooled leather. The paper was thick and rich. The frontispiece, taken from a 1767 engraving, depicted a young, exceedingly handsome duke, much as he would have appeared in, say, 1740. This was followed immediately by a long section entitled *Avertissement*, an exposition on the magnificence of the library, the extraordinary value of its contents, and the reasons why each and every person of any wealth whatever would be almost criminal in neglecting to bid.

The catalog was sent to every major library in France and all over Europe. The auction would comprise 5,668 lots containing some of the most rare and coveted books and manuscripts in the world. Despite all the wealthy commoners who had availed themselves of a catalog, it was nations themselves, through their royal and imperial libraries, who were expected to be the major bidders. For France, this meant the Bibliothèque Royale.

The Bibliothèque Royale was an unusual and enlightened institution for eighteenth-century Europe. While technically the king's own library, it was, in fact, a public establishment, separate from the palaces and châteaus and available to all the scholars of France. It had been founded by Charles IX—he who had screamed, "Kill them all!" and precipitated the Saint Bartholomew's Day Massacre. Public reading rooms had been introduced in the seventeenth century, and the library's contents had come to be considered as much the property of the nation as that of the king. At the auction, the library would be represented by two agents recently engaged for the purpose, l'Abbé Rive and the new assistant curator, Joseph Van Praet.

The auction began on January 12, 1784, and did not conclude until May 5. Kings, queens, and nobles of every sort from every country on the continent sent agents, as did wealthy merchants, lawyers, physicians, and other collectors who had money but not title. When it was over, the auction brought in 464,677 livres (and change), which translates into tens if not hundreds of millions of dollars in today's market. (Two years later, the Marquis de Paulmy purchased 27,000 of the remaining books for 80,000 livres and used them to found another national library, the Bibliothèque de l'Arsenal.)

Curiously, for an auction of this magnitude, most of the items fetched relatively modest prices, 20 to 50 livres. For example, a second edition of Vesalius's *De Humani Corporis Fabrica* went for only 13 livres. A pristine copy of an Aldine work on astronomy fetched only slightly more, 100 livres.

The secondary Servetus material largely followed the pattern. Lots 44 and 45, the Pagnini Bibles, sold for 72 and 121 livres respectively, and the copy of *The Syrups* for only 20 livres. The 1535 edition of the *Geography*, with the unfortunate passage about the Holy Land, sold for 60 livres, and the 1541, which was in superb condition, for 49 livres.

(This latter copy was recently for sale through a major London book dealer. The asking price was forty thousand pounds, or roughly sixty thousand dollars. A thousand to one may not be an accurate conversion from 1784 livres to current dollars, but at least for the major items, it is reasonably close.)

The most important Servetus material, however, was his own theological work. Lot 911, the first editions of *De Trinitatis Erroribus* and *Dialogorum de Trinitate* sold for 700 livres. The next item, the 1546 manuscript copy of *Christianismi Restitutio*, was sold to the Bibliothèque Royale for 240 livres.

Then it was time for Lot 913, what was then thought to be the only surviving copy in the world of *Christianismi Restitutio.* No one knew how high the bidding would go. The price kept going up and up as agents for the competitors sent their surreptitious signals to the auctioneer. Finally, at 4,120 livres, the bidding was over. The winner was once again the Bibliothèque Royale. The treasure had been preserved for France. Immediately after the sale of the Colladon *Christianismi Restitutio,* Lot 914, the Mead reprint, sold for 1,700 livres, also to the Bibliothèque Royale.

The last item in the Servetus section of the theology category was Lot 915, Calvin's *Defense of the True Faith of the Sacred Trinity Against the Hideous Errors of Michael Servetus, Spaniard.*

It was purchased by an unidentified buyer for 19 livres.

‡

ALL IN ALL, the Bibliothèque Royale purchased nearly nine hundred volumes, of which 286 were incunabula and 210 were manuscripts. Five years later, of course, the Bibliothèque Royale, as well as everything else that was "Royale," was caught up in the firestorm of the Revolution. As a repository of national treasures, the Bibliothèque Royale, quickly renamed the Bibliothèque de la Nation, was spared the fury of the mob. The leaders of the revolution even pleaded with local citizens to maintain the library as a public service—the library system had no money, and every other library in Paris had been forced to close.

Soon, however, a debate began over whether to keep the nation's heritage intact or begin history anew. Radicals began a movement, later called *Vandalisme Révolutionnaire,* that attempted to purge France of anything that harkened back to the rot that was the monarchy. Archives and family records of nobles were burned, deeds and town records that supported property claims of nobles destroyed. It was only a matter of time before the radicals got around to books.

In 1792, a mass of portfolios, books, and papers that had belonged to the nobility were taken from the library and burned at the place Vendôme. Rumblings began that the entire contents of the library, an institution of the monarchy, should be put to the torch.

That it didn't happen was largely due not to a French patriot, but rather a Belgian bookworm, l'Abbé Rive's old assistant, Joseph Van Praet.

Van Praet was so apolitical that although he had worked for aristocrats for years, his life was never in danger, even at the height of the Terror. Instead, he ensconced himself at the Bibliothèque de la Nation (soon to be renamed the Bibliothèque Nationale) and not only saved the books they had but used the breakdown of the aristocracy to acquire more—a lot more. Van Praet brought thousands of rare and priceless books, manuscripts, and documents to the library during the Revolution and thousands more during the reign of Napoléon as the Grande Armée swept across Europe, gobbling up aristocratic libraries as it went. (He eventually had to give some of those back after Napoléon's defeat but managed to squirrel away the majority of the most valuable volumes.) Van Praet stayed at the Bibliothèque Nationale until his death in 1837 and was so instrumental in building the nation's collection that the private reading room in the rare book section of the national library's new François Mitterand Center is named for him.

Even Van Praet couldn't save everything. Some material had to be fed to the mob. At Van Praet's suggestion, however, a distinction was made between *titres-monuments,* those items that were important to France, and *papiers vaniteux,* papers or works that merely aggrandized the nobility. Then he showed a remarkably deft hand at getting virtually everything of bibliographic importance placed in the first classification.

‡

AFTER THE BIBLIOTHÈQUE ROYALE, the second most prolific purchaser at the Lavallière auction was the Imperial Library of Vienna. This was not a public institution but rather the personal collection of a

Hapsburg, Joseph II of Austria. The Imperial Library had purchased 350 volumes, of which about fifty were French incunabula, all very rare. The prize that Joseph had sought most, however, had eluded him. It was he who had been the underbidder for the *"example unique"* copy of *Christianismi Restitutio.*

Joseph was grouchy at failing to obtain the book—kings are not used to being denied what they want. His disappointment eventually came to the attention of a member of his court, Count Sámuel Teleki de Szek, himself a book collector of some renown.

Count Teleki, as it happened, was in a position to do something about it. ‡

THERE IS NO GREATER example of the influence of Voltaire than the reign of Joseph II, Holy Roman Emperor and king of Hungary. Joseph's was a regime modeled on the principles of toleration, reason, and fairness expounded by the great French philosopher, and never have theory and the best intentions been put so plainly into practice and failed so dismally.

Joseph was the eldest son of the empress Maria Theresa, whose father, Charles III, cheated of a male heir, had rammed through an edict authorizing women to inherit the crown, thus ensuring unbroken Hapsburg domination of the Holy Roman Empire, or what was left of it, at any rate. Maria Theresa's domain encompassed Austria, Hungary, and the Netherlands. She inherited the crown in 1740 and ruled for forty years, respected by her peers, feared by her enemies, and beloved by her people. She treated both her children and her empire with maternal solicitude. (It was this concern for her children's future security that led her to marry her daughter, Marie Antoinette, to the great French king Louis XVI; luckily she did not live to witness the outcome.)

Joseph, stifled from adolescence by overmothering, rebelled in order to give himself a separate identity. Whatever *she* was, he wasn't. Maria Theresa was a devout, intolerant Catholic who believed that any liberalizing of religion would lead to political anarchy and the destruction of the ruling family. Joseph became a child of the Enlightenment who distrusted the Catholic Church and sought to replace its influence with the moral authority of the state. She was a pragmatist who courted the aristocracy in order to control it. He sought a leveling of the class structure, universal schooling, and an end to serfdom. She saw books as agents of dissent and passed the most stringent censorship edicts possible in order to keep foreign thought out of her empire. He made sure he read extensively, traveled widely, promoted French and German culture, and amassed a private library with extensive sections devoted to science, medicine, and philosophy.

For sixteen years after he was crowned king of the Romans at age twenty-one in 1764—a title noteworthy for its grandeur if not for its actual authority—Joseph had chafed under the restrictions imposed upon him by his mother, who held on to all the real power. It wasn't until she died in November 1780 that Joseph was at last free to act. With a series of sweeping edicts he implemented a reform program astonishing for its boldness and breadth.

No stratum of society was left untouched by Joseph's new ideas. He abolished serfdom, liberalized the penal code so it applied fairly to aristocrats as well as peasants, and abolished capital punishment. He imposed the Edict of Toleration that gave Protestants the same rights as Catholics ("My Empire...has not made victims like Calas and Sirven," he wrote) and even sought protection and relief for Jews. A great believer in education, Joseph set about reforming and reorganizing all the schools in his empire; he allowed scholars to study books prohibited by the *Index librorum* and swept away the restrictions on sales of scientific and foreign books in Vienna. He retained tariffs on imported goods but lowered those on domestic ones in order to encourage local industry; closed monasteries and appropriated the wealth for the state; and attempted to impose uniform regulations on all local bureaucracies. A great admirer of Voltaire's friend Frederick the Great—his mother's archenemy—Joseph decreed that German, not Latin, would be the one official language of the empire, to be used in all government transactions, even though less than a quarter of the population spoke German, and that quarter was not the ruling quarter.

If his sole purpose had been to upset, unsettle, and confuse every man, woman, and child in his realm, he could not have succeeded more admirably. So much change effected so quickly across so many borders and affecting so many different peoples and nationalities was bewildering. Opposition arose from nobles and peasants alike. The Netherlands deposed him in absentia, Belgium announced its independence, and the serfs, sensing their opportunity, rose in armed rebellion in Transylvania and had to be put down forcibly.

‡

IN THIS ATMOSPHERE OF uncertainty, those groups on the fringes of society, like the Unitarian community in Cluj, the capital of Transylvania, felt the insecurity of their position most acutely. Yes, Joseph had issued the Edict of Toleration, but would it hold? Did it apply to them, or just to Lutherans and Calvinists? Would it lead to violence against them? The Unitarian Church had survived the Turks, the reintroduction of Hapsburg rule in 1690, the Jesuits, and the repressive policies of Maria Theresa, but would it survive Joseph's liberalism? The congregation looked around for a means by which to buttress their security.

It so happened that at the time there lived in eastern Hungary, on the very border of Transylvania, a nobleman of some influence by the name of Count Sámuel Teleki de Szek. Count Teleki was the lord-lieutenant of Küküllô and Bihar counties, not far from Cluj, and had in fact been born in Marosvasarhely, in the same province, about fifty miles away.

The Telekis were, and still are, one of Hungary's most distinguished families. Countess Blanka Teleki was a heroine of the Hungarian fight for independence in 1848. Another Teleki was an African explorer who in 1886, at his own expense, mounted a yearlong expedition deep into the interior of northern Kenya. He discovered two large lakes, which he named after the Hapsburg crown prince Rudolph and his wife Stephanie. There is an István Teleki who is active in a political campaign to secure basic human rights for the Hungarian ethnic minority in Transylvania. Perhaps the most famous member of the family was Count Pál Teleki. He was a senior official of the International Boy Scouts who was honored by President Franklin Roosevelt, served as the Hungarian delegate to the peace conference following World War I, and then became prime minister. He was recalled to lead the country in 1938 but committed suicide two years later rather than cooperate with Hitler.

Count Sámuel, the lord-lieutenant, was born in 1739. As a young man, he had been sent abroad for his schooling and attended not only the Sorbonne but also the very best universities in Protestant strongholds such as Basel and Utrecht. When he returned to the family estates in the 1760s, Count Sámuel began a campaign to reform public education, providing a broader, more cultured approach. He even dipped into his own pocket to provide financial aid for local scholars and students studying abroad. In 1774 he was summoned to court and appointed to the lord-lieutenant position by Maria Theresa as part of her program to co-opt the Hungarian aristocracy. When Maria Theresa died, Joseph kept Teleki on as part of the Hungarian bureaucracy.

But above all Count Sámuel, like the Duc de Lavallière and Joseph himself, was a discerning, educated, and impassioned bibliophile.

He had begun collecting books during his school years in Europe, with the goal of amassing one of Europe's great private libraries. He developed a network of dealers, book scouts, and other collectors that he would maintain throughout his life. Through agents, he purchased books from as many as twenty-five European cities. His collection was oriented to early printed texts and the writings of the Enlightenment and included the work of Aldus, Froben, and Estienne. He even married another collector, a countess named Zsuzsanna Bethlen de Iktár, although her passion for books was probably not the only reason for the alliance—Gábor Bethlen had ruled Transylvania in the early 1600s with help from the Turks.

At the time of Joseph's accession to the throne, the Teleki library was fast growing to be the largest and most prestigious in the country. It was well known throughout Hungary and Transylvania that the count was interested in old books.

The Unitarian congregation at Cluj, worried about the future, turned to Count Teleki. Either as a bribe or in gratitude for protection, the head of the congregation, Stephen Agh, gave Sámuel Teleki the single most important and valuable item the congregation possessed. He gave him their copy of *Christianismi Restitutio.*

‡

IT MUST HAVE BEEN LIKE opening a package from some distant relation and finding not a coarse, grotesquely patterned, handknitted scarf, but a long-lost Vermeer. *Christianismi Restitutio* was by this time no obscure little volume. It had only been three years since the Duc de Lavallière's auction, and everybody knew the story behind the book, its rarity, and its value. Indeed, it was common knowledge that the Lavallière copy, now safely and permanently ensconced in the Bibliothèque Royale in Paris, was the only surviving copy in the world.

But not anymore. Now Count Teleki held another copy in his hand.

The temptation to keep it, to make it the centerpiece of his library, must have been powerful. But it is dangerous to advertise that you own something coveted by your sovereign, and, in the end, Count Sámuel made a wise move. He graciously presented the book to Joseph, with his compliments.

Joseph was very pleased indeed. Now *that* was a gift. According to the head librarian at the Royal Library at Vienna, where Joseph deposited the book, Count Teleki "was recompensed for his generosity with the gift of a splendid diamond." The following year, Teleki was summoned once more to Vienna, this time to be appointed chancellor-assistant of Transylvania, a position that required his attendance at court. And in 1791, just after Joseph's death, Count Teleki became chancellor of all of Transylvania.

When Count Teleki died in 1822, his library exceeded forty thousand volumes. Although he did not have *Christianismi Restitutio,* among his books were volumes illustrated by Hans Holbein the younger, Rubens, and Dürer, as well as numerous illuminated atlases, maps, and albums. There were also incunabula, rare prints, and one-of-a-kind editions. All of them went into the Teleki Library at Marosvasarhely (now Tirgu Mures in Romania), one of the first Hungarian public libraries, which the Count had founded in 1802. He left the collection to the people of Transylvania—an immeasurable gift to his country.

As for Joseph II, he died a broken man, just ten years after his mother. Faced with insurmountable political obstacles, he had had to rescind all of his idealistic edicts except the abolition of serfdom. The great experiment in enlightenment had failed—"Here lies Joseph, who could succeed in nothing," he wrote bitterly from his deathbed.

Through it all, the Unitarian church at Cluj survived. It would not be an overstatement to say that Servetus bought them that survival with *Christianismi Restitutio.*

✢

INTEREST IN THE BOOK was spurred by the Lavallière auction and the discovery of a second surviving copy. In 1789, the year before Joseph II died, a German scholar, translator, and bibliophile named Christoph Gottlieb von Murr asked the king's permission to use the newly discovered Vienna copy as the basis for a reprint. Joseph, ever interested in the advancement of knowledge and pleased at the publicity that a reprint made from his copy would generate, readily agreed.

Murr's interest seems to have been bibliographic rather than theological or medical. He had already produced a scholarly essay on the provenance of the two known copies. Murr's notion was to create a facsimile edition, indistinguishable from the original save for a tiny "1790," the year of publication, on the last page.

There had been facsimile editions before, although not produced in the spirit of academic advancement. In 1721, in Ratisbon, Germany, a prominent and enterprising Lutheran clergyman named Georg Serpilius began secretly to reproduce both *Errors of the Trinity* and *Two Dialogues on the Trinity*. Serpilius did not, however, identify his reprints. In fact, they were intended to be all but indistinguishable from the originals, and they were, except for Serpilius's inexplicable use of a single rather than double dash on the title page.

Reprints hot in hand, Serpilius had then contacted book collectors and prominent Unitarians and told them that he had heard of the existence of two extremely rare books by the Spanish heretic Michael Servetus, and that he was willing to act as middleman if the collector wished to purchase them. If the collector agreed, Serpilius sold the reprints as originals. Since the counterfeits were not discovered for some years and there is no record of Serpilius ever having been caught, the scam seems to have been successful.

Murr's reprint, sold as such, became for collectors the next best thing to owning the unobtainable genuine original. The print run seems to have been quite small, since soon afterward it became almost as difficult to acquire a Murr edition as one printed in 1553. There are perhaps twenty left in the world today, virtually all of which are in national libraries or university collections.

Murr may have been a great scholar, but he obviously underestimated the difficulty of translating book knowledge into practical applications, and it cost him dearly. In 1811, at age seventy-eight, after reading a medical manual, he inexpertly attempted to use a catheter on himself and died in both extreme pain and acute embarrassment.

✠

AFTER MURR'S REPRINT HAD been snapped up by collectors, *Christianismi Restitutio* once again seemed doomed to become nothing more than a bibliographic curiosity. Not only were there no more copies of the book to be had, but interest in Servetus himself was fading. The

DE TRINI-

TATIS ERRORIBVS
LIBRI SEPTEM.

Per Michaelem Serueto, aliàs
Reues ab Aragonia
Hispanum.

Anno M. D. XXXL

DE TRINI-

TATIS ERRORIBVS
LIBRI SEPTEM.

Per Michaelem Serueto, aliàs
Reues ab Aragonia
Hispanum.

Anno M. D. XXXI.

Genuine (bottom) and counterfeit title pages of De Trinitatis Erroribus three hundredth anniversary of his execution passed quietly, even among Unitarians, and his contribution to the founding of their movement had become more unspoken than explicit.

So quiescent had Servetus scholarship become that the city of Geneva finally felt safe to release records of the trial, sequestered for more than three centuries. Voltaire had been denied access to these same transcripts when he had wished to write further about Servetus and Calvin in the wake of *Essai sur les moeurs*, but now they were available to any scholar who wished to have a look.

In 1877, a Scottish physician and medical historian named Robert Willis used those records to produce the first serious historical record of Servetus's life and trial in English. Willis had compiled a highly respected translation of the writings of William Harvey (from the Latin) thirty years before and had been interested in Servetus ever since. For the new book, Willis used not only the Geneva records but also those of the Vienne trial, which had been transcribed in 1749 by l'Abbé d'Artigny. The result was a compelling and heartbreaking account of a brave and intelligent man doomed by conscience. In his epilogue, Willis included a bibliographic history of the two surviving copies of *Christianismi Restitutio* and also speculated as to whether a third copy would ever show up.

On April 27, 1878, just five months before his death, Willis received a letter from a correspondent named Sir William Turner. Turner had written to a number of academic libraries, inquiring as to whether or not they had any Servetus materials that he might examine. John Small, the head librarian at the library of Willis's own alma mater, the University of Edinburgh, had replied that he thought they might.

When Small went to the catalog, he came across a listing that surprised him. He had no recollection of it and thought it must be a misprint, so he went to the shelves to check. There was no mistake—the University of Edinburgh library did indeed own a genuine 1553 copy of *Christianismi Restitutio*.

Small removed the book from the shelves. It had a nineteenth-century leather binding, polished calf or brown morocco, with a single gold fillet round the border. On the cover, tooled in gold, was "Donata Bibl. Edinb. a domino D. Georgio Douglasio filio illustriss. ducis de Queenberrie A.D. 1695." Inside, the book had been damaged in a curious way. The first gathering of sixteen pages had been torn out. In their place, someone had substituted carefully copied handwritten pages.

Small, of course, knew the Douglas family well. The current patriarch was John Sholto Douglas, the eighth Marquess of Queensberry, who had given the world both the rules of gentlemanly pugilism and his son, Lord Alfred—"Bosie"—who was soon to initiate the love affair that would bring down Oscar Wilde. Aware of the value of his discovery, Small conducted an intense search of library records but could find no indication whatever of how Lord George Douglas had come to own the book two centuries before.

One thing that was clear was that Lord George could not have donated the book in 1695 because he had died in 1693. In 1695, the Szent-Iványi copy was hidden away in Cluj, and the Colladon copy was sitting anonymously in the library of Karl von Hessen-Kassel, so this would have been the only known copy of *Christianismi Restitutio* in the world. Only years of searching by the most seasoned bibliophile could have unearthed such a find. But at the time of his death, Lord George Douglas had been only twenty-five years old.

☩

LORD GEORGE DOUGLAS WAS born in 1668, the youngest of three sons of the third earl and first duke of Queensberry. His father, William, had lived through the Great Rebellion and as an adolescent seen Cromwell's forces conquer Scotland. The Douglas family, like most of the Scottish nobles, had fought on the side of the Royalists and was forced by the new government to pay a heavy fine. The family fortunes seriously impaired, William was obliged as a young nobleman to forgo certain privileges and entertainments befitting his position. He never got the chance to study abroad, for example, which was all the fashion in those days.

The family recovered with the restoration of Charles II. William, now in his twenties, was rewarded for his loyalty and rose steadily until he had attained the titles of lord high treasurer of Scotland, constable and governor of Edinburgh Castle and, finally, duke of Queensberry, one of the lords of the privy council of both Scotland and England. By the time Lord George was born, William's industry had recouped all of the wealth lost under Cromwell. Still, like a child of the Depression, the first duke of Queensberry never forgot the economy and deprivation of his youth—William was a bit of a penny pincher.

As third son, Lord George could not hope to succeed to his father's titles—those would go to his older brother James—but he was still sent to Glasgow University, the best in Scotland, for training in Latin, Greek, the classics, mathematics, and science. His father was adamant that part of his education be spent studying abroad—no Douglas was going to be denied that particular privilege again—and so in March 1686, at the age of eighteen, the baby-faced, sickly Lord George left for an extended tour of the Continent. William did not feel that his son was sufficiently mature to undertake this adventure alone, so he hired Alexander Cunningham, a brilliant lawyer, classical scholar, and chess master to serve as his son's tutor and companion. William had decided that Lord George should study law while he was away, that being the area of study most valuable to a life spent in public service.

Just at the time that Lord George and his tutor left, William was kilt deep in politics and intrigue. Charles II had died in 1685 and had been succeeded by his brother James. James was already flirting with the idea of reinstating Roman Catholicism as the state religion, much to the fear and consternation of Protestant families like the Douglases. Sure enough, in June 1686, at the instigation of the ambitious earl of Perth, who had recently converted to Roman Catholicism in order to curry favor with James, William was stripped of all of his titles and pro-hibited from leaving Edinburgh.

Stripped, too, of the income associated with his positions and hav-ing recently undertaken large improvements of the family castle—which necessitated equally large expenditures of capital—William, basically under house arrest, squirmed at the bills that his youngest son, now skipping blithely through Europe, was stacking up.

The tour had begun in Utrecht, which boasted one of the best law schools in the world. Unfortunately, Lord George and his tutor arrived in April, well into the school term, too late for a novice to pick up the material easily. Indeed, the two young men seemed to take the whole legal studies aspect of the trip as a vague guideline rather than a strict objective—Cunningham suggested going to Brussels after Utrecht, even though there was no university in Brussels. However, Lord George and Cunningham felt that this deficiency was more than made up for by the gaiety of Brussels, the cheapness of its lodgings, and the ability to get in some decent dancing and fencing without a series of school lectures getting in the way.

But Cunningham's real passion, one that he communicated thor-oughly to his charge, was his love of books. Everywhere they went, Utrecht, Heidelberg (William nixed the Brussels idea), Strasbourg, Basel, Milan, Florence—they haunted the bookstores. They did more than haunt, they bought, and bought prodigiously. They worked with secondhand dealers and bid at auctions. Somewhere along the line, probably at one of the cheaper shops, since there is no surviving in-voice, they picked up an oddity—a book missing its title page, index, and first fourteen pages of text. It might not have even been bound. Whether Cunningham knew it for what it was or was simply attracted by the book's age and condition, no one knows. But soon, along with the other eight hundred books the pair bought, it was packed up and on its way to Scotland.

This profligate spending on old books was an ongoing source of conflict between father and son. No matter how often Lord George and

Cunningham pointed out to William that they were in no way extravagant, that they always got good value, that, in fact, by acquiring all of these books they were actually *saving* him money (the books being much cheaper in Holland, Germany, Switzerland, and Italy than in Scotland), William still put up a fuss. "The Duke of course jibbed at the expense involved, but was met with a number of spirited replies from Lord George, who, while remaining outwardly deferential toward his father, was showing definite signs of that independence of mind so characteristic of the Queensberry Douglases," W. A. Kelly, a biographer, noted.

Such was William's tightfistedness that for a short time Cunningham flirted with a new plan for achieving financial security. While at Heidelberg, the two young men were introduced to two women—one a Welsh widow, the other an English teenager—both rumored to be in possession of large dowries. Cunningham at first suggested that Lord George marry the English girl—she was sixteen—but, finding her father to be not as wealthy as originally thought, he switched his advocacy to the Welsh widow, who, although twenty-nine, was confirmed to be very well off. Lord George, for reasons of his own, did not take to the idea, and the scheme was dropped.

By the time the pair landed in Italy, all pretense of a legal education was dropped. William wrote, urging that Lord George return to Germany and enroll in a university or, at the very least, study at the University of Padua. Cunningham wrote back, assuring his employer that the private course of study that he, Cunningham, was currently providing was eminently preferable to anything a university had to offer. The two continued on their way.

In Milan they visited the famed Ambrosian Library, and in Florence they were given a private tour of the grand duke's library, where they met Gottfried Leibniz, who was on a private tour of his own. They saw the sights in Rome and met all the best people.

In 1689, while Lord George and his tutor were taking in the sights in Italy at his expense, William's position took a decided turn for the better. According to the *Dictionary of National Biography*, his eldest son,

James, had the foresight to be in the vanguard of William of Orange's bloodless coup, the first Scottish nobleman to desert to the Prince of Orange, "and from thence acquired the epithet (among honest men) of Proto-rebel." The new king acknowledged James's support by appointing him colonel of the Scottish horse guards, and with that stroke the earl of Perth was vanquished.

By 1692, when Lord George and Cunningham finally straggled home by way of Leipzig, Dresden, Berlin, Poland, Denmark, and Sweden ("moving in circles which few grand tourists of a later age were able to enter for all their financial resources," Kelly observed), William and James Douglas were in sufficient favor at court to get Lord George invited into the Royal Society—as a seasoned traveler, no doubt—and presented to the king. By January 1693, Cunningham was able to report to William that the king had offered Lord George the ambassadorship to either Sweden, Denmark, or Brandenburg—the choice was his. William evidently wanted a say in this, or at least to see his son before he left the country again, because Cunningham and Lord George had to travel back to Edinburgh before giving their answer. It was January and quite cold; Lord George took ill, never recovered, and died about six months later.

Out of respect for his son, William bequeathed all of Lord George's books to the Advocates Library at Edinburgh, later the Edinburgh University Library. Cunningham compiled the catalog. Two years later, William followed his son to the grave, and James took over the family, becoming the second duke of Queensberry.

After William's death, Alexander Cunningham donated in Lord George's name a book bought on their tour that he'd omitted from the catalog, his now-rebound copy of *Christianismi Restitutio*, the one John Small rediscovered two hundred years later.

‡

WHAT CUNNINGHAM AND the Douglas family could not have known, but Small did, was that the sixteen missing pages were a vital piece of bibliographic evidence. It meant that not only was this volume a third copy of one of the rarest and most valuable books in the world, but that it was Calvin's own, the one he had used to denounce Servetus to the French Inquisition. The sixteen missing pages were those that had been sent to Arneys through Trie. The manuscript pages—there are eighteen—are not an exact copy of the missing printed pages, because Calvin, wanting a complete book and having already removed the first gathering, instructed his secretary to use instead the first section of the 1546 manuscript of *Christianismi Restitutio* sent to him by Servetus, the closest facsimile available.

So Calvin, after ordering every copy of *Christianismi Restitutio* hunted down and destroyed, after threatening anyone who harbored a copy with the same fate as that of its author, could not bring himself to destroy his own. ‡

CHAPTER NINETEEN

WHEN CHRISTOPH VON MURR misdirected his catheter, it epitomized the sort of experimentation that went on in the late eighteenth and early nineteenth centuries (although not always with such disastrous results). It was a period in which the monumental leaps of pure theory by men like Newton, Boyle, and Locke were sounded, digested, and finally applied. Science buzzed with the excitement of research. Watt gave the world the steam engine, Franklin electricity, and Linnaeus the classification of the natural world.

Once again, the progress of science spilled over into other, messier arenas of human affairs. Tinkering with vials and tubes and machinery led to tinkering with economics and politics; tinkering with economics and politics led to the American War for Independence and, later, the cataclysm of the French Revolution. As, by degrees, the laws of the natural world were discovered, people attempted to apply what they had learned to the laws of human interaction. Many once again struggled with the concept of the true nature of God.

The antitrinitarian movement that had begun in the little Italian church in Geneva had now spread to England, where Unitarians were an entrenched, grudgingly accepted minority. Although not allowed to hold public office or attend Oxford or Cambridge, Unitarians and other Dissenters, as they were called, created their own schools that were every bit the intellectual match of their more established counterparts. These schools, which encouraged free inquiry in religion, also encouraged the same approach to science, history, politics, and other academic disciplines. The result was a disproportionate number of Dissenters who became leading scientific minds of the time. One man in particular embodied this quest to reconcile science and the spirit: the great English chemist Joseph Priestley.

Priestley was born on March 13, 1733, in West Riding, Yorkshire, in the English Midlands, a major center for the manufacture of cloth. His mother died when he was six. His father could not care for Joseph adequately and sent him off to live with his aunt, Sarah Keighley, who adopted him when he was nine.

The Keighleys, like the Priestleys, were Calvinists, but, according to Priestley himself in his autobiography, unlike his parents, his aunt made her home "a resort for all the dissenting ministers in the neighbourhood without distinction, and those who were the most obnoxious on account of their heresy were almost as welcome to her, if she thought them honest and good men (which she was not unwilling to do) as any others." At Mrs. Keighley's dinner table, Priestley, who had mastered Greek, Latin, and Hebrew in addition to French, Italian, and Dutch by the time he was sixteen, was exposed to the sort of political and theological questioning definitely outside the experience of the average English family. When it became time for him to go to school, he was sent to the foremost Dissenting academy in England.

Joseph Priestley followed the same spiritual path as had Michael Servetus two hundred years before, tracing the roots of the Trinity to the Council of Nicaea, rejecting all corruption of the religion outside Scripture, and believing in Christ as a man who was made divine by God's word. Priestley was similar to Servetus in temperament as well. Both were outspoken, scathing to opponents, and unable to suppress either their opinions or their passion; both possessed raw genius that extended across academic disciplines. Priestley published essays on history, education, civil policy, government, and philosophy, as well as numerous treatises on religion, and while he always considered himself primarily a theologian, like Servetus he is now mostly remembered for his contributions to science.

Joseph Priestley

Priestley began his scientific career relatively late in life, at age thirty-three, after he met Benjamin Franklin in London in 1766. He asked Franklin for permission to write a history of electricity, which Franklin thought was an excellent idea. While writing the history, Priestley sought to reconcile certain inconsistencies by performing some experiments and, for the purpose, invented an "electricity machine," really a demonstration device in which he showed that graphite conducted electricity. He finished his history the following year and as a result was elected to the Royal Society.

From there, Priestley became an obsessive experimenter. His favorite medium was gas, an interest that developed, he said, "in consequence of living for some time in the neighborhood of a public brewery." Hundreds and hundreds of times, he heated a substance to see what sort of gas was created.

He succeeded in isolating oxygen, nitric oxide, hydrogen chloride, and ammonia. He was the first to put forward and then prove the theory that plants take in carbon dioxide and give off oxygen, and that this is due to a chemical reaction precipitated by sunlight on green leaves. "I find that you have set all the philosophers of Europe to work upon *fixed air* [carbon dioxide] and it is with pleasure I observe how high you stand in their opinion; for I enjoy my friend's fame as my own," Franklin wrote him in a letter.

Like Murr, Priestley frequently tried out his experiments on himself. He diluted his "fixed air" with water and produced ... seltzer. He drank it, liked it, and the soft-drink industry was born. After he had isolated oxygen, he breathed it in through a siphon: "The feeling ... was not sensibly different from common air, but I fancied that my breast felt peculiarly light for some time afterward. Who can tell but that, in time, this pure air may become a fashionable article of luxury?" It took 250 years, but the Oxygen Bars in California finally proved Priestley correct. Not all his experiments were as successful: he once preserved meat in nitric oxide for six months, then tried to eat it. ("He found it horrible, though his friend Magalhaens considered it not so bad," reported his biographer, Anne Holt.)

In 1780, he moved to Birmingham and was at once invited to become a member of the Lunar Society, whose ranks included Erasmus Darwin and Josiah Wedgwood—both of Charles Darwin's grandfathers—and James Watt. The group met once a month for scientific and philosophic conversation at a member's house at the full moon (so they could see to walk home at night). Watt once wrote to Erasmus Darwin by way of invitation, "I beg that you would impress on your memory the idea that you promised to dine with sundry men of learning at my house on Monday next ... For your encouragement there is a new book to cut up, and it is to be determined whether or not heat is a compound of phlogiston [an undetectable substance that many in the eighteenth century supposed existed in all combustible materials] and empyreal air, and whether a mirror can reflect the heat of the fire ... If you are meek and humble, perhaps you may be told what light is made of, and also how to make it, and the theory proved by synthesis and analysis."

Despite what had become an enormous scientific reputation,

Priestley's own genius for indiscretion often got him into serious trouble. In addition to his radical religious opinions, he was an outspoken supporter of the American Revolution at a time when it was even less popular than usual to hold that view in England. He opposed the lucrative slave trade and was an advocate for the repeal of the Test and Corporation Acts, which discriminated against anyone who did not adhere to the articles of the Church of England. He published *The History of the Corruptions of Christianity*, a full-blown attack on the Trinity, and followed it up with *The History of the Early Opinions Concerning Jesus Christ*. Priestley's worst indiscretion was his vocal support of the French Revolution. Detesting tyranny in any form, he viewed the fall of the monarchy as the dawn of a new, brighter day, just as the fall of the tsar, before the coming of Stalin, at first seemed to signal the end of repression in Russia to American political progressives. But even in the early days before the Terror, the French Revolution was perceived as a threat to the English monarchy and established social order, and the public overwhelmingly feared it.

In Birmingham in 1791, those few still supporting the French cause decided to throw a dinner to commemorate Bastille Day, "the auspicious day which witnessed the Emancipation of Twenty-six Millions of People from the Yoke of Despotism, and restored the blessings of equal Government to a truly great and enlightened Nation," the public advertisement, which ran three days before, rather recklessly announced. Any "Friend to Freedom" had to pay only five shillings for a ticket, which included a bottle of wine. There were sufficient rumblings in the town to make the sponsors question the wisdom of the gesture, but the manager of the hotel where the dinner was scheduled to take place (and who presumably had already disbursed funds in anticipation of the profit) assured them that it was perfectly safe. Accordingly, July 14 arrived, and the dinner was held.

The manager was right: the dinner itself was safe. Although a mob gathered, it confined itself to jeering and hooting until around eight o'clock, just after the "Friends to Freedom" had eaten and gone home. Then those in the mob, having drunk no small amount themselves, made up for lost time. They smashed the windows of the hotel before going on to set fire first to the New Meeting House, where the Dissenters prayed, and then to the Old Meeting House, just because it was there. Finding themselves out of public buildings to attack, they decided to move on to private property. The natural choice was the home of the most public Dissenter in England, Joseph Priestley.

Priestley, who hadn't even attended the dinner, was playing backgammon when a friend arrived with a chaise. It was only with great difficulty that he was made to believe that his family was in danger. They got away "with nothing more than the clothes we happened to have on," Priestley later wrote. Because the mob was on foot, the Priestleys at first drove only about a half mile out of town and waited, assuming that that was enough for security.

> It was remarkably calm [he wrote], and clear moonlight, we
> could see a considerable distance, and being upon a rising
> ground, we distinctly heard all that passed at the house, every
> shout of the mob, and almost every stroke of the instruments
> they had provided for breaking the doors and the furniture ...
> one of them was heard to offer two guineas for a lighted can-
> dle, my son ... having taken the precaution to put out all the
> fires in the house ... I afterward heard that much pains was
> taken [*sic*], but without effect, to get fire from my large elec-
> trical machine, which stood in the library.

Priestley lost everything that night—home, library, and worst of all, the notebooks containing the results of unpublished scientific research. Priestley himself spent the better part of the next three days exhausted and on horseback, hunted by a mob that traced his path to a neighboring town and beyond. Eventually, he and his family fled to London in hopes of redress. Birmingham disbursed token compensation for his losses, but it was clear that there was no hope of returning. Priestley wrote a letter to "My Late Townsmen and Neighbours":

> You have destroyed the most truly valuable and useful apparatus of philosophical instruments that perhaps any individual, in this or any other country, was ever possessed of, in my use of which I annually spent large sums with no pecuniary view whatever, but only for the advancement of Science, for the benefit of my country and mankind. You have destroyed the Library corresponding to that apparatus, which no money can repurchase except in the course of time. But what I feel far more, you have destroyed manuscripts which I shall never be able to recompose; and this has been done to one who never did, or imagined, you any harm.

In London, outraged by the French Reign of Terror, the Royal Society ostracized Priestley, and he was forced to resign. He was going to have to leave England. France, which had made him an honorary citizen in 1792, offered him a house and a seat on the National Assembly, but he refused. Instead, in 1794, he and his family crossed the Atlantic and came to America.

‡

THE CHOICE WAS NOT arbitrary. At the end of the eighteenth century, Unitarianism was just gaining a foothold as a religious movement in the United States. Radical antitrinitarian ministers had begun to gain favor, particularly in Massachusetts. In addition to their denial of the Trinity, almost all of them had one other thing in common. They had either corresponded with Joseph Priestley or become followers of his theological works.

Until Priestley's arrival, however, Unitarianism in America had no celebrity. No other Unitarian minister had ever preached to a packed audience that included the vice president (John Adams), or been invited to visit President Washington at his home in Mount Vernon, or claimed the personal friendship of Thomas Jefferson. "As to Unitarianism," Priestley wrote from Pennsylvania, in a letter to a friend, "it is, I perceive, greatly promoted by my coming hither, and the circulation of my publications."

Priestley founded a Unitarian Society in Philadelphia, and his sermons were printed and distributed throughout the country. He was offered a professorship of chemistry at the University of Pennsylvania and the presidency of the American Philosophical Society. There is no telling just how much influence Priestley might have exerted in both science and religion had he remained in what was then the nation's capital. Instead, inexplicably—based, it seems, solely on his wife's distaste for Philadelphia—Priestley relocated to Northumberland, 130 miles outside the city, a town so remote that when a shipment of his books was delivered to a neighboring village in error it took two years to correct the mistake. Mrs. Priestley died the following year.

By 1798, American relations with France had deteriorated greatly— the French were seizing American ships, and Talleyrand, then the French foreign minister, tried to bribe an American diplomatic mission led by John Marshall. Priestley's perceived association with the radicals in France got him in trouble once more. Congress passed the Alien and Sedition Acts, and Priestley, now in his sixties, faced the possibility of deportation under President Adams.

But Joseph Priestley was not deported because the following year Thomas Jefferson was elected president.

‡

JEFFERSON HAD MET Priestley in Philadelphia in 1797. In addition to a broad love of scholarship and science, they had the Lunar Society in common. Jefferson's favorite professor at William and Mary, William

Small, had retired to England, settled in Birmingham, and been invited to join the group. Although Small had died before Priestley arrived, Jefferson, who corresponded with his old mentor until the end, was well aware of the intellectual fervor that was the society's signature.

Small's influence on Jefferson's character cannot be overestimated. Years later, Jefferson would write to his grandson:

> I had the good fortune to become acquainted very early with some characters of very high standing, and to feel the incessant wish that I could ever become what they were. Under temptations and difficulties, I would ask myself what would Dr. Small, Mr. Wythe [brilliant legal scholar and signer of the Declaration of Independence], Peyton Randolph [first president of the Continental Congress] do in this situation? What course in it will insure me their approbation?

From Small, Jefferson had acquired a deep reverence for the Enlightenment and the work of *philosophes* such as Voltaire and Montesquieu, which led directly to the formation of his views on religious freedom. The colonies had inherited England's prejudice in favor of the Church of England—only Anglican ministers received a stipend, paid from public taxes. Dissenters, whom Jefferson estimated comprised two-thirds of the population of Virginia, were not given equal rights under the law. This, to Jefferson, was unacceptable, and so he penned the Bill for Establishing Religious Freedom in 1779.

That statute, although not passed by the Virginian general assembly until 1784, bears great similarity to the proclamation of young King John II of Transylvania over two hundred years before:

> We the General Assembly of Virginia do enact that no man shall be compelled to frequent or support any religious worship, place or ministry whatsoever, nor shall be enforced, restrained, molested, or burthened in his body or goods, nor

shall suffer otherwise on account of his religious opinions or
belief; but that all men shall be free to profess, and by argument to maintain, their opinions in matters of religion, and
that the same shall in no wise diminish, enlarge or affect their
civil capacities.

When Thomas Jefferson later wrote the epitaph that he wished inscribed on his tombstone, he chose three achievements stating that "by
these as testimonials that I have lived, I wish most to be remembered."
Two of them were of little surprise—"Author of the Declaration of
American Independence" and "Father of the University of Virginia." For
the third, however, Jefferson chose neither his presidency nor his role
in the drafting of the Bill of Rights to the Constitution. To Jefferson,
the third most important accomplishment of his life was "Author of the
Statute of Virginia for religious freedom."

Jefferson's own views of religion were complex and evolved over
time. Always an antitrinitarian, in his youth he was a deist, one of those
who applied reason and science to religion and whose conception of
God was simply that of a Supreme Being who created the world as one
would an intricate clock, then left it to tick. As Jefferson grew older, he
continually reexamined the basis and precepts of his own personal
faith.

Even from Northumberland, Priestley had become something of a
mentor to Jefferson. They corresponded frequently, and Jefferson
asked for his advice in organizing the curriculum of the University of
Virginia. Priestley's religious views also affected Jefferson's own. In
1803, in one of his most thoughtful and impassioned analyses of his religious beliefs, Jefferson wrote:

I am a Christian, in the only sense in which he [Christ] wished
any one to be; sincerely attached to his doctrines, in prefer-
ence to all others; ascribing to himself every *human* excellence; and believing he never claimed any other...In the

moment of my late departure from Monticello, I received from Dr. Priestley, his little treatise of "Socrates and Jesus Compared." This being a section of the general view I had taken of the field, it became a subject of reflection while on the road ... The result was, to arrange in my mind a syllabus, or outline of such an estimate of the comparative merits of Christianity... I am averse to the communication of my religious tenets to the public; because it would countenance the presumption of those who have endeavored to draw them before that tribunal, and to seduce public opinion to erect itself into that inquisition over the rights of conscience, which the laws have so justly proscribed. It behooves every man who values liberty of conscience for himself, to resist invasions of it in the case of others ... It behooves him, too, in his own case, to give no example of concession, betraying the common right of independent opinion, by answering questions of faith, which the laws have let between God and himself.

But regardless of his own faith, Jefferson, like Voltaire, always opposed the accumulation of power under the veil of godliness. And again like Voltaire, Jefferson viewed John Calvin as one of history's worst offenders, a tyrant who bred other tyrants in his name. The event that exposed Calvin for what he was, that most epitomized his hypocrisy, was the trial and execution of Michael Servetus.

"The Presbyterian clergy are the loudest, the most intolerant of all sects," he wrote in 1820 to William Short, an American diplomat and former protégé who had served as his private secretary in Paris, "the most tyrannical and ambitious, ready at the word of the law-giver, if such a word could now be obtained, to put their torch to the pile, and to rekindle in this virgin hemisphere the flame in which their oracle, Calvin, consumed the poor Servetus, because he could not subscribe to the proposition of Calvin, that magistrates have a right to exterminate all heretics to the Calvinistic creed! They pant to re-establish by law that holy inquisition which they can now only infuse into public opinion."

Joseph Priestley died quietly and peacefully on February 6, 1806, sitting in a chair in his bedroom in Northumberland. Up until one hour before, he had been dictating changes to a new pamphlet and chastising his secretary for attempting to alter his language. Then he stopped and put his hand in front of his face so that his family, who were present, would not see him die. When his hand dropped, he was gone.

Priestley left a legacy of scientific inquiry and freedom of conscience, but he died unaware that the religious movement that he had all but founded in America was about to explode. But then, he had never been to Massachusetts.

✝

MASSACHUSETTS HAS ALWAYS held a special niche on the continuum of American radicalism. It was Massachusetts that, by its example, polarized the colonies against the British; Massachusetts where the first shots rang out in the War for Independence; Massachusetts that set the tone for a specific kind of American rebel—independent, plainspoken, and in the forefront of the battle of free thought against the tyranny of inherited ideas.

The need to question, to rebel against authority, to replace ceremony with common sense, had become ingrained in the citizenry and found itself without an outlet in the years following the war. Casting about for a new opponent, the rebels of Massachusetts suddenly woke up and discovered a strong dissatisfaction with some of the fundamental tenets of their religion. Having just thrown off the divine right of kings, some young ministers and their followers now turned the fight to the divine right of Calvin.

Calvinism, they concluded, was a cold, repressive doctrine with a view of man that could not be further from the ideals of personal freedom that had been vindicated by seven years of revolutionary struggle.

Man was not a corrupt, damned creature, helpless against his imperfections, nor did he need any intermediary between himself and God. Sermons questioning predestination and the Trinity began to be heard both in the small parishes in the countryside and the large, established churches in Boston. And because the church structure in Massachusetts was decentralized, with no formal mechanism for anyone outside a congregation to remove its minister, every time a liberal was appointed, the movement as a whole gained momentum.

Pivotal in the new thinking was an idea that Servetus had propounded in 1530, that Christ was a man made divine by God's word, rather than a manifestation of God himself. A conservative minister, Jedediah Morse, attempted to force the liberals to admit that they were Unitarians, which at the time meant not only rejecting the Trinity but also the divinity of Christ. Such an admission would allow conservatives to force the liberals out of the Church. The liberal ministers refused to take the bait. They denied being Unitarians, insisting that a rejection of the Trinity was supported by Scripture and a separate issue from Christ's divinity.

The stalemate continued until 1803, when David Tappan, the Hollis Professor of Divinity at Harvard, died and the six members of the corporate board of the college were charged with naming a successor. The position was of immense importance, effectively determining the course of education for future ministers of Massachusetts churches. The board was split 3–3 between Henry Ware, a liberal, and Jesse Appleton, a conservative. Ware was an avowed antitrinitarian but, like his colleagues, denied being a Unitarian. After a year of deadlock, the board finally voted for Ware, and the Harvard Board of Overseers, the highest authority at the college, ratified the choice. As soon as Ware assumed his post, every conservative member of the Board of Overseers resigned. The following year, a liberal, Samuel Webber, was chosen as Harvard's president.

Shut out of Harvard, Morse and his allies established the Andover

Theological Seminary, which would adhere to strict Calvinist principles. Morse also founded his own church in Boston and pressed his attacks on the liberals through pamphlets.

Cheap and short, pamphlets were the talk shows of their day. The public gobbled them up. Anyone who wanted to get out a point of view or dose of propaganda could do so almost instantly through a pamphlet. Records of congressional proceedings were produced in pamphlets, as were accounts of criminal or civil trials. It was regular practice for the sermons of an important minister to be reprinted as pamphlets and sold on street corners.

In 1815, Jedediah Morse issued a pamphlet in which he reprinted a section from an English biography that claimed that the Unitarians in England considered the liberals in Massachusetts as part of their movement. Morse then went on to charge that the liberal ministers refused to acknowledge their true beliefs because they were engaged in a conspiracy to spread their doctrine in secret and undermine the Protestant religion.

Morse's pamphlet sold all over Massachusetts and demanded a reply. The liberals chose the acknowledged leader of their movement, William Ellery Channing, a Boston minister and Fellow at Harvard. No longer able to convincingly deny his Unitarianism, Channing instead claimed that there was no conflict between Unitarianism and mainstream Christianity. Morse responded, Channing answered, and the pamphlet wars continued for another four years.

Finally, in 1819, Channing decided the time had come to accept the inevitable and define the movement. He used as his platform a speech delivered at the ordination of a new minister in Baltimore. A large group of liberal Bostonians made the four-hundred-mile journey to hear Channing's sermon, entitled "Unitarian Christianity," in which he argued for the use of logic and common sense when reading the Scriptures. Anyone who did so, Channing insisted, would see that Christianity *was* Unitarian. Although it was later reported that almost no one in the packed church could hear the speech, the pamphlet version, which went through eight editions in four months, became one of the most widely read sermons in the United States. By 1822, all but one of Boston's churches were Unitarian, and the movement was acquiring followers as far away as Charleston, South Carolina, prompting Thomas Jefferson to write, "I confidently expect that the present generation will see Unitarianism become the general religion of the United States."

For a decade, Jefferson's prophecy seemed likely to come true. Even Morse's son, Samuel F. B. Morse, inventor of the telegraph, became a Unitarian. Yet years of defending themselves against the conservatives had left a mark. To prove that they were not in fact Unitarian, the liberals had turned to the Scriptures, finding passage after passage to demonstrate that one could deny the Trinity and still remain a mainstream Christian. They had gotten so used to dissecting, parsing, and endlessly reinterpreting biblical phrases that they stopped doing anything else. The movement, which had been so spiritual for most of its existence, became coldly pseudoscientific, almost Scholastic.

The person who arrested this tendency, who shifted the emphasis back from the mind to the soul, was the poet and orator Ralph Waldo Emerson, perhaps the most famous Unitarian America has ever produced. Emerson was a Unitarian minister who had attended Harvard during the years of the pamphlet wars. Channing was his own minister.

Emerson became pastor of Boston's Second Church in 1829 but resigned three years later, finding it increasingly difficult to perform his duties with the sense of inspired enthusiasm that he felt the office required. He began a new career as a public lecturer and turned his considerable intellect to the question of what had caused him to quit his pastorate. He decided that "the blame for his failure as a minister lay not with himself but the institutions of organized religion, which he declared could no longer command respect." Probing further, he discovered that it was the trend toward intellectualism and formality that was deadening the spirit and turning religion away from its purpose.

In 1838, he was invited to address the graduating class at the Har-

vard Divinity School and used the occasion to deliver a sermon decrying common church practice and putting forward his own views of the
remedy, which came to be known as transcendentalism. Emerson's
transcendentalism had nothing to do with India or meditation. Man's
essence, he argued, was not formed simply through a series of sensory
experiences. Instead, there were aspects of the human essence—the
most important aspects, in fact—that transcended anything we might
have seen, heard, or reasoned. Without awareness of this, life becomes
empty and purposeless. It was this transcendence that man sought in
religion.

Emerson when on:

> Whenever the pulpit is usurped by a formalist, then is the wor-
> shipper defrauded and disconsolate... My friends, in these er-
> rors, I think, I find the causes of a decaying church and a
> wasting unbelief... In the soul, then, let the redemption be
> sought... Faith makes us, and not we it, and faith makes its
> own forms... the remedy is, first, soul, and second, soul, and
> evermore, soul.

Emerson's sermon was roundly denounced within the established
Unitarian community. "I did not like it at all," said Edward Everett Hale.
"Mr. E held that the Christianity of the present day is little better than
none."

But young Unitarians came away with a far different view. One in
particular, a poor farmer's son named Theodore Parker, was inspired to
take Emerson still further. He denied that Christianity held any unique
mandate on religious truth. The Bible was merely a written history, no
more or less valuable or reliable than any other history. "Christianity
does not rest on the infallible authority of the New Testament," Parker
said in a sermon. "I cannot see that it depends on the personal authority of Jesus. He was the organ through which the Infinite spoke."

This was too much for many established Unitarian ministers. The

Boston Association of Ministers took up the question of what to do about Parker. So inflammatory were Parker's ideas that they resurrected an epithet that in the past had only been used against them—heresy. It was decided that Parker should be invited to a meeting to discuss the problem in the hope that he could either be persuaded to recant his views or prevailed upon to resign his ministry. Parker accepted the invitation, and the planned meeting took place in January 1843.

To those familiar with the Servetus trial and the general treatment of dissenters through the ages, the Boston Association's handling of the Parker controversy marked a watershed in the annals of religious toleration. Parker met with a number of important ministers, including Dr. Frothingham of the First Church, who cited their objections to Parker's views. Parker responded but refused to recant. He was then asked to voluntarily withdraw from the Association and resign his pastorate. Parker refused, stating that he believed that the right of free thought had never before had limitations placed on it within their movement. As the eminent Harvard Unitarian scholar, Conrad Wright, wrote:

> It then became apparent that, while the members would have been very much relieved if Parker had taken the hint and resigned, they were not disposed to prescribe a doctrinal test for membership... So several of the members said kind things about Parker's sincerity; he burst into tears... Dr. Frothingham shook him cordially by the hand and expressed the hope that he would come to see him soon; and the closest the Unitarians ever came to a heresy trial was over.

The 1840s and '50s would mark the peak of Unitarian influence in America. However, the very spirit of inclusion and free inquiry that had allowed the movement to encompass so many disparate and conflicting philosophies as to the nature of God and His relationship with man worked against a strong, unified front. Unitarians splintered into factions.

While Unitarianism never fulfilled Jefferson's prophecy, the words of Emerson live on, as does the record of the decency with which the movement treated Theodore Parker.

‡

WITH EMERSON AND PARKER, Unitarianism moved back to its spiritual roots. In their words are the echoes of Michael Servetus, who, at age twenty, wrote, "God himself is our spirit dwelling in us and this is the Holy Spirit within us. In this we testify that there is in our spirit a certain working latent energy, a certain heavenly sense, a latent divinity and it bloweth where it listeth and I hear its voice and I know not whence it comes nor whither it goes."

But even as the vision of Servetus had finally found expression, Servetus himself had been relegated to an afterthought—if even that—in the movement he had inspired.

It would take William Osler, a member of the religious mainstream, an Episcopalian and admirer of John Calvin, to gain Servetus at least some of the credit that his extraordinary life deserved. ‡

WILLIAM OSLER WAS the most famous doctor of his time, and today there are many who still call him the greatest physician in history. He was the youngest professor of medicine ever at Canada's elite McGill Medical School; he was one of four doctors, memorialized in a portrait by Sargent, to start the Johns Hopkins Medical School; he was appointed Regius Professor of Medicine at Oxford, the only Canadian to achieve this honor. His patient list included Walt Whitman; Edward, Prince of Wales; Henry and William James; and Sir James Murray of *Oxford English Dictionary* fame. ("See that fine old man over there? He's Sir James Murray. The University pays me my stipend as Regius Professor to keep him alive till the *Dictionary* is finished," Osler once told a friend.) Upon being informed that Dr. Osler had been knighted, one of his patients, a twelve-year-old girl, said, "Too bad. They should have made him king."

Osler was born on July 12, 1849, in the wilds of the Ontario frontier. His father, Featherstone Lake Osler, was an English naval officer who had the distinction of being the man who turned down the position of naturalist aboard the *Beagle* just prior to its being offered to Charles Darwin. When the British government changed hands in 1832 and the Whigs came to power, Featherstone, a Tory, found himself without a ship. His naval career stymied, he decided to enter the ministry, fully expecting to lead a quiet life in an English country parish. Instead, as a result of his seafaring background, he was assigned to the British colonies north of Toronto, the most remote outpost in North America.

He and his wife Ellen went unwillingly; life in much of Canada was primitive, cold, bleak, and desperate. In England, the phrase "to go to Halifax" was slang for dying.

The Oslers, who began their new life in a tiny one-room shed that had originally housed a horse, persevered and were rewarded with success and social position that would have been unattainable had they stayed in England. William was the eighth child born to the family, and the youngest son. He planned to become a minister like his father, but his life turned when, at seventeen, a sporting injury forced him to spend a winter in bed. While he was convalescing, one of his teachers, Reverend William Arthur Johnson of Trinity College, introduced him to the world of natural science.

Johnson had a microscope, a rarity in western Canada in 1867. He and the school physician, Dr. James Bovell, who was treating Osler's leg, often met to examine slides that Osler had helped prepare during the long months of enforced rest. When his leg improved, the three went tramping through riverbanks and in marshes collecting shells, rocks, worms, algae, and other interesting specimens. Additionally, Bovell had one of the best medical libraries in Canada, and Osler spent many evenings with the doctor and his books. "That winter gave me a good first-hand acquaintance with the original works of many of the great masters," Osler wrote.

In 1868, Osler enrolled in the Toronto School of Medicine. He was drawn immediately to the potential of autopsy in the advancement of medicine—he would regularly eat his lunch in the dissection room. After two years at Toronto he switched to McGill, and at twenty-two he graduated. His senior thesis, a report based on twenty postmortems he had conducted, illustrated with specimen slides, was so impressive that the school urged him to stay on and teach, but he elected instead to continue his medical studies in Europe. He attended the University of London and afterward schools in Berlin and Vienna, where he was instructed by some of the finest teachers in Europe. When he returned home, McGill made him a full professor even though he was only twenty-five and younger than some of his students. They called him the Baby Professor.

Medical school salaries were small at McGill—Osler earned just over one thousand dollars a year—and professors were expected to supplement their incomes by becoming practicing physicians. In 1874, Osler took a job as physician in the smallpox ward at Montreal General Hospital. (This paid six hundred dollars. He spent the money on fifteen microscopes from Paris for his students.) Although by this time a vaccine was available, many in Montreal refused to take it, and hundreds died from the disease each year. "Doctors feared and hated smallpox almost as much as the general public did," wrote Osler's most recent biographer, Michael Bliss. "Being a smallpox doctor, a physician in the pesthouse, was to practice on the bottom rung of the medical ladder." Osler treated more than eighty patients over a two-year period, observing the disease in all of its stages, trying to help those for whom he knew there was no help. He performed many postmortems, and worked with patients with open sores in an attempt to forestall the ravaging effects of the disease. As a result, he caught smallpox himself, although he had previously been vaccinated, which saved him: "My attack was wonderfully light," he wrote. His old teacher, the Reverend Johnson, was not so lucky; he died from smallpox a few years later.

Over the course of the next ten years, Osler's reputation grew. He delivered papers at international conferences and published lectures. He traveled widely, keeping abreast of developments in Germany and spending time in Boston at the Harvard Medical School. He was held in such high esteem that when the chair in clinical medicine at the University of Pennsylvania fell vacant, the trustees unanimously invited Osler to accept the position.

‡

WHEN OSLER CAME TO AMERICA, medicine was just emerging from a dark age. Medical hygiene in particular had remained medieval in the

United States. Despite centuries of evidence, from men like Richard Mead, of the role that sanitary conditions could play in preventing infection and disease, physicians in nineteenth-century America were often stupendously unsanitary. They didn't wear masks or wash their hands or instruments between patients. Surgeons, whose chief experience in most cases had been treating war wounded, sometimes smoked cigars in the operating room. Death from infection was far more widespread than death from primary disease or injury. In fact, it was considered preferable to perform surgery in a patient's home, often on a table in the kitchen, rather than in a hospital, where postoperative infection was a far greater hazard.

Medical education reflected the practice of medicine. With the exception of a few high-grade schools, doctors received their training in glorified butcher shops. In most states, medical schools were privately operated and unlicensed, answerable to no standards but their own. There was little or no clinical training, and the bulk of learning was acquired through apprenticeships with practicing physicians—an ongoing source of cheap labor for the doctor.

As the nation grew, so did the demand for doctors. Since all it took to open a medical school was a hall and a group of physicians willing to lecture—with students required to buy tickets to those lectures—the profit potential in opening a medical school was substantial. Forty-seven medical schools opened between 1840 and 1875—more than the total number previously in existence—most with no academic admission requirements at all. Schools attracted brawlers and drunkards. It was not uncommon for some of these budding doctors to be illiterate. In 1870, the president of Harvard, the nation's finest medical school, wrote, "The ignorance and general incompetency of the average graduate of American Medical Schools, at the time when he receives the degree which turns him loose upon the community, is something horrible to contemplate."

Government was no help. American medical students were not much better off than Vesalius. Until 1830, the dissection of human corpses was illegal in every state in the union. Students had to sneak their own cadavers into school in order to study the body. Colleges sometimes put body snatchers on the payroll. Even after Massachusetts legalized autopsies in 1830, it took decades for dissection to become a widespread tool.

There were intermittent stabs at raising standards. In 1847, the respectable side of the medical profession created its own organization, the American Medical Association. As one of its first acts, the AMA set up a committee to study medical education. Soon afterward it issued a report advocating extending the school year from four months to eight, establishing a minimum requirement of seven faculty members of different specialities to open a medical school, observing more rigorous standards for admittance, and adopting a more intensive curriculum. The two medical schools that attempted to institute the recommended changes suffered a disastrous drop in enrollment and would have been forced to close had they not returned to lower standards.

The Civil War was a boon to the medical profession, but not to upgrading the practice of medicine. Demand for physicians overwhelmed supply. With virtually every physician and surgeon pressed into service, regardless of skill or training, even the maintenance of low professional standards became a laughable impossibility. Still, the war was not without its benefits. Doctors near the front often received more clinical experience after one battle than they would get for the rest of their lives. As with Galen at the gladiatorial school, the horrible wounds that modern weapons such as the lethal Minié-ball bullet produced gave many of them their first real opportunity to look inside the human body. But the mass-production cutting and stitching and the enormous numbers of amputations did little to advance science. When these doctors left the army, many turned to teaching as a means of increasing the often meager income that came from the treatment of patients.

Medical schools again boomed, more than tripling between 1860 and 1900. Competition for students became more acute. As had happened after the AMA report, anytime a school tried to raise its stan-

dards, it saw enrollment shrink as students switched to a less demanding curriculum. Thus student bodies became a mishmash of the motivated and the venal, the qualified and the dregs.

Writing in 1885, a member of the faculty at Rush Medical School
in Chicago described his class:

> The students were of all types. The refined well-educated,
> neatly dressed, well-to-do student, twenty-one to twenty-
> three, who had high ideals concerning his chosen career,
> might sit next to a poorly dressed, thirty-year-old man, who,
> likewise with high ideals, was working his way through col-
> lege. Or his neighbor might be a rougher specimen who, after
> twenty or thirty years as a teacher, druggist, traveling sales-
> man, or western farmer, had given up his former occupation
> because he believed he could make more money as a doctor.
> In my class of 1888, there were only seven men out of the one
> hundred thirty five who could show diplomas from colleges of
> literature, science, and arts.

In fact, of the over sixteen thousand medical students in the
United States in 1890, fewer than eight percent had college degrees.

Even in the better medical schools, such as those at Harvard or
Yale, the curriculum was overwhelmingly weighted toward lecture and
classroom study. It was possible even in these institutions to graduate
without ever having actually seen a patient. Other facilities were far
worse. As late as 1903, most medical education was, as reported by the
AMA's Council on Medical Education, "absolutely worthless," with
some schools "no better equipped to teach medicine than is a Turkish-
bath establishment or a barbershop."

It was William Osler, more than any other physician, who revolu-
tionized the practice of medicine as well as the way new doctors were
to be trained in America.

From his trips to Europe, Osler came to realize that the classroom lectures that dominated American medical education were no substitute for clinical experience. Medical students in Germany, Austria, France, and Britain spent a large portion of their training dealing directly with patients. Osler opposed the prevailing ethos in America that clinical training was harmful because students would rarely encounter diseases in textbook form, and many diseases might not be encountered at all. At the University of Pennsylvania, he immediately intensified the clinical training of his students.

Osler also placed heavy emphasis on dissection in his teaching curriculum. When there were insufficient cadavers for autopsy from the wards, he took groups of students to the Blockley Dead House of the Philadelphia Hospital. There, in the cavernous building where the city's unclaimed cadavers were deposited before burial, he dissected the corpses of charity cases. Osler worked while his students stood over

William Osler teaching at the Blockley Dead House

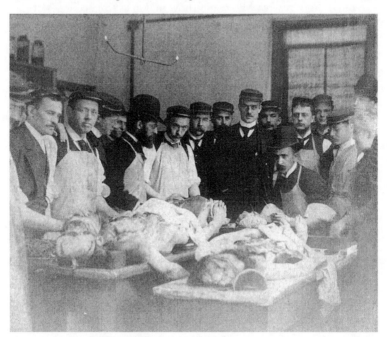

him, watching. No one wore masks or gloves, and Osler often contracted "cadaver warts," tubercular sores on his hands from contact with diseased tissue.

He kept voluminous records of the results of autopsies, particularly those of his own patients, thereby matching diagnosis against actual cause of death. Occasionally, Osler found himself faced with one of his own mistakes—a condition he had failed to detect or one disease that had masqueraded as another—but he never denied his errors or tried to rationalize them away.

Teaching and treatment were everything to him. Later in his life, when asked what he would like for an epitaph, he replied that he would prefer "He brought students into the wards."

Osler thrived in Pennsylvania, gaining a reputation as the finest professor of clinical medicine in America (a position for which, in truth, there was not that much competition). Still, his vast abilities had yet to be tapped by a system that largely continued to resist his approach and tenaciously clung to methods that didn't work. In order to fully mature into the teacher and clinician that he could be, Osler needed an institution that was prepared to allow him to set his own curriculum.

He got it in 1889.

‡

IN 1873, A WEALTHY Baltimore Quaker died. He was an abolitionist who had made a fortune, first in the wholesale grocery business, then in railroads. Upon his death, he created two trusts of $3.5 million each. The first was to be used to establish a premier university in his home city, the second to establish a hospital. Part of the plan was to create the finest medical school in America, with the most up-to-date teaching facilities, as a part of the university and served by the hospital. The Quaker's name was Johns Hopkins.

The university opened in 1876, but the hospital was not ready until 1885. The board of trustees was composed of other Quakers, and they refused to dip into the principal of the endowment. According to Hopkins's instructions, the hospital was "in construction and arrangement [to] compare favorably with any other institution of like character in this country or in Europe," so the project moved forward slowly.

Although the university began to organize the medical school in 1884, it took four years before the administration was ready to hire heads of the departments. Osler, "the best man to be found in the country," according to William Welch, head of the new medical school, was hired in early 1889 as physician-in-chief at the hefty sum of $5,000 per year, and then appointed Professor of the Theory and Practice of Medicine at the university. At forty years of age, William Osler had just secured what was certainly one of the most important medical positions in the United States.

Osler's counterpart as head of surgery, William Stewart Halstead, was even younger, with a reputation almost as towering, but his salary was only $2,000 per year. While investigating the potential of cocaine as a local anesthetic—the use of anesthesia during surgery was one the great advances of the second half of the nineteenth century—he and some other pioneers had sampled the product sufficiently to become full-blown addicts. Halstead had recently emerged from his second months-long hospital stay for treatment of his condition. Nobody talked about this to anyone outside the profession—even in 1889, people might have tended to shy away from a surgeon who was a drug addict—but the reduced salary reflected the increased risk the school felt it was assuming by hiring him.

(Halstead did all right in the end, though. Not only did he stay at Hopkins for over twenty years, he supplemented his income with a private practice in which his fees often ran to $10,000 or more per patient. And that was 1890 dollars—with no income tax. By comparison, Osler's top private fee was $3,000 to Frederick Pabst, the Milwaukee brewer, for a four-day house call. "I'm off to Milwaukee to put a bung in old Pabst," he told a friend.)

It took another four years to get things completely ready, but in

1893 the Johns Hopkins School of Medicine enrolled its first class, eighteen students, three of whom, in a groundbreaking development, were women.

The appointment of Osler turned out to be a brilliant move. Hopkins secured Osler's reputation, and Osler was the one teacher who made the school. He was knowledgeable, insightful, and funny. He had had so much experience in the wards that he could diagnose a patient from the doorway of his hospital room. Students worshipped him, forty or fifty trailing after him on his rounds.

Living in an age before photomicrography or any detailed documentation of many of the diseases and conditions that he needed to describe to his students, Osler enhanced his teaching with a command of language rare in scientists. For example, when describing mitral stenosis, a narrowing of the mitral valve extremely difficult to detect with just a stethoscope, he said, "Imagine that you are in Paris. It is three o'clock in the morning and the streets are empty. There is a dense fog in the air that descends all the way to the cobblestoned streets. Suddenly, a coach turns the corner. The sound of wheels on the cobblestones is mitral stenosis."

Osler combined his encyclopedic knowledge, clear thought, and language skills in a textbook, *Principles and Practice of Medicine*, which ran to over a thousand pages and was a compendium of his personal experience and all that he had seen in Europe and America. Almost from the date of publication in 1892, *Principles and Practice* became the seminal textbook of disease, diagnosis, and treatment. Osler personally supervised seven editions, and the book itself, updated by others, eventually ran to sixteen. It stayed in print until 1947 and was then reissued in 1968. *Principles and Practice of Medicine* was the primary textbook used in medical schools for decades and became almost as famous as its author.

Also in 1892, he married for the first time. His new wife was a widow, Grace Linzee Revere Gross, a direct descendant of Paul Revere. Three years later, the couple had a son, Edward Revere Osler. Between his Hopkins salary, fees for private patients, and royalties from the text-book, Osler, who despite his professional successes had never been able to save very much money, became a rich man. Finally he could afford to begin to indulge his other passion—book collecting.

‡

OSLER'S INTEREST IN DEVELOPING a library dated from his first introduction to James Bovell's collection of medical and classical works back in Toronto. During his later trips overseas, he had visited the private libraries of many European physicians and seen the breadth of their collections. He now used his new wealth to buy rare and unusual books detailing the history of the development of medical science, to the point where he became as well known to the famous booksellers of his age as to other doctors.

During breaks at Hopkins, he regularly traveled to Europe, buying books wherever he went. He bought a first-edition Vesalius, a first-edition Harvey, and rare editions of Galen and Avicenna. He collected Champier, Paracelsus, Aquapendente (Harvey's professor), and Colombo. He had books, manuscripts, documents, letters. He also had perhaps the most extensive collection of Servetus material in the world.

Osler had first become interested in Servetus when he came across a series of articles, by a Magdeburg pastor named Henri Tollin, in a German medical journal called *Virchow's Archiv für pathologische Anatomie und Physiologie.* Tollin, although a Protestant, defended Servetus and denounced his execution. Then, after Robert Willis published *Calvin and Servetus: A Study of an Important Epoch in the Early History of the Reformation* in 1877, Osler's interest intensified. He read and acquired Wotton and other books and articles written about Servetus and became particularly fascinated by the passage on pulmonary circulation.

Almost immediately he began to seek out a copy of *Christianismi Restitutio.* An original was out of the question, of course, but even the

Murr 1790 reprint turned out to be virtually unobtainable. Osler enjoyed joking about its rarity. When friends traveling to Europe asked if there was anything he'd like them to get for him, he would answer, "Oh yes. Could you pick me up a copy of *Christianismi Restitutio* while you're over there?" "Of course," they would reply, pleased that there was something their friend wanted that he didn't already have.

The story of Servetus's tragic life and obsession with pursuing truth as he saw it captured Osler's imagination, and his interest in Servetus became more than bibliographic. He began to mention Servetus in talks and letters and eventually became well known for his desire to help the Spanish physician secure his rightful place in medical history.

His advocacy, like that of Voltaire in a previous century, spurred a good deal of interest and attention, particularly in Europe. As the 350th anniversary of the execution approached, a number of Servetus supporters around the world thought to place a monument in Geneva to commemorate the occasion. A group was formed called the *Comité du Monument Michel Servet*, led by a French senator, Auguste Dide. Osler readily lent both his name and support to the effort.

The *Comité* moved with the glacial speed that *comité*s are wont to do, raising some money here and there and trying to decide what sort of monument could best glorify Servetus's memory. Hearing of the project, members of the Protestant clergy and other Calvin supporters in Geneva proposed a preemptive monument of their own. Their idea was a simple stone tablet placed in Champel. However, instead of the Plateau de Champel at the top of the hill, where the execution had actually occurred, the Calvinists proposed a more obscure spot farther down the hillside. The stone was to be set between two streets at the back of the hospital.

The city council of Geneva leapt at the plan, even renaming a tiny adjoining street "rue Michel Servet." On October 27, 1903, the stone was dedicated. At the ceremony, there was a good deal more said about Calvin's greatness than Servetus's martyrdom. The rear inscription on the stone stated:

*Duteous and grateful followers of Calvin our great
Reformer, yet condemning an error which was that
of his age, and strongly attached to liberty of
conscience according to the true principles of his
Reformation and the Gospel, we have erected this
expiatory monument. Oct. 27, 1903.*

The front inscription, the only place where Servetus's name and the fact that he was burned at the stake actually appear, was impossible to read without hiking twenty feet up a steep incline through grass and weeds. Almost no one, therefore, who passed the monument on the much more easily accessible rear side, would have the slightest idea what the duteous and grateful followers of Calvin were atoning for.

Members of the *Comité* were outraged and more determined than

The front side of the stone monument to Servetus in Geneva in 1908. Weeds largely obscure the monument today

ever to erect their own monument. They intended it to be a good deal more compassionate and far less forgiving of Calvin—to say nothing of placing it where people could see it. They finally raised the money they needed and commissioned a local artist, Clothilde Roch, to sculpt an affecting image of a wretched Servetus suffering in prison in the days before he was condemned, clothes in tatters, hands clasped in despair. The entire process took over three years, but finally, in late 1907, everything was ready.

When Dide and the *Comité* requested permission to mount the sculpture on a large pedestal and place it in the public square on the Plateau de Champel, however, the council harrumphed and said merely that it would consider the request. Then, after dithering about for months, in May 1908, just days before the *Comité*'s proposed dedication ceremony, the council rejected the sculpture on the grounds that the city had already dedicated a monument to Servetus.

Rather than fight it out in Geneva, Dide offered the sculpture to the town of Annemasse, four miles southeast of the city, just across the French border in Haute-Savoie. The mayor, Joseph Cursat, accepted instantly. The monument was placed in the main town square in front of city hall and dedicated on October 25, 1908.

The rectangular pedestal on which the sculpture was mounted contained an inscription on each side. One of them was from Voltaire:

> *The arrest of Servetus in Geneva, where he did neither*
> *publish nor dogmatize, hence he was not subject to its*
> *laws, has to be considered as a barbaric act and an*
> *insult to the Right of Nations.*

On another side was inscribed an excerpt from Servetus's letter to the Council of September 15:

> *I beg you, shorten please these deliberations. It is clear*
> *that Calvin for his pleasure wishes to make me rot in*

this prison. The lice eat me alive. My clothes are
torn and I have nothing for a change, no shirt, only
a worn out vest.

Dide said at the dedication, "Glorifying Servetus we honor...what is the most precious and the most noble in our human nature: a generosity of heart, independence of the spirit, heroism of convictions."

While all this was going on, the town fathers of Vienne, not to be outdone, decided to erect their own monument to Servetus, to be unveiled in August 1909. The town even sponsored the production of a particularly awful, overwrought play entitled *Michel Servet: episode dramatique en deux actes en vers (Michel Servet: A Dramatic Episode in Two Acts in Verse)*. The playwright, Fernand Raymond, had all the characters right, but was prone to throw people together for dramatic effect who had either never met or were not both present at the moment Raymond describes. Guillaume de Trie, for example, was placed in Vienne to personally accuse "Dr. Villeneuve," and Calvin was present

The original 1907 sculpture of Servetus in rags by Clothilde Roch. It was melted down for scrap by the Germans in World War II and replaced in 1960 by a facsimile cast from the original model.

at Champel to again denounce Servetus (in verse) just before the fire
was lit.

Despite all the public relations, the Vienne sponsors were unable
to raise nearly enough money for a monument. They then appealed to
known Servetus supporters in England and America.

Osler was by now in England. He had remained at Hopkins for
twelve years, but just after the turn of the century, he was offered the
chair of Regius Professor at Oxford, the highest honor that Great
Britain could bestow on a physician. With his Canadian roots, Osler
had always felt more English than American, and he accepted.

Of those whom the Vienne sponsors contacted, Osler was the only
one who agreed to help. He was made *Membre du Comité de Patronage*,
wrote letters of appeal to the *Lancet* and the *British Medical Journal*,
contributed a hefty sum of his own money to the project, and offered
to be present at the unveiling of the monument.

As the months stretched on and no work was done, the *Comité de
Patronage* tried to persuade Osler to underwrite the entire project. In
June 1909, they wrote, "Please excuse our insistence. We were hoping
that you could find some more money in England and America. We are
very embarrassed to have to ask." Two months later, they wrote, "There
is nothing more on the monument to Servetus at Vienne. The statue is
ordered, the artist is ready to work...but the money is not there."
Eventually, Osler, nobody's fool, washed his hands of the affair. As a
Christmas card that year, he sent many of his friends a photograph of
the sculpture on the monument at Annemasse.

Vienne finally finished its monument in 1911. Osler was invited to
attend the unveiling but declined.

‡

DURING THE PERIOD WHEN he was actively supporting the monument efforts, Osler immersed himself in historical records to prepare a
lecture on Servetus. In April 1908, he traveled to Vienna to see the

Szent-Iványi copy at the national library, and in December of the same year went to the Bibliothèque Nationale to view the Colladon copy. While he was in Paris, he read trial transcripts and city records and corresponded regularly with the bibliophile L. L. Mackall, who was eventually to uncover the truth about Mead's ownership of the Colladon copy and his role (or lack of it) in the commissioning of the reprint. The more Osler read, the more fascinated he became. "His lectures on Judicial Astrology scandalized all the Faculties," he wrote to Mackall, "and they had to make it a Parlement (de Paris) matter."

Curiously, during the bulk of his research, he was unaware of the Edinburgh copy, even though it had been thirty years since it had been discovered on the shelves and Willis and Turner had published an article on it shortly afterward. In a letter in 1908, he noted that he had gone to Vienna, "anxious to see the copy of *Christianismi Restitutio* . . . in which for the first time lesser circulation is described. This is one of only two copies in existence." He would remain ignorant of Calvin's edition for another year, until David Cuthbertson, an associate librarian at Edinburgh, prepared a small book on Servetus and the third copy.

Osler had continued to search "high and low" for the 1790 reprint with no success. Even the world-famous booksellers with whom he regularly did business, such as Maggs Brothers and Bernard Quaritch, had been unable to locate an available copy. It wasn't until 1910, when a friend and fellow collector, J. F. Payne, the Harveian librarian at the Royal College of Physicians at Oxford, died and bequeathed him his copy, that Osler finally had his book.

So enormous had his collection become, over ten thousand books and manuscripts in all, that for the last ten years of his life, Osler worked on a massive annotated listing, the *Bibliotheca Osleriana*. The completed catalog ran to almost eight hundred pages in folio. By the time of his death in 1919, Osler owned the Murr reprint, both a genuine first edition and a counterfeit copy of *De Trinitatis Erroribus*,

Syrups, a first-edition *Geography,* a first-edition Pagnini Bible, and a copy of almost everything that had been published about Servetus in any language. He left his entire library to McGill University.

✝

IN MAY 1909, Osler completed his research and gave his lecture on Servetus at the Hopkins Historical Club in Baltimore. It was published in pamphlet form that same year. He would later refine the lecture and deliver it regularly to medical students in both America and England.

Osler's lecture recounted the story of Servetus's life and detailed both the significance of his scientific discovery and the principles upon which he based his philosophy. Osler very specifically attempted to portray the man as a whole rather than depicting him as a symbol or victim, not glossing over the flaws in his personality or the lapses in his critical thinking. He opposed the use of the Servetus case for political purposes. After the Vienne unveiling, a friend sent him some newspaper articles about the event. "Thanks for your cuttings about Servetus, over whom they seem to have poured a good deal of oleo-margarine," he wrote back in a letter. "The difficulty is that the liberals use him as a stick with which to beat the clericals."

Osler was one of the few champions of Servetus who was himself a Protestant and an admirer of Calvin. In the lecture, he said:

> Much scorn has been heaped upon the great reformer, and one cannot but regret that a man of such magnificent achievements should have been dragged into a miserable heresy hunt like a common inquisitor...But let the long record of a self-denying life, devoted in an evil generation to the highest and the best, wipe for all reasonable men this one blot. Let us, if we may judge him at all, do so as a man, not as a demi-god. We cannot defend him, let us not condemn him.

Still, Osler was most responsible, even more than Voltaire, for gaining some measure of credit, at least among medical historians, for Servetus and his discovery.

> The modern world [is finally recognizing] the merits of one of the strangest figures on the rich canvas of the sixteenth century. The wandering Spanish scholar, the stormy disputant, the anatomical pro-sector, the mystic dreamer of a restored Christianity, the discoverer of one of the fundamental facts of physiology, has come at last to his own. There are those, I know, who feel that perhaps more than justice has been done; but in a tragic age Servetus played an unusually tragic part, and the pathos of his fate appeals strongly to us... he remained faithful unto death to what he believed was the *Truth*.

Osler's son Edward was killed in the trenches of France in 1917. He was only twenty-two years old. A number of Osler's friends were serving in the medical corps when Edward was wounded by shrapnel, and they tried desperately to save him. When he died, they hesitated before informing Osler. He was sixty-eight and in weakening health, and his son was the most important thing in his life. Two years later, a shattered William Osler was dead.

With Osler gone, Michael Servetus once more dipped below the waves of history. ‡

THE GROWTH OF human knowledge has always depended on individuals of immense talent and passion who have struggled to evoke fundamental change in the way we see our world. Those who succeeded, like Einstein, Newton, Shakespeare, or Picasso, have become our most respected figures. We often forget, however, that in many cases those changes we now so unconditionally embrace were resisted fiercely by the reigning orthodoxies of their times, and that many of those whom we now consider visionaries were ridiculed and reviled until the force of their vision overwhelmed the concentrated ignorance around them.

But there were also those, no less brilliant, who did not succeed, whose ideas could not take root before they were crushed. Their vision and passion were no less intense, and what they had to say no less vital to the human spirit. It was only circumstance that separated them from the others.

Michael Servetus was one of those great, overlooked figures. With kinder turns of fate, he might well have changed the course of history in not one but two fields—first, by ushering in a simpler, purer, and more generous Christianity and, second, by prompting a more curious and effective medical science. Instead, Michael Servetus was hunted down and burned at the stake.

His execution marked a turning point in the quest for freedom of expression. Although thousands had been executed for heresy before him and others would be executed after, the extraordinary nature of both Servetus the man and Servetus the representative of honest and passionate dissent rippled through Europe in ways that his enemies had never foreseen.

Servetus's detractors, and indeed some of his supporters, have denounced him as an extremist—obsessed, inflexible, and blind to the forces around him. Yet it was these very qualities that compelled his refusal to compromise his beliefs even unto death. And it was that refusal, in turn, that drove his enemies to drop their mask of righteousness and exert the full force of repression to silence him. And so the Servetus trial stands with other, similar affairs like the Dreyfus case and the Scopes trial as a testament to courage of conscience. These cases become starting points at which other champions of justice and fairness may draw a line and say, "This was wrong."

Even so, had he lived just a century earlier, Servetus might have ended up a forgotten figure, or at best a myth. The difference for him was the development of printing and the spread of books. The three copies of *Christianismi Restitutio* that survived virtually became surrogates for their author, going into hiding and relying on secret supporters for protection until, centuries later, they could be safely read and appreciated. The book kept alive the spirit of the man and the evidence of his genius, so that other men of similar spirit and genius—Leibniz, Voltaire, Priestley, Jefferson, and Osler—might draw inspiration from Servetus's unsparing quest for truth. Today, 450 years later, we are richer for it.

✠

THE UNIVERSITY OF PARIS Medical School building where Servetus followed Vesalius as Guinter's assistant still stands on the rue de Bûcherie. It is now owned by the city of Paris and is used as a center to provide various public services to the populace. The surgical theater in which both men performed the dissections that propelled anatomy into the modern age is now part of a travel agency for senior citizens. The room is clean, freshly painted white, and bare save for a circular display stand in the middle containing vacation brochures.

In Geneva, in a park just outside the walls of the old city, there is a famous monument to the Reformation, to which thousands of tourists make a pilgrimage every year. In the center are four figures, each about fifteen feet high, cut from pinkish stone. Second from the left, slighter taller than Farel to his right and Knox and Beza to his left, is the dominant figure of Calvin, glowering down on visitors. There are stone murals to either side depicting other heroes of Protestantism, and there are two large blocks of stone at either end, one inscribed *Luther* and the other *Zwingli*. The monument is spotlessly clean, and a small moat has been set in front to prevent anyone from giving in to the temptation to add a touch of graffiti.

On the walls of the Hôtel de Ville (city hall) in the center of the old city is a series of murals depicting the stages of Genevan history, the most prominent being that which commemorates Calvin's Geneva welcoming the flood of refugees from Catholic oppression in the mid-sixteenth century.

Streets in Geneva are named for the city's heroes and luminaries. There is a rue Jean Calvin, of course, and a rue Guillaume Farel, both in the center of the old city. There is, however, no rue Berthelier or rue Perrin, even though each of those families was instrumental in overthrowing the rule of Savoy and gaining the independence without which Calvin's efforts at reform would have been impossible. In fact, there is little evidence at all that a great and brave struggle for freedom ever took place here. For most visitors, seeing only the huge sculpture of Calvin or the murals on the Hôtel de Ville, it would seem that Genevan history began in 1536.

The stone tablet memorializing Servetus still stands. It is so well hidden amidst untended trees and bushes that in the reference volume in Geneva's own tourism agency, it is called "the lost monument." To discover Servetus's name still requires the twenty-foot hike up the steep hill through the weeds. The rue Michel Servet survives as well. It is a grimy, two-block-long thoroughfare running down from the Plateau de Champel, past a gas station and the backs of some buildings, toward the hospital. Underneath Servetus's name reads simply, "Spanish physician." The Plateau de Champel is now a small public park. There is a fountain with a number of signs that forbid bathing, and it is advisable to keep to the paths because local residents assiduously ignore the many admonitions to curb their dogs.

After the fall of France in World War II, the monument to Servetus in Annemasse was taken down by order of a mayor appointed by the Vichy government. After numerous efforts by the Roch family in Switzerland to buy back the sculpture, it was eventually melted down for scrap the following year. The stone panels were destroyed. In 1956, the town organized a committee to reerect the monument. Two years later, 411,500 francs had been raised, most of it from area residents. Two years after that, the new monument was ready. The mock-up that Clothilde Roch had used as the model for the original had been retained by her family, and this was used to recast the sculpture. Three of the four panels were recut exactly as the originals. The rear panel, however, which had previously contained the quote from Voltaire, was replaced by one that read, "Erected for the first time in 1908, given over to the Germans in 1942, this statue was reestablished by public subscription and dedicated once more on 4 September 1960." It now stands, as had the original, in an open, attractive plaza in front of city hall.

Voltaire's château lies just outside the center of Ferney-Voltaire, as the town is now named, a small, toney little hamlet, with shops such as La Lingerie and Rodier lining the main street. The château is a museum and the grounds are often used for plays or concerts. On the tour, the Calas case is described in detail, but there is no mention of Servetus. The mountainside leading down to Lake Geneva is covered with tall pine trees rather than the vineyards of Voltaire's time, so it is no longer possible to see the city or the Plateau de Champel from the windows.

The Unitarian Church in the United States is small, with only about 200,000 active members, but it is an accepted and vibrant part of American religious life. Michael Servetus is considered the spiritual inspiration for the movement, and almost every important history of Unitarianism begins with his story.

The Unitarian community in Cluj, Transylvania, continues to persevere.

‡

HISTORY IS AN OCEAN that books help us to navigate. It is the permanence of the printed word that has allowed ideas to travel from place to place, from age to age. It is easy to dismiss the sixteenth century as the distant past, but Servetus, Calvin, Luther, Erasmus, Charles, Francis, and the rest were dealing with the forces of an emerging technology much as we are today. The power of unleashed expression is not unique to the electronic age.

Today, the three copies of *Christianismi Restitutio* can still be found at the Österreichische Nationalbibliothek in Vienna, the Bibliothèque Nationale in Paris, and the library of the University of Edinburgh. ‡

BIBLIOGRAPHIC   NOTES

FOR A FIGURE as ignored by history as Michael Servetus, there is a
wealth of material to be had, both by and about him. In 1953 the theological historian Roland Bainton published *Hunted Heretic: The Life and
Death of Michael Servetus (1511–1553)*, a biography on which he
worked, on and off, for thirty years. Marian Hillar, in 1997, published the much more comprehensive *The Case of Michael Servetus
(1511–1553): The Turning Point in the Struggle for Freedom of Conscience*.
Hillar, a Polish expatriate and Socinian scholar, is vitriolic in his denunciations of both Calvin and the Catholic Church, but there is no
doubting the depth of his research. Still, perhaps the most useful work
on Servetus remains the 1877 *Servetus and Calvin* by Robert Willis,
M.D., which provides an extraordinary record of the trial at Geneva,
taken from city records, and that of Vienne, from the transcription by
l'Abbé d'Artigny in 1749. Further records of the trial are provided in *An
Impartial History of Michael Servetus, Burnt Alive at Geneva for Heresie*
penned anonymously in 1724 by an author whose identity was never
firmly established, although his information was confirmed by later
scholarship.

Lesser works abound. Servetus has fascinated scholars for centuries, and there is no shortage of commentary on his life and work.
Osler's lecture has been transcribed and published, and there are articles and citations too numerous to mention. Of particular utility to us
were David Cuthbertson's *A Tragedy of the Reformation*, a history of the

Edinburgh copy of *Christianismi Restitutio*; John F. Fulton's *Michael Servetus: Humanist and Martyr*; *Michael Servetus and the Discovery of the Circulation of the Blood* by John Knott; and *Michael Servetus, His Life and Teachings* by Carl Theophilus Odhner.

As for Servetus's own work, there is an equal wealth of sources. The Unitarian scholar Earl Morse Wilbur translated both *Errors of the Trinity* and *Two Dialogues on the Trinity* in their entirety, and these provide the most concise and revealing source for insights into Servetus's points of view about the nature of God, His role in our lives, the sanctity of the Scriptures, and the distortions perpetrated on them by one Catholic or Protestant theologian after another. These arguments, set down when Servetus was nineteen, remained the cornerstone of his beliefs for his entire life. Charles D. O'Malley translated, in whole or in part, a number of Servetus's other works, among them the *Syrups*, the *Geography*, the *Apology for Fuchs*, and, most importantly, the section of *Christianismi Restitutio* in which pulmonary circulation was first discussed.

With the exception of the original *Christianismi Restitutio*, copies of Servetus's actual work are also widely available. We were fortunate to live within a half hour's drive of Yale University, which, between the Beinecke and the Whitney/Cushing Medical Library, has one of the best Servetus collections in the world.

As for Servetus's nemesis, John Calvin, the range of available material is obviously even greater. In addition to Émile Domergue's compendious seven-volume biography *Jean Calvin*, there are a number of one-volume works that were quite useful. Hugh Y. Reyburn's vastly underrated 1914 study, *John Calvin: His Life, Letters, and Work*, was of particular utility in that the author walked a middle ground between the fawning apologies of Calvin's supporters and the blind denunciations of his detractors. Among the former, T. H. L. Parker's *John Calvin: A Biography* provided a good deal of personal history, while John T. McNeill's *The History and Character of Calvinism* was an excellent source of philosophic and theological background information. Quirinus Breen's

John Calvin: A Study in French Humanism provided insights into Calvin's formative years. Calvin's own work was invaluable, of course. Virtually everything he wrote has been translated. In addition to *Institutes of the Christian Religion,* we made great use of *The Register of the Company of Pastors in Geneva in the Time of Calvin,* translated by Philip E. Hughes, a detailed record of city ordinances and legislative and judicial decisions from 1541 through 1566, which also contains a large section on the Servetus affair.

For the origins and early days of printing, the British Library publishes a number of useful works, including S. H. Steinberg's *Five Hundred Years of Printing* and *The Gutenberg Bible* by Martin Davies. While just about every work on the history of books, reading, or printing contains some amount of material on Aldus, Paul Grendler's monograph *Aldus Manutius: Humanist, Teacher, and Printer* and Martin Lowry's *The World of Aldus Manutius: Business and Scholarship in Renaissance Venice* paint the most vivid pictures of both the man and the world in which he toiled.

As to the two ferocious adversaries Charles V and Francis I, three works stand above the rest—William Robertson's brilliant and timeless classic *The History of the Reign of the Emperor Charles V,* which has not been matched in over two centuries; R. J. Knecht's *Renaissance Warrior and Patron: The Reign of Francis I;* and Francis Hackett's *Francis the First: First Gentleman of France.* Of the latter two, the first is notable for its detail and the second for its wit and tone, which capture uncannily the spirit of an absolute monarch who often thought and behaved like a petulant eight-year-old.

The genesis and growth of the Unitarian movement were chronicled in depth by Earl Morse Wilbur in *Our Unitarian Heritage* in 1925. More recently, David Bumbaugh, a professor at Meadville-Lombard University in Chicago, has provided a shorter but eminently readable volume entitled *Unitarian Universalism: A Narrative History.* The work of Conrad Wright, professor emeritus at Harvard, is always worth reading, as is *The Epic of Unitarianism,* edited by David Parke, a compilation of excerpts by the most prominent figures of the movement. For an overall picture of theological dissent and the development of liberal Christian ideology, see J. M. Robertson's excellent *A History of Freethought: Ancient and Modern to the Period of the French Revolution.*

An overview of the history of medicine can be found in Fielding H. Garrison's *An Introduction to the History of Medicine.* For the evolution of medical education in the United States, see *American Medical Schools and the Practice of Medicine: A History* by William G. Rothstein and *The Education of American Physicians: Historical Essays* edited by Ronald L. Numbers. For earlier medicine, Charles D. O'Malley's *Andreas Vesalius of Brussels* paints a vivid portrait of the great anatomist and his times.

For the life of William Osler, two biographies rule the field. They are Michael Bliss's recent *William Osler: A Life in Medicine,* which, as the title implies, leans heavily toward Osler's professional life, and Harvey Cushing's massive 1925 Pulitzer Prize–winning *The Life of Sir William Osler.* Cushing, a brilliant brain surgeon in his own right, undertook the project to honor his friend and compiled virtually every letter, note, and scrap of paper written by, to, or about Osler, producing a some-times elephantine chronicle. Still, wading through Cushing's work often provides glimpses into Osler's character, perspective, and sense of humor that the shorter book cannot. Osler's original work, the famed textbook *Principles and Practice of Medicine,* but also *A Way of Life* and, of course, his essay on Servetus, are useful not simply for content but also for the feel they provide for a man who was a mix of Victorian gentleman and single-minded reformer. ‡

SELECTED BIBLIOGRAPHY

Aiton, E. J., *Leibniz: A Biography* (Bristol, England, 1985; Adam Hilger).

Aldridge, A. Owen, *Voltaire and the Century of Light* (Princeton, N.J., 1975; Princeton University Press)

Allen, Gay Wilson, *Waldo Emerson* (New York, 1981; Viking)

Bainton, Roland, H., *Erasmus of Christendom,* (New York, 1969; Charles Scribner's Sons)

——, *Here I Stand: A Life of Martin Luther* (New York, 1950; Abingdon-Cokesbury Press)

——, *Hunted Heretic: The Life and Death of Michael Servetus (1511–1553)* (Boston, 1953; Beacon Press)

Beales, Derek, *Joseph II* (Cambridge, 1987; Cambridge University Press)

Bell, Mary I. M., *A Short History of the Papacy* (New York, 1921; Dodd, Mead)

Beloff, Max, *The Age of Absolutism* (London, 1954; Hutchinson.)

Benson, George, A Brief Account of Calvin's Burning of Servetus (London, 1743; *The Old Whig*)

Blanning, T. C. W., *Joseph II* (London, 1994; Longmans)

Bliss, Michael, *William Osler: A Life in Medicine* (London, 1999; Oxford University Press)

Boorstin, Daniel, *The Discoverers* (New York, 1983; Random House)

Breen, Quirinus, *John Calvin: A Study in French Humanism* (Hamden, Conn., 1968; Archon Books)

Brodie, Fawn M., *Thomas Jefferson: An Intimate Portrait* (New York, 1974; W. W. Norton)

Brooks, Richard A., *Voltaire and Leibniz* (Geneva, 1964; Librarie Droz)

Bumbaugh, David, *Unitarian Universalism: A Narrative History* (Chicago, 2001; Meadville-Lombard University Press)

Calvin, John, *Selections from Institutes of the Christian Religion*, trans. Henry Beveridge (Chicago, 1952; Encyclopaedia Britannica)

——, *The Catholic Encyclopedia* (New York, 1914; D. Appleton)

Chauffpie, Jaques George de, *The Life of Servetus* (London, 1771; R. Baldwin)

Coq, Dominique, *Le Parangon du Bibliophile Français: Le Duc de la Vallière et sa Collection* (Paris, 1988; Promidis)

Cushing, Harvey, *The Life of Sir William Osler* (Oxford, 1925; Clarendon Press)

Cuthbertson, David, *A Tragedy of the Reformation* (Edinburgh, 1912; Oliphant, Anderson & Ferrier)

Davies, Martin, *The Gutenberg Bible* (London, 1995; British Library)

De Rosa, Peter, *Vicars of Christ: The Dark Side of the Papacy* (New York, 1988; Crown)

Drummond, William H., *The Life of Michael Servetus* (London, 1848; John Chapman)

Duffy, Eamon, *Saints and Sinners: A History of the Popes* (New Haven, 1997; Yale University Press)

Durant, Will, and Ariel Durant, *The Story of Civilization* (New York, 1957; Simon & Schuster)

Faludy, George, *Erasmus* (New York, 1970; Stein & Day)

Fulton, John F. *Michael Servetus: Humanist and Martyr* (New York, 1953; Herbert Reichner)

Gargett, Graham, *Voltaire and Protestantism* (Oxford, 1980; Voltaire Foundation)

Garrison, Fielding H., *An Introduction to the History of Medicine* (Philadelphia, 1914; W. B. Saunders)

Glendinning, Victoria, *Jonathan Swift: A Portrait* (New York, 1998; Henry Holt)

Grendler, Paul, *Aldus Manutius: Humanist, Teacher, and Printer* (Providence, R.I., 1984; John Carter Brown Library)

Hackett, Francis, *Francis the First: First Gentleman of France* (Garden City, N.Y., 1935; Country Life Press)

Hale, John, *The Civilization of Europe in the Renaissance* (New York, 1994; Atheneum)

Harvey, William, *On the Motion of the Heart and Blood in Animals*, trans. Robert Willis (Frankfurt, 1847)

Hemmeter, John C., *Michael Servetus: Discoverer of Pulmonary Circulation* (Leyde, 1915; E. J. Brill)

Hillar, Marian, *The Case of Michael Servetus (1511–1553): The Turning Point in the Struggle for Freedom of Conscience* (Lewisburg, N.Y., 1997; Edwin Mellen Press)

Hohnel, Ludwig von, *Discovery of Lakes Rudolf and Stephanie: A Narrative of Count Samuel Teleki's Exploring and Hunting Expedition in Eastern Equatorial Africa in 1887 and 1888* (London, 1894; Longmans, Green)

Holt, Anne, *A Life of Joseph Priestley* (London, 1931; Oxford University Press)

Hunter, Michael (ed.), *Robert Boyle by Himself and His Friends, with a Fragment of William Wotton's Lost Life of Boyle* (London, 1994; William Pickering)

An Impartial History of Michael Servetus, Burnt Alive at Geneva for Heresie (London, 1724; printed for Aaron Ward)

Kelly, W. A., *The Library of Lord George Douglas* (Cambridge, 1997; Libri Pertinentes Publications)

Kesten, Hermann, *Copernicus and His World* (New York, 1945; Roy Publishers)

Knecht, R. J., *Renaissance Warrior and Patron: The Reign of Francis I* (Cambridge, 1994; Cambridge University Press)

Knott, John, *Michael Servetus and the Discovery of the Circulation of the Blood* (New York, 1911; William Wood)

Koch, Adrienne, and William Peden, *The Life and Selected Writings of Thomas Jefferson* (New York, 1944; Modern Library)

La Vallière, Louis César de la Baume Le Blanc, duc de, *Catalogue les Livres de la Bibliothèque de feu monsieur le duc de La Vallière*, 3 vol. (Paris, 1783; Guillaume de Bure)

——, *Prix des Livres de la Bibliothèque de Monsieur le duc de La Vallière* (Paris, 1784; Guillaume de Bure)

Lázár, István, *Transylvania: A Short History* (Budapest, 1997; Corvina)

Livermore, Harold, *A History of Spain* (New York, 1958; Farrar, Straus & Cudahy)

Lowry, Martin, *The World of Aldus Manutius: Business and Scholarship in Renaissance Venice* (Ithaca, 1979; Cornell University Press)

Mackall, Leonard Leopold, *Servetus Notes* (New York, 1919; P. B. Hoeber)

Manchester, William, *A World Lit Only by Fire: The Medieval Mind and the Renaissance: Portrait of an Age* (Boston, 1992; Little, Brown)

Manguel, Alberto, *A History of Reading* (New York, 1996; Viking)

McBrien, Richard P., *Lives of the Popes: The Pontiffs from Saint Peter to John Paul II* (San Francisico, 1997; HarperSanFrancisco)

McNeill, John T., *The History and Character of Calvinism* (Oxford, 1954; Oxford University Press)

Meade, Richard H., *In the Sunshine of Life: A Biography of Dr. Richard Mead 1673–1754* (Philadelphia, 1974; Dorrance)

Numbers, Ronald L. (ed.), *The Education of American Physicians: Historical Essays* (Berkeley, 1980; University of California Press)

Odhner, Carl Theophilus, *Michael Servetus, His Life and Teachings* (Philadelphia, 1910; J. B. Lippincott)

O'Malley, Charles Donald, *Andreas Vesalius of Brussels 1514–1564* (Berkeley, 1964; University of Californis Press)

Orcutt, William Dana, *The Kingdom of Books* (Boston, 1937; Little, Brown)

Osler, William, *A Way of Life* (1913 reprinted Philadelphia, 1992; J. B. Lippincott)

——, *Bibliotheca Osleriana* (Oxford, 1929; Clarendon Press)

——, *Michael Servetus* (Oxford, 1909; Oxford University Press)

——, *Principles and Practice of Medicine* (New York, 1892; D. Appleton)

Parke, David (ed.), *The Epic of Unitarianism: Original Writings From the History of Liberal Religion* (Boston, 1985; Skinner House Books)

Parker, T. H. L., *John Calvin: A Biography* (Philadelphia, 1975; Westminster Press)

Pepys, Samuel, *Diaries* (New York, 1955; Heritage Press)

Priestley, Joseph, *The Autobiography of Joseph Priestley* (Teaneck, N.J., 1970; Fairleigh Dickinson University Press)

Randall, Willard S., *Thomas Jefferson: A Life* (New York, 1993; Henry Holt)

Reddaway, W. F. et al. (eds.), *The Cambridge History of Poland (to 1696)* (Cambridge, 1950; Cambridge University Press.)

The Register of the Company of Pastors of Geneva in the Time of Calvin, trans. Philip E. Hughes (Grand Rapids, Mich., 1966; William E. Eerdmans Publishing)

Reyburn, Hugh, *John Calvin: His Life, Letters, and Work* (London, 1914; Hodder & Stoughton)

Roberts, J. M., *A History of Europe* (London, 1996; Allen Lane)

Robertson, J. M., *A History of Freethought: Ancient and Modern to the Period of the French Revolution* (London, 1936; Watts.)

Robertson, William, *The History of the Reign of the Emperor Charles V* (London, 1772; Strahan & Cadell)

Rothstein, William G., *American Medical Schools and the Practice of Medicine: A History* (New York, 1987; Oxford University Press)

Sanders, Joan, *La Petite: The Life of Louise de Lavallière* (Boston, 1959; Houghton Mifflin)

Sedgwick, Henry, *Ignatius Loyola: An Attempt at an Impartial Biography* (New York, 1923; Macmillan)

Servetus, Michael, *Christianismi Restitutio and Other Writings*, trans. Charles D. O'Malley (Birmingham, 1989; Classics of Medicine Library)

——, *The Two Treatises of Servetus on the Trinity*, trans. Earl Morse Wilbur (Cambridge, 1932; Harvard University Press)

Steinberg, S. H., *Five Hundred Years of Printing*, ed. John Trevitt (London and New Castle, Del., 1996; British Library & Oak Knoll Press)

Stephen, Leslie et al., *Dictionary of National Biography* (London, 1885–1901; Smith, Elder.)

Tallentyre, S. G., *The Life of Voltaire* (New York, 1905; G. P. Putnam's Sons)

Temkin, Owsei, Was Servetus Influenced by Ibn an-Nafis? (Baltimore, 1940; *Bulletin of the Institute of the History of Medicine*)

Tuchman, Barbara, *The March of Folly* (New York, 1884; Alfred A. Knopf)

Wedgwood, C. V., *The Thirty Years' War* (London, 1938; Jonathan Cape)

White, Andrew Dickson, *A History of the Warfare of Science with Theology in Christendom* (New York, 1905; D. Appleton)

Wilbur, Earl Morse, *Our Unitarian Heritage* (Boston, 1925; Beacon Press)

Willis, Robert, *Servetus and Calvin: A Study of an Important Epoch in the Early History of the Reformation* (London, 1877; Henry S. King)

Winship, George Parker, *Printing in the Fifteenth Century* (Philadelphia, 1940; University of Pennsylvania Press)

Wotton, William, *Reflections upon Ancient and Modern Learning* (London, 1694; J. Leake for Peter Buck)

——, *Reflections upon Ancient and Modern Learning*, 2nd ed. (London, 1697; J. Leake for Peter Buck)

A C K N O W L E D G M E N T S

We had a good deal of help in writing this book. Many people took the time to speak at length with us, both to help us find obscure references and to provide background that was not available in print. Miriam Mandelbaum at the New York Public Library first set us on the trail. Toby Appel, the librarian at the Cushing/Whitney Medical Library at Yale, and Mona Florea, her assistant, were consistently patient, enthusiastic, and invaluable. Time after time, they helped us find what we were looking for, even when we weren't sure ourselves, and let us have access to an amazing variety of materials, from a genuine first edition of *De Trinitatis Erroribus* to the catalog of the Lavallière auction, complete with the almost impossible-to-find price list. At the Beinecke Rare Book and Manuscript Library, curators Christa Sammons and Vincent Giroud were always willing to take the time to fill in a blank for us, send us in the right rather than wrong direction, or translate a passage.

As for Unitarian history, John Tolley and Dean Grodzins at Meadville-Lombard University were generous with their time and knowledge, as was the Reverend Barbara Fast at the Unitarian congregation of Westport. Dr. Géza Jeszenszky, the Hungarian ambassador to the United States, and a former professor of history, was of enormous assistance in helping us trace both the Teleki and Szent-Iványi families. As to the former, Paul Teleki gave us further details of his remarkable family, and for the latter, István Szent-Iványi, a member of the Hungarian parliament, and his sister Ilona helped us trace the history of theirs.

On the book front, we are deeply indebted to Geneviève Guilleminot-Chrétien at the Bibliothèque Nationale de France for her help in learning more about the Duc de Lavallière and Joseph Van Praet, but mostly for allowing us a private viewing of the Colladon copy of *Christianismi Restitutio*. And without the help of Claudia Oudey and François Giraud of Room Y at the BNF, we would never have had the opportunity of speaking with Mme. Guilleminot.

Also in Paris, the staff of the Village Voice bookshop, specifically Odile Hellier (owner), Michael Neal (wizard of the Bibliothèque Nationale), and Aude Samarut and Barbara Bessat-Lelarge (ways and means of the French post office), obtained photoreproductions for us in the face of enormous odds. Without Don Bell ("Don the Bookman") none of it would have been possible.

Monika Kiegler at the National Library of Austria took the time to send rare material on the Teleki copy of *Christianismi Restitutio*, as did Jean Archibald at the Edinburgh University Library for the Douglas copy. Murray Simpson, director of Special Collections at the National Library of Scotland, helped us with the history of the Douglas family, as did David Wright of the Faculty of Divinity at the University of Edinburgh.

We'd like to include a special thank-you to Lewis Leist, who was kind enough to send a book that was very enlightening on the life and times of Gutenberg. Robert Fleck of Oak Knoll Books was quite helpful in filling in details of the early history of printing, and Ross King helped us understand the fate of the great aristocratic libraries of the sixteenth and seventeenth centuries. Christine Ruggere at Johns Hopkins helped with the evolution of medical education in America, and Dr. Albert Klainer contributed some priceless anecdotes about William Osler.

Our editor at Broadway Books, Gerry Howard, not only immediately saw that this was a good story, but more importantly envisioned the telling as we did. He shared our enthusiasm and helped guide us to producing a better book. Thanks also to Jay Crosby at Broadway, who was consistently patient and helpful. Our agent, Jed Mattes, let two strangers walk into his office one day, then sat with us for two hours discussing a project that he could not have known would come to fruition. Not only has he always been supportive, but he is a thoroughly kind and decent man. As Erasmus said of Froben, he is a man with whom you can play dice in the dark.

Finally, we want to thank our daughter, Emily (age ten as this is written), who was patient and understanding during a period when she did not get the attention she deserved, and who helped her parents resolve an embarrassing number of fights about just whose prose was more turgid or whose research more thorough.

INDEX

ILLUSTRATION CREDITS

Frontispiece—Servetus woodcut (Cushing/Whitney Medical Library, Yale University)
Erotic illustration from the Hypnerotomachia (Beinecke Rare Book and Manuscript Library, Yale University)
Dolphin anchor logo (Beinecke Rare Book and Manuscript Library, Yale University)
Erasmus (Cushing/Whitney Medical Library, Yale University)
Francis I (Réunion des Musées Nationaux/Art Resource, NY)
Marguerite d'Angoulême (Réunion des Musées Nationaux/Art Resource, NY)
Charles V at 16 (Réunion des Musées Nationaux/Art Resource, NY)
Coronation at Bologna (Beinecke Rare Book and Manuscript Library, Yale University)
Calvin drawing by student (Centre d'Iconographie genevoise, Collections Bibliothèque publique et universitaire, Genève)
Map from the Geography (Cushing/Whitney Medical Library, Yale University)
Vesalius (Cushing/Whitney Medical Library, Yale University)
Title page of the Fabrica—1553 (Cushing/Whitney Medical Library, Yale University)
Title page of Syrups (Cushing/Whitney Medical Library, Yale University)
Map of Geneva (Centre d'Iconographie genevoise, Collections Bibliothèque publique et universitaire, Genève)
Title page of Christianismi Restitutio (Bibliothèque nationale de France)
Servetus's last letter from prison (Cushing/Whitney Medical Library, Yale University)
Pulmonary circulation passage from CR (Bibliothèque nationale de France)
Loyola in armor (Réunion des Musées Nationaux/Art Resource, NY)
Servetus passage from Wotton (Cushing/Whitney Medical Library, Yale University)
Colladon's notes (Bibliothèque nationale de France)
Leibniz (Cushing/Whitney Medical Library, Yale University)
Title page of Impartial History (Authors' collection)
Louise de la Vallière (Réunion des Musées Nationaux/Art Resource, NY)
Duke de Lavallière (Cushing/Whitney Medical Library, Yale University)
Errors of the Trinity, genuine and counterfeit (Cushing/Whitney Medical Library, Yale University)
Priestley (Cushing/Whitney Medical Library, Yale University)
Blockley dead house (Osler Library of the History of Medicine, McGill University)
Geneva stone monument (Authors' collection)
Servetus sculpture (Cushing/Whitney Medical Library, Yale University)

NANCY GOLDSTONE is the author of several works of fiction and nonfiction. She has written for the *New York Times,* the *Washington Post Magazine,* and the *Boston Globe Magazine.*

LAWRENCE GOLDSTONE has written both fiction and nonfiction, and won a New American Writing Award for his first novel, *Rights.* Together, they are the authors of *Used and Rare, Slightly Chipped,* and *Warmly Inscribed.* They live with their daughter in Connecticut.

GAYLORD'S